WHAT THE
GREAT PHILOSOPHERS
THOUGHT ABOUT
GOD

By

MAX FISHLER

PLATO · ARISTOTLE · ST. AUGUSTINE
SHANKARA · MAIMONIDES · ST. THOMAS AQUINAS
SPINOZA · KANT · HEGEL
KIERKEGAARD

UNIVERSITY BOOK PUBLISHERS

Copyright © 1958
by Max Fishler
and W. L. Abt

UNIVERSITY BOOK PUBLISHERS
4320 Los Feliz Boulevard, Los Angeles 27, Calif., U.S.A.

PRINTED IN THE U.S.A.

CONTENTS

PREFACE

There is a popular notion that philosophers do not believe in God. This is far from the truth. Most philosophers are led, inevitably, to the idea of God, in their attempt to explain the nature of reality. Philosophy thus supplies a rational basis for religion. Hence the founders of religious dogma have sought philosophic grounds in substantiation of their beliefs. Among these are two of the pillars of Christian Theology and Dogma, St. Augustine and St. Thomas, who turned to the ancient Greeks for guidance in these matters, the former, to Plato, and the latter, to Aristotle. Maimonides, too, father of Jewish Theological Doctrine, appealed to the pagan Aristotle for rational support of his theology.

The philosopher achieves a unique insight into divinity, and it is this insight that the present volume seeks to explore and clarify.

The idea of writing this book was suggested to me by Dr. Maurice Sachnoff who, despite his iron-lung existence, found inspiration in the metaphysical depths of Spinoza's thought and in Spinoza's conception of God. He therefore proposed that I make a better understanding of "What the Great Philosophers Thought About God" available to all.

I have chosen ten men who dealt exhaustively with the subject of God and who are, I believe, representative of the great philosophers of our race.

PREFACE

It is hoped that this undertaking will also result in a truer appraisal of the speculations of the great philosophers on God — the supreme object of religion and theology, in the prime sense of these terms. I am happy to contribute thus to the eternal quest — man's unending search for the divine.

My thanks are due to the following: to my wife, Gisella, for her boundless love and devotion; to my dear friend, Cybelle Abt, for her inspiration, her love of philosophy and loyalty to ideals; to Harriet Neu, for her patience, care and affection in typing the manuscript of this book, and to Dr. William L. Abt, whose generosity made the book possible and who, in his search for spiritual truth, did not fail to detect the portion contained herein.

"In the mind of man there dwells the idea and ideal of the divine. In God there necessarily abides the sublime vision which man craves.

The separation of the two — that which dwells in the mind of man as a necessary idea and the vision of that divine idea which is the prerogative of God alone — the separation of these two is difficult for the seeker after truth; he knows not for certain whether God Himself be not man's creation even as man is God's noblest handiwork." — from "Reflections on the Nature of God"

— By the Author

INTRODUCTION

Ever since the dawn of human reason man has sought to know God. And, for countless centuries, philosophers have striven to comprehend the infinite nature of the divine. Some have succeeded more, others less; but the philosopher's aim has always been to dispel the mists that enshroud the nature of divine Being. Philosophy, is therefore, in this regard, rational speculation on what, for religion, is immediate experience.

But the fruits of the philosophic mind are almost as varied as the fruits of nature. Some philosophers thought they could arrive at God through reason. These are the rationalists.

One inevitable result of such a rationalistic approach is a refinement upon the notion of divinity. The philosopher, in shedding the light of reason upon the concept of God, or upon the "object" of that concept, alters its very character; so that the idea of God becomes identical with infinite and eternal Being; hence no longer a transcendent deity but a divinity immanent *in* all things. Other changes, too, follow for the rationalists; but whatever is lost in immediacy and intensity through rational reflection, is gained in scope, breadth and comprehensiveness.

In addition to the rationalistic approach to the divine, however, there are others; and these have different methods of arriving at God, such as intuition, or through some form of unique religious experience. Those who employ these methods are the mystics and saints.

For a number of prominent thinkers, again, the idea of God is an indispensable prerequisite for man's *ethical* being; these are the moral philosophers. And there are the aestheticians, for whom God is revealed in beauty and makes Himself known through the aesthetic experience. They should all be heard.

It is important to remember, also, that the philosophic quest for the divine is not merely theoretical and speculative, but practical as well; because the concept of God, distilled and purified through philosophic reflection, may serve to cure man of error, superstition, hate and fear.

Indeed, by avoiding the customary pathways to divinity we may learn to travel on the highway of enlightened vision, where looms a divine expansiveness such as the philosophic spirit alone can discern. And this may be the religion of the future, leading to a nobler humanity which, perhaps, only an adequate conception of God can fashion and appropriate as its very own.

Be that as it may, the ideas of these men, comprising their quest of the divine, should yield an intellectual feast; because, for them, the search for God is not a mere intellectual pastime; rather is it the result of an inner struggle, and pursued with great effort. We find, therefore, that human reason is here seasoned with such devotion, love and understanding that, in the very act of seeking the divine, these men become, in a measure, themselves divine.

Finally, a word about the biographical material relating to these philosophers. A little about the life of each man may help us to understand his thought; though, in the end, all reasoning must rest upon its own firm foundations. But we can sometimes learn even from the temporal lives of men what in them there was to give substance to their ideas; for what a man does often reveals the measure of his thoughts. It is well, therefore, to know to what extent the earthly aspect of their lives reflects the inner brilliance of men's spiritual selves.

These philosophers were extraordinary men. Indeed, so unique was their vision that they were often regarded as divinely inspired — as in the case of Plato, Aristotle, St. Thomas and Spinoza; but sometimes, they were considered as being merely eccentric, with the idiosyncrasies of genius, which sees life by way of unsuspected avenues and reaches God through undisclosed paths, forbidden to other men.

And they lived, thought and loved with an intensity far surpassing that of ordinary men. At some point or other, they saw where others failed to see. They peered into nooks and corners concealed from common sight, and their vision was illumined by a light which would have blinded lesser men had they been privileged to behold as these men did.

I have therefore inserted just so much about the life of each philosopher as I felt might cast some light upon the peculiar character of his thought. For this I beg to be excused in a book dealing with the nature of God; though it is perhaps not needful to plead for that which is, after all, the main aim of all books, namely, life itself. We need not cover up the lives of great men;

INTRODUCTION

rather ought we to view them in all their human weakness
and power, for then we may learn how we, too, can rise
to greater heights than our ordinary humanity permits
us to hope we can attain.

PLATO

PLATO

(427-347 B.C.)

I

Among the great thinkers of the West, the first who is the source of much later speculation regarding the nature of God, is Plato. Many of the subsequent arguments for the existence of God may be found, in essence, in this great philosopher. A survey of Plato's views on deity is consequently indispensable for an understanding of the guiding theological notions and ideas of Western man.

Plato's thoughts on God, which are among the most difficult to comprehend, found their way into both the Christian religion and Western philosophy. This could not take place however, until the *Idea of the Good* of Plato had been transformed into the *One* of the neo-Platonists and then adapted to the Christian religion by St. Augustine, Origen, Dionysius the Areopagite, John the Scot, and other key figures of the Christian Church.

A complete evaluation of Plato's contribution to Western philosophy does not lie within the province of this chapter. It is Plato's notion of divinity alone that we shall try to elicit from his complex vision imbedded in his voluminous writings.

Plato's conception of divinity, however, cannot be understood apart from the times in which he lived and the notions current in his day, which he was instrumental in refashioning. The life of the average Greek of the 4th or 5th Century B.C., was governed by many gods; and his fortune, good or ill, was the result of the will of the gods who presided over the destinies of men. This was Greek polytheism.

The gods were beings much like ourselves, only of larger dimensions and passions; and their pleasure or displeasure could easily be aroused. They were therefore to be propitiated or appeased through offerings and prayers.

The gods understood human wishes and desires and could take sides in issues of momentous importance, such as wars, political contests, or in the arts. Like humans, these gods had their own wars. They possessed all of the vices of man, and committed almost all human crimes. They could be moral too, on occasion, just like human beings; but on these moral occasions they dispensed justice on earth with a divine righteousness superior to man's. Hence it was important to keep them well disposed. And this could be achieved through proper offerings, libations, and the observance of feasts and ceremonies.

Many of the gods had a social function too, in being attached to a particular locality. The various city-states, each had their special patron god or goddess, such as

Athena, who presided over the fortunes of Athens. Hence, to displease the god of the city-state or to fail to acknowledge his benevolent guidance in the affairs of one's community, was tantamount to treason. This is why the charge against Socrates was so serious: "denying the gods that the state worships and worshipping other gods instead" — for which Socrates had to drink the hemlock and pay with his life for "irreligion."

In short, both as an individual and as a member of his community, the Greek was in close relation to the gods and in constant contact with them. And, there had accumulated over the years a complex tradition as to how one can invoke the favor of the gods; festivals were therefore celebrated with the most careful attention to all the details of the religious observances.

All this was for the *average* Greek.

For the Greek of exceptional intelligence and education, however, there were the works of the tragic poets and naturalistic philosophers who stood, each in their own way, in direct opposition to this naive, popular polytheism. Thus we find Xenophanes, the reputed founder of the Eleatic school (b. 570 B.C.), saying:

> "Mortals think that the gods are born as they are and have perceptions like theirs, and voice and form . . . if oxen and lions had hands, and could paint and produce works of art as men do, horses would paint the forms of the gods like horses, and oxen like oxen. In place of these imaginary beings let us adore the one infinite being who bears us in his bosom, and in whom there is neither generation

nor corruption, neither change nor origin . . .
There is one God . . . comparable to mortals
neither in form nor thought."

The tragic poets, on the other hand, were the first to
draw the attention of the Greeks to the immoral character of the gods. Some renounced their polytheistic
religion because of the injustices that went unpunished
by the gods:

"Does anyone say that there are gods in
heaven? No! there are none, unless one is
fool enough to believe an old tale . . . see
for yourselves . . . tyranny slays thousands
and despoils their goods, and men who break
their oath and cause cities to be sacked are
happier than those who walk quietly in the
ways of piety . . . And . . . small states,
where the gods are honored, are overpowered
in battle . . . and become subject to greater
states that are far less god-fearing."

(Euripides)

Finally, the Greek naturalistic philosophers, or Cosmologists, ventured on a quest of *natural causes* —
primordial physical elements, such as water, air, fire,
to explain the world of phenomena along purely physical
lines.

Between these two extremes, Plato steered an ingenious
metaphysical course. Against the background of these
two anti-religious forces, Plato propounded his teleological
metaphysics and metaphysical theology.

Plato's God is the cause of all that exists and all
that transpires in the world, but his is a divine *principle*

PLATO

— the *Idea of the Good,* for the fulfillment of which all things strive; a *final purpose* rather than a person or a compelling force or power; he is an *ideal goal,* the *eternal, perfect type of existence.*

It is ironical that this most abstract of deities should be the creation of him who sometimes speaks of many gods, and often employs myths to explain his metaphysical theories. But this does not detract from his main aim, and, was probably designed also to secure him against charges of irreligion.

Plato's deity is the World-Soul, the Idea of the Good — the One — or the Ideal of perfection. This is the divine principle toward which all things strive, and, in their *becoming,* here on earth, imitate.

Hence it is in the relationship of means to end that all temporal things exist. This relationship of all things for the sake of their ideal purpose or "final cause," is the supreme principle, the *teleological* principle which was to govern Plato's metaphysics and theology. All things exist for the sake of the Idea which they imperfectly exemplify; all ideas exist for the sake of the Idea of the Good. And this *teleological causality* takes precedence, for Plato, over the *mechanical causality* of the world of perception which so impressed the naturalistic cosmological thinkers, and it also supersedes the anthropomorphic conception of the gods of the accepted state religion.

To understand Plato's deity we must know and understand his world of perfect Being which is the realm of Ideas, the world of *true Being,* as opposed to our world of imperfect, temporal *non-being, or becoming.*

Plato's philosophy represents not only a metaphysical doctrine to be mentally grasped, but also a way of life to be actively pursued. And his God is the ideal of perfection of this ideal life.

————

II

In turning from the temporal to the eternal, from imperfect realities in process of *becoming* to perfect and changeless *Being*, Plato was only voicing what was at the heart of the Greek spirit — the quest for perfection and an immutable reality. The Greeks wanted to immortalize themselves, and they contrived to do so through the creation of eternally beautiful art-works. They loved perfect form, and their works of art, as well as their tragedies and poetry, were the expression of that love of form and desire for eternity.

Now, if we transfer this desire for perfection, for immutable being, from the realm of art to the sphere of philosophy, we may see how the sublime conceptions of Plato's mind were born and how his world of Ideas took shape. Plato did for philosophy and the quest of truth, what the poets, sculptors and artists of Greece had achieved for the beautiful: he clothed philosophy in raiments of everlasting Forms. The result is Platonic Idealism, and the world of Ideas, the highest of which is the Idea of the Good, the most perfect of all the Forms, the *divine Form*, or the *Deity*.

PLATO

Greek philosophy begins with the search for something abiding in the flux of things, something which underlies all variety and survives all change — "deathless" and "ageless."

What is this great and mysterious ocean of change, decay and death? they speculated. Could it be that amid all the endless flux and change there is nothing abiding?

The naturalistic philosophers (Thales, Anaximenes, Heraclitus) searched for this universal and abiding factor in the material world (in water, air, fire); the Pythagoreans thought they had discovered the abiding in the unchanging nature of numbers and the truths of mathematics; the Eleatic philosophers struggled to attain it through the concept of pure Being; the artists and poets tried to lay hold of it in their perfect creations.

Plato came and saw deeper than any of his predecessors. He had himself been a poet in his youth, and had destroyed his poems because they did not lead directly to truth; and his master, Socrates, had warned him against depending upon merely physical antecedents and causes, which was the method of naturalistic science. Plato adopted that which was common to all the poets and philosophers: their quest of the changeless amid the changing, the eternal amid the temporal. What was this? *It was the perfection of true Being,* the realm of eternal Ideas. There were perfect Forms for all things, with the Idea of the Good, the most perfect Form, the divine Form, at their head, giving life and reality to all the other Forms.

There are Ideas for everything possible: Ideas of things, and qualities, and relations; of the good, the beautiful, and the true, as well as of the ugly and the bad. Everything exists for the sake of its Idea or perfect Form which the thing imperfectly represents; and all Ideas exist for the sake of the Idea of the Good — the absolute end of all reality.

Plato thus instituted *teleology* in place of the anthropomorphisms of the older religion and he rejected the physical explanations of the Greek Cosmologists regarding the mechanism of nature's workings. His teleology was intended to prove that the world is ruled not by jealous gods nor by mechanical principles, but by *a purpose, an end* — which is the *chief good, the ideal of perfection* towards which all things are drawn as the lover by the image of the beloved. This was the view involving a final purpose to creation, a divine cause for which all the worlds in space exist.

Human actions are the best examples of the operation of the teleological principle because in them a purpose is at work. However, the cosmic Purpose is Purpose in relation to the Good, or the Idea of the Good, not to be found in the realm of becoming or in individual objects. Hence, while the Good has enormous power and objective existence, it cannot find a home or completed manifestation in individual things; it can be fully realized only in the Idea. Whenever anything in the world therefore is called "good," a bond is immediately established between the world of becoming and the realm of perfection or the Idea of the Good, the "good" thus *participating* in the ideal of goodness. That is what we mean when we say: "this is good." We imply that it possesses something which will find verification in a state of perfect existence. As an element in the becoming process, it tends towards that ideal state, its perfect Idea. Therefore, "it is good."

To understand this, Plato's new type of "causality" — teleological causality — positing a purpose towards which all things and actions are directed as their ideal end, and to distinguish it from the other causality of the physicists, naturalists and empiricists, Plato makes it clear that his *new* causality which is the *final cause,* or the Idea of the Good, is also the divine Reality which makes all things become, and become *real.* For, insofar as anything manifests its Idea, it works towards the realization of the final cause, the Idea of the Good, the divine Idea, or the principle of divine Being in the world.

And the difference between the world that truly *is* and the world that is only in process of *becoming,* between the higher world and the lower, is the same as that between the archetype and that which is but a copy or image of the archetype.

The world of becoming in space and in time is only an *imitation* of the archetypal world of the eternal Forms, where the deity or divine principle is to be found.

The oft-quoted Allegory of the Cave is indicative of this upward striving from darkness to light, from shadow to reality, from non-being to being:

"And now . . . Behold! human beings living in an underground den, which has a mouth open towards the light . . .; here they have been from their childhood, and have their legs and necks chained so that they cannot move, and can only see before them, being prevented by the chains from turning round their heads. Above and behind them a fire is blazing at a distance, and between the fire and the prisoners there is a raised way; and you will see, if you look, a low wall built along the way . . .

"I see."

"And do you see, I said, men passing along the wall carrying all sorts of vessels, and statues and figures of animals made of wood and stone and various materials, which appear over the wall? Some of them are talking, others silent."

"You have shown me a strange image, and they are strange prisoners."

"Like ourselves, I replied; and they see only their own shadows, or the shadows of one another, which the fire throws on the opposite wall of the cave?"

"True, he said; how could they see anything but the shadows if they were never allowed to move their heads?"

"And of the objects which are being carried in like manner they would only see the shadows?"

"Yes, he said."

"And if they were able to converse with one another, would they not suppose that they were naming what was actually before them?"

"Very true."

"And suppose further, that the prison had an echo which came from the other side, would they not be sure to fancy when one of the passers-by spoke that the voice which they heard came from the passing shadow?"

"No question, he replied."

"To them, I said, the truth would be literally nothing but the shadows of the images."

"That is certain."

"And now look again, and see what will naturally follow if the prisoners are released and disabused of their error.

"At first, when any of them is liberated and compelled suddenly to stand up and turn his neck round and walk and look towards the light, he will suffer sharp pains; the glare will distress him, and he will be unable to see the realities of which in his former state he had seen the shadows; and then conceive some one saying to him, that what he saw before was an illusion, but that now, when he is approaching nearer to being and his eye is turned towards more real existence, he has a clearer vision, — what will be his reply? . . . will he not be perplexed? Will he not fancy that the shadows which he formerly saw are truer than the objects which are now shown to him?"

"Far truer."

"And if he is compelled to look straight at the light, will he not have a pain in his eyes which will make him turn away to take refuge in the objects of vision which he can see . . . ?"

"True, he said."

"And suppose once more, that he is reluctantly dragged up a steep and rugged ascent, and held fast until he is forced into the presence of the sun himself, is he not likely to be pained and irritated? When he approaches the light his eyes will be dazzled, and he will not be able to see anything at all of what are now called realities."

"Not all in a moment, he said."

"He will require to grow accustomed to the sight of the upper world. And first he will see the shadows best, next the reflections of men and other objects in the water, and then the objects themselves; then he will gaze upon the light of the moon and the stars and the spangled heaven; and he will see the sky and the stars by night better than the sun or the light of the sun by day?"

"Certainly."

"Last of all he will be able to see the sun . . . but he will see him in his own proper place, and not in another; and he will contemplate him as he is."

"Certainly."

"He will then proceed to argue that this is he who gives the season and the years, and is the guardian of all that is in the visible world, and in a certain way the cause of all things which he and his fellows have been accustomed to behold?"

"Clearly," he said, "he would first see the sun and then reason about him."

"And when he remembered his old habitation, and the wisdom of the den and his fellow-prisoners, do you not suppose that he would felicitate himself on the change, and pity them?"

"Certainly, he would."

"And if they were in the habit of conferring honors among themselves on those who were quickest to observe the passing shadows and to remark which of them went before, and which followed after, and which were together; and who were therefore best able to draw conclusions as to the future, do you think that he would care for such honors and glories, or envy the possessors of them? Would he not say with Homer:

'Better to be the poor servant of a poor master', and to endure anything, rather than think as they do and live after their manner?"

"Yes, he said, I think that he would rather suffer anything than entertain these false notions and live in this miserable manner."

"Imagine once more, I said, such an one coming suddenly out of the sun to be replaced in his old situation; would he not be certain to have his eyes full of darkness?"

"To be sure, he said."

"And if there were a contest, and he had to compete in measuring the shadows with the prisoners who had never moved out of the den, while his sight was still weak, and before his eyes had become steady (and the time which would be needed to acquire this new habit of sight might be very considerable), would he not be ridiculous? Men would say of him that up he went and down he came without his eyes; and that it was better not even to think of ascending; and if any one tried to loose another and lead him up to the light, let them only catch the offender, and they would put him to death."

"No question, he said."

"This entire allegory, I said, you may now append, dear Glaucon, to the previous argument; the prison house is the world of sight, the light of the fire is the sun, and you will not misapprehend me if you interpret the journey upwards to be the ascent of the soul into the intellectual world according to my poor belief, which, at your desire, I have expressed — whether rightly or wrongly God knows. But, whether true or false, my opinion is that in the world of knowledge the idea of good appears last of all, and is seen only with an effort; and, when seen, is also inferred to be the universal author of all things beautiful and right, parent of light and of the lord of light in this visible world, and the immediate source of reason and truth in the intellectual; and that this is the power upon which he who would act rationally either in public or private life must have his eye fixed."

"I agree, he said, as far as I am able to understand you." *(Plato's Republic: Jowett Translation)*.

III

One important result of this Platonic view of the world is that Mind as the principle of reasonableness, orderliness, harmoniousness, and perfectability, is woven into the very structure of Reality and is so universally diffused as to allow no particle of reality to remain unaffected by it.

Mind or Reason is in control of the universe. And Plato invokes a principle, midway between Mind and the physical universe, the "Demiurge," to create and fashion the world in imitation of the perfect, eternal Ideas or Forms. And since the cosmos manifests abundant evidence of design, purpose, and Reason, a *divine* craftsman *must* be at work — hence the divine "Demiurge," who makes the universe conform as closely as possible to the eternal pattern.

In the dialogue "Timaeus" Plato gives this as a "most likely" explanation as to how the world came to be in space and in time.

Volumes have been written about the "Timaeus" in which Plato expounds his views regarding God and creation. Generations of scholars have sought to explain this important aspect of Plato's thought.

The divine Demiurge may be said to correspond in the nature of universal being to an artisan or craftsman in our physical world. Instead of a single specific idea which the human craftsman seeks to make objectively real, however, the divine craftsman — the "Demiurge" — makes manifest and gives embodiment to the most comprehensive of all Ideas, the Idea of the Cosmos, in all its multifarious being.

The divine craftsman makes Reason or Mind manifest in creation. But he is hampered by an obstructing principle — namely, Necessity. The *necessary* opposes the *rational* in the Universe: that is Plato's contention. But the whole problem of creation is veiled in obscurity because of the problem of time. At one point in his life Plato contended that the world could not have been created or have originated in time; since time, according to Plato, comes into being along with the Cosmos and hence could not be present or conceivable prior to the

Cosmos. In the "Timaeus" however, the argument is *for* the creation of the Cosmos in time.

However that may be, the problem, here as elsewhere with Plato, is to prove: 1. That physical necessity, of itself, is insufficient to account for the Cosmos and Man; 2. that a divine end or purpose (teleology) must be invoked to account for the nature of Reality; 3. that the entire world-process was pregnant with meaning insofar as the purposefulness in the Universe was for the realization of the Good; and 4. that a Creative Intelligence was necessary to account for the urge to the actualization of the divine Ideas.

In another Dialogue, the "Philebus," Plato explains that the world of perception is a "mixture" of the "unlimited", i.e. space, and "limitation", i.e. the mathematical forms of things; and that the cause of this mixture, which is the highest divine principle in the Cosmos, is the Idea of the Good. Space assumes mathematical shape and form in order to imitate, and thus as far as possible to become like, the world of Ideas. Mathematical configurations, forms and structures are the intermediate links by which empty space which "is not," is able to imitate the pure Forms or the Ideas, in the world of phenomena. Therefore it is that mathematical knowledge, along with philosophical knowledge, deals with abiding essences; and the phenomenal world is in reality a limitation of space, formed in imitation of the Ideas; while space is the "nothing" out of which the world of phenomena is formed for the sake of the Idea of the Good or the Deity.

Thus, the Ideas are the final cause of phenomena; all occurrence in the world is for the sake of the Ideas;

all Ideas exist for the sake of the Idea of the Good; and the world of *becoming* (or non-being) exists for the sake of that which truly *is*.

This constitutes the teleological metaphysics of Plato.

IV

Plato was born in the year 427 B.C. and died, at the age of 80, in 347 B.C. He stemmed from two of the most illustrious families of Athens, and it seems quite certain that he met Socrates through Critias, the cousin, and Charmides, the brother of his mother, both of whom were leading reactionary politicians of their day and close friends of Socrates; thus he had probably known Socrates since boyhood.

As a young man, Plato was contemplating a political career; at the age of 24 he was courted by the reactionaries to join their party and enter public life under their banner. But Plato waited to see how they would act when in power; and this was soon to be. Their extravagant terroristic methods repelled him and he eagerly awaited the restoration of the democracy in Athens. When this took place and he saw Socrates "the wisest, best and justest of men" being condemned to death and forced to drink the hemlock, democracy too disgusted him. He was convinced, as A. E. Taylor says, that "there was no place for a man of conscience in active politics", nor, for that matter, any room for such a man of conscience in Athens; so he and other friends and followers of Socrates fled the city. They took refuge in the home of Eucleides at Megara. Plato spent some of the following years in extensive travels through Greece, Egypt and Italy.

Returning to Athens about the year 387, he founded the *Academy* for the study of philosophy and for scientific research. All during the rest of his life he was its head, bringing it into prominence as the center not only of philosophy but also of mathematical, juridical and other scientific knowledge and research.

He later intervened in the political life of Syracuse, having been summoned to become the tutor of the successor of Dionysius I who had died in the year 367. Plato, always dreaming of a state with a philosopher at the helm, went to Syracuse to train and instruct Dionysius II in philosophy and science, in order to fit him for the duties of a constitutional king, according to Plato's ideal of this high office. The whole enterprise, however, was doomed to failure because, again, political life was unsuited for Plato's idealism. Intrigue, banishment and finally murder overwhelmed the fortunes of the royal house and Plato once again was destined to see his ideal of the philosopher on the throne turn into an unmitigated disappointment.

In addition to his monumental philosophic legacy which gives Plato the well-earned title as "the greatest of philosophic writers", his influence upon subsequent thought through his pupils, friends and co-workers at the Academy, is inestimable and greater beyond measure than that of any one man or school in all history.

PLATO

In mathematics, mechanics, natural history, biology, botany, jurisprudence, it was Plato's friends, relatives and pupils (headed by Aristotle, of course) who made the most significant contributions for centuries to come. In fact, almost all the exact sciences, as well as the humanities, find their inception in this first great University of the West.

And in the realm of practical legislation we have it on the authority of Plutarch that Plato and his associates were actively involved in some of the most important political and martial events of the day.

And yet, the influence of Plato is *most* marked in realms farthest removed from practical life — in the Ideal Realm, the world of ideas. It was as a great teacher of mankind and as a leader in the perennial struggle of man's higher self with his animal nature — it is here, in the realm of ideas and ideals, that Plato is unquestionably the most potent influence of all time, and in all countries.

For, Plato, and the Platonists who followed him, realized, as Dean Inge says, that "the soul is the wanderer of the metaphysical world . . . The psychical man is therefore unstable. He may rise to the spiritual man, or he may sink to the carnal man, or, as most of us do, he may fluctuate uneasily between the two." *(Mysticism and Religion)*

Plato depicts man as the meeting ground of the two antagonistic principles in the world — Reason and Necessity — which clash throughout the realm of nature but are in man united in one and the same being. For man is that marvelous creation of the gods, or of the powers of creation in the Cosmos, wherein a part of the divine harmonious substance of the World-Soul is immortally entrenched; but his soul has its mortal parts too — the passions; and, of course, there is also his organism of flesh and blood, wherein physical necessity reigns supreme.

However, the very position and the functions of the various organs of the human body are calculated to insure that what is "good" should be given preference, even as to their particular location in the human body, so that the reasonable may control the less reasonable factors.

Thus, according to Plato, the purpose for which both the eyes of man and his power of speech were created is to arouse in him the desire for philosophy; this is their primary function; for, "the sight of day and night, of the months and the revolutions of the year, have created number, and have given us a conception of time, and the power to inquire regarding the nature of the universe; and from this source we have derived philosophy; than which no greater good ever was or will be given by the gods to mortal man."

Thus does the teleological principle operate throughout the universe, manifesting a divine purposiveness — first, in the Universe as a Whole, and in certain features of the physical aspect of the heavens: God, Plato tells us in the *Timaeus*, resolved to form a moving image of eternity which is Time . . . "and when he set in order the heaven, he made this image *eternal but moving*, according to number, while eternity itself rests in *unity*; and this image we call *time* . . . the past and future are created species of time, which *imitates eternity* and revolves according to a law of number."

The seven planets, through their motion, preserve the remembrance of time, and the sun was created to afford a measure of their swiftness.

This same divine purposiveness appears in the quantitative, numerical relationship among the elements out of which the parts of the cosmos were made, and finally, through the diffusion of the World-Soul as the active principle throughout the universe. Principally, the divine Purpose makes its presence felt in the mind and soul of man as the source of the beautiful, the moral, the rational, the orderly and the harmonious; all of which elements work for the one Purpose, the supreme End, the actualization of the Good — until that Purpose meets its opposite, Necessity, in brute Matter, devoid of Soul, devoid of Mind or Reason; for "Creation is mixed, being made up of Necessity and Mind"; but the divine Craftsman using "Persuasion" achieves his ideal purpose — since "Mind overrules Necessity by persuading her to bring the greater part of created things to perfection." *(Timaeus)*

At the level of Soul-Existence, enormously powerful forces are set in motion in the Universe for the realization of the Good; these forces produce those teleological aspects of life made manifest in law, government, morality, art, philosophy and all the other products of the Mind of Man which evidence the psychical and the divine, functioning in the world for the final and absolute end and aim of all creation: the actualization of the Idea of the Good.

V.

Plato's views, on the whole, are difficult to track down with certainty, because he was constantly revising and remodelling his notions over a period of half a century; and, in addition, we have his own wise admonition in these matters pertaining to the nature of God:

> "The father and maker of this Universe is beyond discovering, and even if we did find him, to tell of him to all men would be impossible." *(Theat.)*

Plato is not only an example of a great philosopher who discoursed freely on the nature of God and was aware of the extreme importance of this subject for philosophy, but he was also convinced of the vital role of religion in the life of a community:

> "The demonstration (of God's existence) would be the best and noblest prelude to all our laws."

Hence in the *Laws* he embarks upon an elaborate theological exposition. Indeed, he has been accused of sanctioning "religious persecution" in order to safeguard his city from atheistic theories which, he felt, would endanger the very safety of the commonwealth where, according to Plato's later notions, severe measures should be taken to guard against the dangers of atheism, atheists being now regarded by him (in the *Laws)* as dangerous political offenders.

But the laws he wants enacted would insure the adoption of *his* theological notions, because these seem to him able to stand the test of reason, and his philosophic arguments in support of them are intended to offer convincing proof, such as to merit the endorsement of all rational men. The demand by the State for assent to them therefore would be justified, which would not be the case if the Olympic gods or the established religion were in question.

Plato's purpose throughout is to lead us to an idealistic interpretation of Nature through the function of a Soul everywhere in the world. (The details are left uncertain — whether there be one soul or whether many souls inhabit the Cosmos — and uncertain this must of necessity be). Plato seeks to indicate that whatever and no matter how varied Soul may be in the nature of things, it is always — whether as one or many — evidence of the workings of a divine Intelligence manifested in the Order and Rationality of created things and in the World as a Whole.

It is in the *Laws*, the last of Plato's masterworks, however, that we find an explication of the total function of the Soul in the Universe. The manifestations of that which is Soul, he now tells us, are present in every phase of the visible world; nothing anywhere occurs wherein a Soul does not play a determinant role.

Plato's tremendous power of transfiguration asserts itself, in the *Laws*, when, in the last years of his life, he seeks a final synthesis of his life-long strivings. It is here, in this last great work, that Plato is more anxious than ever to prove the primacy of the Soul, and to demonstrate the priority of the spiritual over the material elements everywhere in the world.

His whole life was spent in teaching the primacy of the Spiritual over the material and physical. This primacy he tried to establish through his doctrine of the eternal

Ideas which were the perfect patterns or Forms for all existences. Now he seeks the *connecting link* by which the spiritual gains a foothold in the material and physical. This link is the Soul and the activity of Soul in the universe.

Soul is prior to matter — the spiritual, moral and intellectual take precedence over the material and the physical. In Plato's own words:

> ". . . thought and mind and administration
> and art and law are prior to that which is
> hard and soft, heavy and light" . . . "characters
> and morals, wishes and reasoning, true opinions,
> and recollections are prior to length, breadth,
> depth and strength of bodies."

In the *Laws*, Plato makes it abundantly clear that the intellectual activities and the characteristics in nature and in man which bear upon the aspects with which art and law, morality and philosophy deal, are in the very nature of things, in the Cosmos as a Whole, as well as in the realm of values, prior to all material processes, qualities and entities. His life-long desire to establish this priority of the spiritual over the material, the intellectual over the physical, the moral over the emotional, now finds a final consummation.

Here, again, endless battles have been waged by opposing camps of scholars as to just how Plato could make the transition from the realm of *Being* to that of *Becoming*, from the world of eternal Ideas to the order of time and change; the more so since Plato himself devotes several dialogues (five to be exact: *Thaetetus, the Sophist, the Statesman, Parmenides and Cratylus*) to explain or resolve the conflict between the One and the Many, or the philosophy of Being and eternal Ideas, on the one hand, and the philosophy of Becoming and the phenomenal world of sensuous reality, on the other. In these dialogues Plato attempts to solve the problem of the antithesis of Permanence vs. Change, Being vs. Becoming, Sameness and Rest vs. Alteration and Motion.

In one of these — *the Sophist* — Plato becomes aware of the important truth that Life, Motion, Process and Change, must be present in the nature of Being. Hence the Theory of Ideas as well as its opposite, materialism, cannot account for "Being-in-its fullness." The material and the psychical, the phenomenal and the noumenal are equally necessary for a complete view of the Cosmos. The Soul, in the World as in Man, bridges the gulf between the material and the psychical aspects of reality. In fact, the function of God or the Deity is to insure participation by the objects of this world in the realm of Ideas. God's work consists in imbuing the realm of becoming with characteristics and qualities of the higher and eternal realm.

And Plato develops the idea of the activity of Soul in the nature of reality through a more and more complete realization of the various types of movement manifest in creation, which are finally systematically classified in Book 10 of the *Laws;* movement reaching up to the most perfect of all movement which is that of the Soul, movement from within, self-induced, eternal, and the only movement without a prior cause for its existence.

Indeed, once the world has been created, almost every

aspect of its existence can be accounted for through the
function of a Soul. Hence it is that matter, motion, physical attributes alone are insufficient to explain the world.
We cannot understand the nature of things through
their spatial and physical characteristics alone. A principle
of Life must be added to the principle of Motion to make
reality intelligible. And this means that we must invoke
the notion of Soul to explain the world. There is no
reality without a Soul. The Universe is soul-full, full
of the spark of divinity, which is Soul or Life, functioning in the nature of existing things; wherefore mechanistic, materialistic, "naturalistic" interpretations, will not
suffice. The Laws of Nature must be evaluated in their
full and divine significations as the expression of God
in the Universe through the action of Soul as the principle of Life and Spirituality in the Real.

The Platonic view of divinity is therefore intimately
connected with his life-long quest for the supremacy of
the spiritual, moral and intellectual in the Cosmos, a
view of the world which modern man has lost and which
he is now striving to regain. The autonomy of the moral,
political and artistic is thereby also established; for these
are phases of that which is ultimately the Divine and
they become dominant factors in the Cosmos as well
as in the nature of man.

The universe reflects the divine through the Life,
Order, Beauty, Harmony, Form, Law in the world; and
the cultural activities of man, too, all the varied phases
of character and intellect are manifestations of this divine spiritual activity.

Thus, while God makes himself manifest in the very
structure and order of the heavenly bodies, He is also

to be observed actively involved in whatever displays the working out of the Principle of the Good, the desire for perfection in the creation of beautiful form, in the mind of the genius, in the actions of the morally good, and in the actualization of the good achieved through statesmanship which strives for the ideal commonwealth of man.

Plato's God, then, is the result of his consuming quest of the ideal in the nature of the real. Always on the alert for spiritual truths, with a keen eye for the beautiful, the sublime and the moral, Plato contrived to universalize his master's, Socrates', search for the morally true, until it widened into the revelation that the divine is a universally diffused active spiritual essence throughout the Universe.

Plato's deity is the cause of harmony, justice, orderliness and goodness in the world; and the source of that overflowing measure of the purposeful in things, which overrules all materialistic necessity in the universe.

So closely related is this Platonic conception of God to the nature and structure of the universe, that his God sometimes appears merely as the essence of reality itself; the Platonic Ideas are the logical essences of things, and God is the highest of these logical essences. Hence the Ideas are not really existing entities at all; they do not exist independently but are part of the objects they inhabit. And the Idea of the Good, or God, is, similarly, the Universe in its essential Being. But a closer approximation to the Platonic view is that which holds that, for Plato, there are three levels of being or reality: the level of sense-experience, the level of the eternal Ideas, and the level of the Idea of the Good or the Divine level.

VI

This interpretation makes the Soul, which plays so prominent a role in Plato's conception of reality, intelligible. The Soul exists on earth as a result of its having fallen from its original divine status. Previous to its earthly existence, it had its being in another sphere, a heavenly abode. From the Orphic and Pythagorean philosophies Plato accepts the doctrine of re-incarnation; and he gives us an elaborate description of what happens after death. For a long time, perhaps a thousand years, the Soul clings to its personality and retains its identity. Then comes a period of complete extinction wherein the soul loses contact with the memory of itself and hence loses its individuality.

Now the souls are told that they can choose whatever life they desire. Actually, however, they cannot choose whatever life they desire because the very life they show preference for is determined by their previous existences. Hence there is no real freedom of choice here. Each soul must choose the sort of existence that conforms to its status, the better souls desiring always a better type of life, and evil ones choosing, of necessity, inferior existences. When the new incarnation is attained, all ties with the past are broken and forgotten; but a continuity of essential character remains.

Another favorite idea of Plato's, useful to him in

this respect, is that of the unity of opposites; from which it follows that even as life involves death, so does death involve life. Death must turn into life, for if death prevailed, the universe itself could cease to be. Death can never be the end. Life must follow death even as death follows life. Indeed, we have a *recollection* of the soul's existence prior to its present state. Mathematical truths, as Plato shows in his dialogue *Meno*, and our knowledge of the eternal Ideas, constrain us to postulate the pre-existence of our soul because here, on earth, all we can gain is relative and temporal knowledge while these mathematical truths are absolute and eternal.

Hence philosophy, which strives for knowledge of the absolute and eternal, requires the tendance of the soul, or a way of life and an appreciation of true and enduring values by which means proper care is taken of the soul "not only in respect of the portion of *time* which is called *life* but of *eternity!*" The danger, says Plato, "of neglecting her from this point of view does indeed appear to be awful."

Here we meet the strain of pure Platonism which distinguishes it from all other idealisms, philosophic and religious. Plato is not so much concerned with personal salvation, as were the later Christian Theologians for instance, but with the search for that which is true and abiding in the nature of Being. And the Soul is the instrument for the attainment of that end. Therein lay its proper use: to help us to a union or re-union with the divine; for, to absorb a true vision of reality, to become emancipated from the limitations of the senses, to see life under the aspect of eternity, to identify our-

selves with the principles of absolute beauty and truth
in the Universe — this means for us to remain untainted
by time, and to attain immortality; and this, too, is our
pass-key to divinity.

But at the opposite pole to the Soul stands formless
space, which, though formless, has the potentiality of
receiving Forms, and hence provides a home for created
things. Space, the principle of non-being, confronted God
at the very beginning of creation, resisting through its
physical matter the rational functions of the Forms.

The material principle which fills space is responsible
for the evil in the world, for it is this that resists the
tendency of the Soul toward the Forms.

Two conflicting causes are thus at work in the universe. The first is the Divine Cause, the teleological
cause. The second is the Necessary Cause — purposeless,
and contained in unformed matter.

On the one hand — the *realm of the perfect Forms,*
eternal and immutable; on the other hand — the sphere
of *materiality*, representing constant change, illusion and
evil in the world. Here we strike that dualism in Plato's
thought which, through the neo-Platonists' interpretation,
became so dominant a factor in medieval philosophy.
For the neo-Platonists, the world of the senses presents
a mixture of Being and non-Being: it *is,* insofar as it
is a part of God, and as such it is *good;* it is *not,*
insofar as it is matter, and *evil.*

Evil is negation of being: materiality; the corporeal
world is evil because it is formed out of matter, and
souls may be called "evil" when they give themselves
over to matter. But, for the neo-Platonists, it belongs to
the essential nature of the soul to find entrance into

matter because there alone is the shining forth of the
deity made possible. Thus, participation in matter, and
therefore participation in evil, is, for the soul, a natural
necessity as it proceeds or issues forth from the
divine. However, since it is only through the
function of Soul upon matter that anything in the world
of sense exists at all, Soul or Spirit is that which *really*
exists even in the nature of matter.

The conception of Nature and the World of the neo-
Platonists comprises this spiritualization of the corporeal. The material part is but the outer shell; inside
the shell is the active reality of souls and spirits. A
body is the *copy*, or, as the neo-Platonists would have
it, the *shadow* of the Idea, in which the Idea had
shaped itself in its matter; the true nature of a thing is
this spiritual or intellectual essence which appears as
phenomenon when perceived by the senses.

Beauty involves the shining forth of this ideal essence.

There streams forth a spiritual light which makes the
entire world of sensuous phenomena beautiful.

In the *Enneads* of Plotinus we thus come upon the
first attempt in the history of Western thought at a
metaphysics of aesthetics, based upon the philosophy of
Plato. Only once before this an attempt was made at
formulating the conception of the beautiful as an independent and absolute reality; and that was by Plato
himself in the *Symposium*. In Plotinus, the beauty which
the Greeks had given birth to and which they so loved
to enjoy, is, for the first time, recognized as the victo-
rious power of the spirit even in the sensuous world.

Greek art and the Hellenic worship of pure beauty
was this apotheosis of the spiritual in the material. But

for Plotinus, the metaphysician and mystic, *all* of the phenomenal world is the *Natural* viewed in terms of the *Psychical*; for neo-Platonism nature itself is real only insofar as it manifests the psychical.

Each soul, released from the universal Soul, is one of the countless forms in which that World-Soul unfolds; and each personality, cast into the sensuous body out of a pure, pre-existent state, is strangely drawn to the void and the vain; hence the task of each soul is to attain release from its bodily frame and material essence. This is the way of "purification" and thus can the soul begin its backward and upward journey through the stages by which it has issued forth from the deity and so *return to* the deity.

This process, which is the *world-process*, is without beginning or end, an eternal necessity. Plato's rationalistic spiritualism thus ends in neo-Platonic mysticism for which God himself does not exist without the streaming forth of his essence; and thus is the world of matter created, and real only as an emanation of the divine being. All of this may be likened to the nature and power of light which shines forever into darkness but could not appear except for the darkness in which it shines.

And Plotinus recounts the stages by which the soul passes through its own intrinsic life to divinity — through knowledge and contemplation of the beautiful, which finds a reflection of the ideas in the world of the senses; then, achieving release from matter, the soul rises from the sensuously beautiful to the spiritually beautiful; and finally to the ecstatic rapture in which

the individual finds union with the ground of all Being
—until the beautiful and the true and the real mingle
in the divine as the individual sinks in the All-One.

This is the salvation of the neo-Platonists, drawing
out, as they did, the full implications of the dualism of
the Platonic philosophy, the duality of the two worlds:
the world of eternal Ideas which is the divine world,
and the phenomenal world of the senses derived there-
from. With this came also the negative morality of
Platonism and its flight from the world, the withdrawal
from the material and sensuous.

The neo-Platonists only followed in the footsteps of
their master, Plato; for, all of their teaching is but an
echo of the Platonic original in mystical garb. Plato, too,
held that the senses hold man in bondage; that the
objects of the ordinary world which present us with flux
and change are not real and not true; that, as rational
beings, we cannot attain happiness until we reach the
realm of abiding reality, the eternal Forms. In the cave
of sense-illusion we live amidst shadows and unreality.
In the intelligible realm of the Ideas we obtain a knowledge of eternity, and the quest of this realm constitutes
the life of the philosopher, the seeker after truth and
wisdom.

Because of this, Plato was referred to as "the divine
Plato" all through the Middle Ages. His constant striving to reveal a divine essence in man and the world
gained him the appellation "divine."

Plato believed in eternal existences, the source of all
temporally existing things; these were intelligible essences,
pure, unblemished, perfect — and real, though transcen-

dent to all sensuous or temporal things. These eternal essences or Forms were approachable only by philosophic thought and could be contacted only by reason, even as the mathematical figures which no eye hath seen: the perfect circle, the perfect square, the perfect right-angled triangle.

Plato was infatuated by this vision of the sublimely real — the eternally real — the perfect — the unchanging — the ideal. His reason had been his staircase; he was reaching higher, toward the divine essences, toward divine Being itself. With more perfect understanding came ever greater illumination. He was in the presence of ideas which life hath not known nor mind visioned! Reason was the ladder — it had led him upwards, to this high altitude. Could he push away the ladder now and rest in pure intuition? Plato was ever hesitating; but his followers, the neo-Platonists, took the decisive step: Plotinus pushed away the ladder of reason. But Plato would not dispense with that wonderful instrument which had brought him to the very brink of divine illumination. He strove rather to perfect reason itself into "dialectic", and so to achieve a converse of the rational soul with the source of creation.

The history of all succeeding thought bears eloquent witness to the vast influence which Plato exerted on Western man. Aristotle, the neo-Platonists, Stoicism, Christianity, the Mystics of the Middle Ages, Hegel, the Cambridge Platonists, the New England Transcendentalists — all borrowed and developed Plato's original insight into the nature of man, the universe, and God. And his "Republic" has been the archetype for all social idealisms — Cicero's "De Republica," St. Augustine's "City of God" and Sir Thomas More's "Utopia," all of which found their original inspiration in Plato's ideal of the perfect State. It has been truly said of him that, like the philosopher of his own creation, "Plato was the spectator of all time and all existence."

In the words of Goethe: "Plato's relation to the world is that of a superior spirit, whose good will it is to dwell in that world for a time. It is not so much his concern to become acquainted with the world — for the world and its nature are things which he presupposes — as to communicate to the world that which he brings with him, and of which it stands in so great a need. He penetrates into its depths, rather to replenish them from the fulness of his own nature than that he may fathom their mysteries. He scales its heights as one yearning after renewed participation in the source of his being. All that he utters has reference to something eternally complete, good, true, beautiful, whose furtherance he strives to promote in every bosom."

ARISTOTLE

ARISTOTLE

(384 B.C.-322 B.C.)

I. LIFE

Closely associated with Plato in the Academy was Aristotle, the most famous of Plato's pupils and perhaps the most influential thinker of all time.

Dante, the poet of Medieval Scholasticism, calls Aristotle "the master of those who know;" and, indeed, for scope of interest, breadth of philosophic and scientific vision, and depth of logical penetration, Aristotle holds a pre-eminent position as the dominant intellectual figure in the Western world for over two thousand years. Down the corridors of time his fame resounds as the most comprehensive thinker on metaphysics, logic and science the world has ever known. He is reputed to have written several hundred volumes, covering almost every phase of human knowledge, thought and conduct. Whether it be in the twentieth century, in the seventeenth, or in the twelfth, Aristotle's is a name to reckon with, for he perpetually provokes thought and stirs the imagination.

It is the fashion today, in some circles, to deride

Aristotle. His science, we are told, is outdated, his logic superseded, and his philosophy discarded. The marvel of it is that though this seems apparently true, Aristotle is still very much with us; like the premature report of Mark Twain's death, Aristotle's demise has been "grossly exaggerated."

A glance at the history of Western philosophy and science will make Aristotle's contribution to both philosophy and science abundantly clear. He coined not only many of the ideas, — the "topics" of future philosophy and science — but the very terminology of Western thought; and his name echoes down the centuries as the "father of Formal Logic," for he discovered the science of logic and invented the syllogism. But our concern is primarily with Aristotle's conception of God. Closely related as Aristotle's thought in general is to that of Plato, his notion of the deity is even more so, being a mere variation of the Platonic theology. But the differences are important, and these we shall soon note.

Of all the pupils of Plato, Aristotle was the most troublesome and the most beloved. When he first applied for admission to Plato's Academy in the year 366 B.C., he was a youth of seventeen, a cultured young gentleman, full of wit and humor. He had been brought up as an aristocrat — polite, graceful, "the very model of sartorial and ethical propriety,"* for his father was court physician to Amyntas II, king of Macedonia, the grandfather of Alexander the Great.

It is said that Plato complained that Aristotle paid too much attention to his clothes — for a philosopher he

* Living Biographies of Great Philosophers
  by Henry Thomas and Dana Lee Thomas.

seemed too worldly! But time was to prove Plato's fears unfounded; Aristotle was destined for a dual immortality: he was to become not only the most eminent of Greek philosophers, but the intellectual backbone of Catholicism as well!

Perhaps the most remarkable feature about Aristotle is the fact that no phase of human life or thought escaped his keen curiosity and analytical scrutiny; metaphysics, theology, logic, natural history, ethics, biology, astronomy, mathematics, rhetoric, history, psychology, politics, drama, poetry, physics, medicine — all found in him a penetrating student and observant researcher; also, a universal interpreter. Plato himself later boasted that his Academy consisted of two parts — the body of his students and the mind of Aristotle.

Plato died in 347 B.C. Aristotle was then thirty-seven years of age. He had been the shining light of Plato's Academy for twenty years. It was only natural for him to expect to be chosen as the head of the school. But the post went to an Athenian. Aristotle was a "foreigner," from the "barbarian" North. (He was born at Stagira, a Greek colonial town several hundred miles to the north of Athens.) The Athenians did not like foreigners. Plato's nephew Speusippus succeeded him as head of the Academy.

Aristotle was grievously disappointed. A former fellow student, Hermias, who had become lord and master of a large strip of land in Asia Minor, but had not forgotten his Platonic training, gathered about himself the two most illustrious of Plato's pupils, Aristotle and Xenocrates. These were joined by Theophrastus, who came to them from the neighboring island of Lesbos, and others who joined them to form the nucleus of a school of which Aristotle was the teacher for three years. Hermias became one of Aristotle's pupils after donating the town of Assus to his Platonic friends, in gratitude for their common Platonic lineage.

But Hermias, it appears, was also desirous of making an experiment in good government, and invited Aristotle to help him govern wisely. Actually, it is said that Hermias only wanted Aristotle "to teach him how to reconcile abstract justice with concrete plunder."* Aristotle failed in this venture. The ideal of justice was not yet ripe for realization.

He did, however, marry Pythias, the niece and adopted daughter of Hermias, whom he loved, it is said, not only for herself but also because of her handsome dowry. For complete happiness, Aristotle taught, man needs also external good fortune, health, and "a fair measure" of earthly goods. So he married Pythias, and on his honeymoon went collecting sea shells in order to prove certain of his scientific theories in marine biology.

Soon the Persians were to invade the country of Hermias, who was taken prisoner, brutally tortured, and killed. Aristotle himself might have been enmeshed in great difficulties had not Philip, king of Macedonia, invited him to come to the royal palace and instruct his son, Alexander.

The news that Hermias had been seized and killed reached Aristotle when he was already settled in the royal palace at Pella, and engaged in the in-

* Living Biographies of Great Philosophers
by Henry Thomas and Dana Lee Thomas.

struction of the young Alexander. He had the satisfaction of knowing, however, that something of the essential teaching of Plato — the eternal worth of loyalty — must have taken a deep root in the soul of Hermias; for, despite the brutal torture and final crucifixion to which he had been subjected, Hermias died with the words on his lips:

"Tell my friends and companions that I have done nothing unworthy of philosophy."

Whereupon Aristotle composed a beautiful ode to the memory of Hermias and his immortal valor.

But he now had other troubles on his hands; for it was an impossible task that Aristotle had undertaken — his attempt to instill philosophic tranquillity into the seething blood of the boyish and brutal Alexander whose pastime was taming horses that no one else could tame. Nor was the royal Macedonian atmosphere conducive to philosophic inquiry and meditation. King Philip's court was no fit place for the rearing of a philosopher-king.

Nonetheless, Plutarch tells us that "Alexander loved and cherished Aristotle as if he had been his own father; saying that though he had received life from the one, the other had taught him the art of living." And, in a moment of gratitude and affection for his teacher, Alexander writes to Aristotle: "for my part, I had rather excel in the knowledge of what is good than in the extent of all my power and dominion."

But suddenly, his father Philip was murdered. Aristotle was, for the moment, forgotten, and Alexander set out to conquer and plunder.

When Aristotle returned to Athens, in the year 334 B.C., to establish his own school, the *Lyceum*, he did not find it difficult to attract many students, despite his Macedonian leanings. He was overwhelmed by followers who flocked to him for instruction and inspiration. A very unique school this was! The students, most of whom were scholars, would eat their meals in common with the master; and they would imbibe wisdom and learn metaphysics and logic as they followed Aristotle who, as he lectured, paced up and down along the Walk called Peripatos, the field of the Lyceum, which was part of the temple Apollo Lyceus. Hence the name "Peripatetic" or walking school which has become synonymous with Aristotelianism. At any rate, as they thus followed Aristotle on his lecture-walks, these Peripatetic students and philosophers took notes of all that Aristotle desired to teach them. These notes, and his actual writings, are said to have comprised hundreds of volumes, some ancient writers say four hundred, others say one thousand; his unparalleled speculative mind and his unprecedented researches in human and animal biology, as well as natural phenomena, comprising a wealth of knowledge such as the world had not known before.

Pliny tells us that Alexander had, through his hunters, fishermen and gardeners, supplied Aristotle with all sorts and varieties of animal and plant life; and from other sources we learn of the immense number of men who had been dispatched to collect animal and botanical specimens which were gathered together for Aristotle's zoological garden — in all probability the very first in the history of the world. Alexander also subsidized Aristotle's biological and other scientific researches with several millions of dollars (in modern purchasing power). We know, further, that from materials compiled by many assistants, Aristotle drew up the outlines for one hundred and fifty-eight constitutions. It was Aristotle, again, who persuaded Alexander to send an expedition for the purpose of exploring the sources of the Nile and the causes of its overflow.

We must remember under what severe limitations all of these ventures had to be carried out. Aristotle was compelled, according to Zeller, "to determine time without a watch, to compare degrees of heat without a thermometer, to observe the skies without a telescope, and the weather without a barometer . . . all the facts on which the physical theories of modern science are based, were as yet almost wholly undiscovered." And yet, with relatively so little he could achieve so much!

Aristotle's scientific researches, in brief, were confined to *observation;* the weapon of modern science, which is *experimentation,* is scarcely to be found here.

For twelve years Aristotle labored unceasingly to establish his school, the Lyceum, in Athens. Then, Alexander, in his thirties, suddenly died! Revolution broke out in the restive city. Demosthenes, with patriotic eloquence and fervor, aroused the Athenians to a proclamation of independence, while Antipater, who had been summoned to the side of Alexander, marched upon the city.

Aristotle had always sided with the Macedonians. He was now practically alone in Athens among those who had been the champions of Macedonianism. But no one, it seemed, dared touch him — for a while. Soon, however, Aristotle was charged with having taught that prayer and offerings were futile and useless. He sensed the danger of his position. "I will not give Athens a chance to sin a second time against philosophy," he said, remembering the fate of Socrates, and left the city. He fled to his mother's home in Chalcis, on the island of Euboea. Here, according to one report, Aristotle was plagued by ill health, but according to Diogenes Laertius, the adverse turn of events so affected the aging philosopher that he committed suicide by drinking hemlock, just as Socrates had done. Thus ended the life of the self-exiled and immortal Aristotle in 322 B.C., at the age of 62.

Now, a word as to the relationship of Plato and Aristotle on which much speculation has been expended. It is said that while Plato recognized and appreciated the genius of Aristotle, and Aristotle was no less aware of the endowments of his teacher, quarrels arose between master and pupil nonetheless, when Aristotle's own ideas began to assert themselves.

But there were deep, underlying reasons for the cleavage between them, differences of philosophic temperament that caused Friedrich Schlegel to make his famous observation that "every man is born either a Platonist or an Aristotelian;" so great is, in one sense, the difference between the two philosophers, and so close, also, is their relationship, that they seem in these very words of Schlegel to have divided the philosophic world between them: one is born either a Platonist or an Aristotelian; there is no other choice!

Perhaps the best estimate of this situation is offered us by J. B. Mayer, in his *Ancient Philosophy from Thales to Cicero,* who makes the pertinent observation that "there seems to be every reason to believe that tradition has preserved the spirit, if not the precise facts, of the relationship between Aristotle and Plato when it attributes to Plato the saying that Aristotle was the intellect of his school and to Aristotle the epitaph in which Plato is described as 'one whom it would be profanity in a bad man even to praise'."

II. THOUGHT

Aristotle rejects the purely mechanistic interpretation of materialistic science. There is, for materialism, no end or purpose towards which our universe is tending; it is governed solely by mechanical laws. But, for Aristotle, mechanical causes are secondary ones — they explain only with reference to the behaviour of bodies in space. What Aristotle desires is a formal, teleological (purposeful) explanation to supersede the mechanistic one.

For Aristotle there is something in nature which is *essential*, and something which, by contrast, we may call *accidental*. The essential can be cognized by thought; but there is also a remainder, something *material* and *mechanical* in the individual physical phenomenon which is foreign to thought, foreign to reason or conception; and this appears in the individual thing as a result of the *matter in which the conception realizes* itself.

Aristotle disclaimed, on principle, any scientific insight, such as modern science attempts to find, in the individual and particular, apart from the universal imbedded in it. The individual instance was, for Aristotle, purely *accidental*, not to be explained conceptually; and he limited true science to that which is valid *universally*.

In short, the ideal of materialistic science was, for Aristotle, the quest of the non-essential, the accidental or merely incidental in the order of nature. But thought is in quest of the *essential* even in the accidental; thought conceives a *telos*, an *end*, aim or purpose to these mechanical sequences. And since all things have their *telos*, their end, purpose, or reason-for-being in themselves, the *entelechy* is the chief principle of the organic development of beings.

The *essence* is realized in every *phenomenon;* and this realization of essence in phenomenon, Aristotle calls *entelechy*. The cosmic processes aim at just this: the realization of the *essence in the phenomenon,* or of the *form in matter*. The fundamental relation in the universe is, for him, not a mechanical but a formative one, and he finds this formative relation best exemplified in the development of organisms and in man's artistic creations.

The aim of true science, then, is to discover *the universal in the particular, the essential in the accidental, form in matter, the essence in the phenomenon.*

Now, the Being which we grasp in conception is the *essence,* the general or *universal;* and this *general essence* realizes itself *in* the particular phenomenon. The entire process leads from potentiality to actuality and is a-chieved through motion. Evolution, or the principle of development, is, for Aristotle, the means whereby things attain their metaphysical status, from the lowest formation of matter to the highest forms.

Aristotle's aim was to discover the inherent structural and functional characteristics of the creative processes in the world. This meant, in each instance, to discover the form or Idea in the individual, for the form or Idea expressed that in a thing which made it what it was. There is no matter purely as such; all matter is matter only for a particular form. Unformed matter is nothing! Pure or unformed matter may arise as a limiting notion in our minds, but in reality, all matter is, in some way, formed; and this form becomes the matter for the next higher form. From form to higher form, we finally arrive at an ultimate Form, an end which is not itself subject to any higher end. This is the metaphysical goal of Aristotle's physics!

Matter, according to Aristotle, is merely *possible* or *potential,* and it has not, in itself, nor can have, the principle of motion or generation. Motion does not belong to matter; it belongs to form plus matter in process of formation. The characteristic of true Being is *action of form upon matter,* and this is the cause of motion in the world. That is how things come to be: 1. through an *impulse to be formed,* inherent in matter; and 2. through the *purposive motion, proceeding from the form.* Without these two essential factors of the development process, there would be no process at all.

Now motion, which is the means by which the process from matter to form, from potentiality to actuality, is constantly being realized, must have a primary and original source. As we go higher and higher in the scale of Being, we finally reach the notion of *pure Form,* absolute actuality without any admixture of matter — that which is unchangeable, immovable — independent and separate from all that moves and changes, and which is yet the cause of all generation and change; the *perfect Being* in which all possibility is at the same time actuality, the highest of all existences, and the best — the deity; this is the ultimate aim and end of all rational explanations and aspirations.

At every stage of development, the form which has become actualized in a particular material manifestation becomes the matter for the next higher form which is now striving for actualization. The form is the moving principle at every level of existence, and each stage of actualized form becomes the material for a still higher form which it strives to develop into; which higher form again becomes its moving principle, and so on and on until we reach a first form, a *pure Form*, matterless Form, the first link in the chain of motions, the first cause of motion, itself unmoved. Thus are we driven to the conception of a pure, perfect, motionless Form as the first cause or the principle of motion in the world. Motion would not be possible and could not be understood unless the chain of its causes had a *first cause* in the *pure Form*, which itself is not moved. This is Aristotle's *Prime Mover* — God — operating upon matter by exciting in matter the impulse to form itself, with the Prime Mover as its *first* as well as its *final cause*. God, through his absolute actuality, is thus the cause of all the upward striving in the universe; and the development of all things from the potential to the actual is achieved *not by any act of creation,* for the First Form or Prime Mover remains ever unmoved. Rather is there a natural tendency which all things have towards God; the world is drawn towards God as the lover towards the beloved—since God is the absolutely Real, the absolute Form, the absolutely

Good, the end of all effort and all desire. This is the reason for the tremendous influence of Aristotle on subsequent European thought: his was the first conceptual formulation of monotheism, *monotheism conceptually formulated.* From the pantheism of Xenophanes, through Plato, the stream of Greek theological speculation attains, with Aristotle, the *theistic* and *transcendental* form which was to permeate all later Western theology and religion; for the God of Aristotle is a self-conscious being, distinct from the world, an absolute Mind or Spirit; hence we have here *spiritual monotheism* as the end-result of Greek philosophic speculation.

For Aristotle, "God ... is the transcendental unmoved mover, who guides the world as its final cause by reason of the perfection of his pure thought . . ." *(Werner Jaeger: "Aristotle").*

But this idea of the Unmoved Mover is Platonic in essence. Plato's transcendental Form as a final cause of motion in the same way as the beloved moves the lover, is, in fact, the principle of the Unmoved Mover, which is the same power described by Plato as the longing of the sensible world for the perfect Ideas.

Thus it is Plato's teleological metaphysics that is the starting-point of Aristotle's metaphysics and theology — a position which he never abandoned.

> "The divine spirituality is conceived of by Aristotle in a purely intellectual manner; its essential nature is solely thought directed upon itself. All doing, and willing, has as its aim an object, distinct from the doer or the willer, but divine mind, being pure form, needs no

object; he is self-sufficient, and his knowledge of himself, which has no other goal than itself, is his eternal blessedness. He acts upon the world . . . through the longing which the world has for him. The world, and all that transpires in it, arises from the *longing of matter after God.*

"Matter (which is the merely potential) is that which is moved without itself moving anything; God (the solely actual) is that which moves without itself being moved; between these two extremes, the entire order of things exists . . . and these, in their totality, Aristotle calls "Nature", or the "world", according to present usage. Nature is, accordingly, the *connected system of living beings viewed as a unity*, in which matter, developing ever higher, from form to form, through all its manifold particular shapes, approaches the motionless Being of the Deity, and imitating this, takes it up into itself potentially." *(Windelband: "A History of Philosophy")*

The universe itself is eternal, a perfect sphere whose circumference is composed of a divine element, the ether; and the sphere is carried around in circular motion through the immediate influence of the Deity. In it are the fixed stars, themselves, in a measure, divine. Above all this is the abode of divinity, in which there is no movement, no body, no space and no time. The lower planetary spheres have a less perfect movement. Still, throughout space all is ordered with perfect regularity according to natural law. Only in the sublunary region, extending from the moon to the earth, which is furthest removed from the First Mover, does irregularity appear through Spontaneity and Chance, which impede the working of Nature. Yet, even here we find a constant and progressive movement from inorganic to organic, from plant to animal, from life which is only nutritive and sensitive to life which is locomotive, and, finally, *rational* in man.

The human soul is a microcosm, uniting in itself all the faculties of the lower orders of life, and possessing, in addition, the divine and immortal faculty of *reason.* Each thing attains its specific end by fulfilling the work for which it is designed by nature. Man achieves his happiness by the unobstructed exercise of *his* special endowment, the *rational* and *virtuous* part of his nature; happiness is the natural accompaniment of such rational activity.

Virtue, which may be described as perfected nature, belongs potentially to man's nature, but it becomes actual by the repetition of acts performed in accordance with reason. It can be intellectual and it can be moral, depending on whether the activity relates to the purely rational part of the soul or to the emotional part, in which case it is capable of being influenced by reason but is not, in itself, rational.

To return to Aristotle's theology however. The Aristotelian God is no cold, inert and uninspiring deity. He is more than an intellectual Idea, a mind-created Object. An element of genuine religiosity, in the modern sense of the term, enters here, perhaps for the first time in Western theological speculation.

"The attitude," says Gomperz, "which the Stagirite assumed towards the great riddles of the universe may be described as monotheism tinged with pantheism . . . His conviction of the strict unity of all nature, drove him to the notion of one Director of the universe." (Theodor Gomperz: *Greek Thinkers*)

Gomperz speaks also of "the deep earnestness with which Aristotle . . . tried to bridge the gulf between the conflicting claims of emotion and intellect."

Hence he could bestow deep religious feeling, often rising to a level of religious fervor, upon the Object of his intellectual construction, the Unmoved Mover, or First Cause of all the motion, life and rationality in the universe. The first Uncaused Cause, the source of motion and creative unfoldment in the world, is also the divine goal of all that has purpose in Nature. Drawn by the inherent power of their divine essence, all things are inclined towards the divine; and the inner direction of things, like the mystical attractive power which the lover feels in the presence of the beloved, shapes the destiny of man and the universe. His God thus has a definite spiritual significance which impelled Aristotle to adoration of Him.

But the knowledge of God is also, and at the same time, for Aristotle, a good criterion for earthly values. All the goods of life, he tells us in his *Eudemian Ethics*, have moral value insofar as they help man to know God.

Furthermore, there arises, for Aristotle, a new *science,*

wherein the ethical sphere comes into contact with the theoretical: this is "Metaphysics" and it is also "Theology" — the science of first principles and of a unified world-view.

Much has been made of Aristotle's devotion to science and scientific inquiry, and some have tried to make of him a pure exponent of scientific method and theory. It has been pointed out that his interests lay primarily in the observation and elucidation of scientific facts, while metaphysics and theology were of secondary interest to him. But this view ignores the far-reaching consequences of his unifying intellectual aim which, on the one hand, as scientific, would not relinquish a single scrap of evidence, and, on the other hand, would not omit the metaphysical and theological. Aristotle relegated each to its proper realm, but the priority always went to the metaphysical — whether it be in the universe or in man.

In this connection it may be well to quote Aristotle's own words on the subject, from the introduction to his work *On the Parts of Animals:*

Aristotle was now immersed in scientific study and the analysis of empirical data. Yet, here is what he tells us:

> "Of things constituted by nature some are ungenerated, imperishable, and eternal, while others are subject to generation and decay. The former are of incomparable excellence, and divine, but not as readily accessible to knowledge. The evidence that might throw light on them,

and on the problems which we long to solve
concerning them, is furnished but meagerly by
generation; whereas concerning perishable plants
and animals we have abundant information,
living as we do in their midst, and ample data
which may be collected concerning their various
kinds, provided we apply ourselves to them
with sufficient effort. Both departments, however, have their special charm. The meager
conceptions to which we can attain of celestial
things give us, by their excellence, more pleasure than all our knowledge of the world in
which we live; just as a half glimpse of persons that we love is more delightful to us than
a protracted view of other things, whatever
their number and size. On the other
hand, as regards certainty and completeness,
our knowledge of terrestrial things has the advantage. Their greater nearness and affinity
to us balances somewhat the loftier interest of
the heavenly objects of the higher philosophy.
Therefore, having treated of the celestial world,
as far as our conjectures could reach, we now
proceed to animals, without omitting, to the
best of our ability, any member of the kingdom, however ignoble. For if these have no
graces to charm the senses, yet even these, by
disclosing to intellectual perception the artistic
spirit that designed them, give immense pleasure to all who can trace causal links and are
inclined to philosophy."

ARISTOTLE

This reveals to us the spirit of Aristotle's thought and his unswerving devotion to whatever reveals the infinite and divine in the world.

We find here again support for the theory that the underlying principle of Aristotle's philosophy, natural or divine, was to trace from the meanest of things to the most sublime aspects of the universe, a purposeful, designing intelligence, revealing and unfolding itself before the eyes of the intelligent observer as well as for the mind of the mystical aspirant. It is for this reason that the minutest of details never escape him. The long arm of his metaphysical quest reaches out to the most insignificant of things, to the most tender emotions, to the celestial heavens and the body and soul of man — always searching, but with a view to their organic unity and ultimate teleology, until the universal absorbs the particular in the very act of explaining it. This is the reason for Aristotle's consuming desire, expressed through infinite patience and with the most meticulous care, to reveal all that nature will yield to the inquiring mind. Thus, while for Plato the primary objective was the archetypal world of Ideas away from and beyond the world of appearances, for Aristotle the supremacy of the mental over the material revealed itself to the inquiring spirit of man in each and every particle of reality and in the smallest as well as in the most universal parts of creation.

This is the all-important aspect to Aristotle's thought that those who are enamoured of "Aristotle's scientific spirit" seem to forget; and it is the aspect which it is the glory of the great Aristotelian scholar, Werner Jaeger, in our day, to have brought to light:

"All the lines of Aristotle's philosophy", he writes, "run together in his metaphysics, while it, on the other hand, stretches out into all other disciplines . . .

"Aristotle builds the Platonic world . . . into the actual world, and gives it the highest position therein, the place from which the light of the eternal shines upon this world . . ."

(Werner Jaeger: Aristotle)

Plato's teleological theology thus forms the starting point of Aristotle's metaphysics. But the metaphysical was natural to Aristotle's thought while his specific views shaped themselves as a result of a conflict between the religious and the cosmological convictions that he had inherited from Plato.

His own mind is perhaps predominantly analytical and scientific. He believes however, and firmly, in something that transcends the limits of human experience though it shines through every aspect of that experience.

The main problems, therefore, that troubled the minds of the medieval religious philosophers—Christian, Jewish and Islamic — were to be found in Aristotle, rationalistically approached. Thus he became, in the middle ages, the light to all those who searched for a rational vindication of their religious needs: they found in Aristotle intellectual anchor and mooring. Those who found themselves torn by a conflict between faith and knowledge turned to Aristotle for sustenance and support. This conflict between faith and reason was, in fact, something which was utterly foreign to the Greek spirit, but it found its first expression in the Greek Aristotle. So deeply grounded are both religious fervor as well as the desire for intellectual verification in Aristotle's thought! Despite the intellectual severity of his conception of the divine Being therefore, he could arouse a deep faith which no analytical scrutiny could attack. The philosophers and mystics of the Middle Ages saw this clearly. Hence Aristotle became their human god. And therein lies the secret of his immortality.

III. THE ROMANCE OF ARISTOTLE'S INTELLECTUAL LEGACY

There is no more astonishing chapter in the history of thought than the fabulous odyssey of Aristotle's spiritual progeny, the literary fruits of his fertile mind. Lost for many centuries under the blanket of the dark ages, his works were discovered and rediscovered, translated and retranslated by Arabs, Jews and Christians — until all the gold of his mental mine was extracted, examined, re-examined, and finally assimilated with all that was most precious to Western man, first in logic and philosophy, then in religion, and finally, in science.

For almost a thousand years the thoughts of Aristotle lay buried under the weight of Plato's far more powerful influence which, especially in the mysticism of the neo-Platonists, survived as a force of great spiritual importance. The Paripatetic school carried on the tradition of Aristotle, but little of Aristotle's own work was preserved intact; and, as might be expected, with the later

Paripatetics, there was more misinterpretation than interpretation of the original Aristotle!

With the submergence of the classical world in the floods of Christianity, at about the year 500 A.D., the earlier and more elementary parts of Aristotle's "Organon", in a Latin translation and commentary by Boethius, began to be circulated as the backbone of what in medieval times was called "Dialectic" which, along with "Grammar" and "Rhetoric", formed the three subjects of the *Trivium* or mainstay of medieval learning. The schools attached to cathedrals and the Benedictine monasteries thus depended, between the years 500-1200 A.D., on Aristotle's *Logic* for the more solid fare of their learning; for it was "Dialectic", with Aristotle's Logic as a base, that was the chief instrument of thought, and therefore, outside of the purely theological studies, the main source of learning in the Middle Ages.

Then, in the twelfth century, a new chapter begins in Aristotle's growing influence; for logic, and dialectical thinking, are no longer studied as a separate discipline but are applied to the problems of theology! The solution of theological problems seemed to depend in large measure upon whether one accepted the Platonic "Ideas" or the Aristotelian "Forms"; and there arose a warfare between the nominalists (who held that the universals of thought were mere names) and the realists (who believed in the objective reality of universals). In the meantime, more and more of Aristotle's works became available through the Crusades, which brought to the West the almost complete body of Aristotle's works, preserved in Arabic translations, and the era of Scholasticism began,

which strove to reconcile the teachings of Aristotle with
Biblical revelation and the inspired wisdom of the Church
Fathers.

Between 1200 and 1270 the general body of Aristotle's
writings began to be imported from the two great centers
of Arabic learning, Cordova and Constantinople, into the
Universities of Paris, Oxford and Cambridge.

The physical, metaphysical and psychological treatises
of Aristotle became the objects of Arabic study and
scholarship from about 800 A.D., after the conquest of
Syria by the Arabs, in the 7th Century. There had arisen,
among the Arabs, great Aristotelian commentators, especially Ibn-Sina (known as Avicenna) who died at Hamadon
in 1037 A.D. and Ibn-Roshd (known as Averroes) who
died at Cordova in 1198, and Arabic translations of Aristotle began to penetrate the Latin West towards the
year 1200.

These were the result of two, three, sometimes four,
derivative translations — Latin translations made from
Hebrew versions of Arabic manuscripts which in turn
were based upon intervening Syriac versions of the original Greek text. And these translations and commentaries
were in each case made to suit the Arabic, Syrian or
Hebrew commentators. They were consequently suspected
of being detrimental to the Church and to true Christian
orthodoxy. For a time, a Papal edict forbade the learning
or teaching of Aristotle. But the number of "Aristotelians" grew by leaps and bounds; and Aristotle's works
found their way into the laps of scholars despite the
Papal edict against them.

Then, in the year 1204, during the fourth Crusade,

when Constantinople fell to the Christians and Latin clergy settled in the Byzantine Empire, two of them (both Dominicans), William of Moerbecke and Henry of Brabant, translated, at the behest of the great Dominican scholar, St. Thomas Aquinas, and in collaboration with him, many of the works of Aristotle from the original Greek (1260-1270 A.D.).

Thus began that great study of Aristotle initiated by St. Thomas in his masterwork "The Summa Theologica", consisting of commentaries and attempts at reconciling and co-ordinating the theology, the science and the metaphysics of Aristotle with the teachings and wisdom of the Christian religion and the Church.

In St. Thomas, the miracle of the resurrection of Aristotle was literally achieved. Sixteen hundred years after Aristotle's death, his thought lives anew in the legacy of St. Thomas Aquinas. Not in St. Thomas alone, however, but in all medieval thought — Christian, Hebrew and Arabic — wherever the flame of metaphysical inquiry was kept burning in the leading representative thinkers of the day, Aristotle survived, and his teachings inspired men to a rationalistic approach to universal problems.

There is a deeper Aristotle, who shines through his scientific research, logic and metaphysics, as well as through his sublime conception of the divine being. It was this Aristotle who so enthralled generation after generation of scholars and philosophers in the middle ages. Always in quest of the magic point of equillibrium between intellect and emotion which spells the perfectly balanced individual and issues in the happiness of the well-regulated life, Aristotle reveals in himself such a

ARISTOTLE

well-balanced mind. Despite his absorbing interest in
science, he aimed at the joys of the highest intellectual
ventures, which reach beyond sense and logic and enter
the celestial sphere of metaphysical theology. Because of
this he has been accorded immortal life in the minds
of men.

ST. AUGUSTINE

ST. AUGUSTINE

(354-430)

O Beauty, so ancient and so fresh . . .
What do I love when I love Thee? . . . I
asked the earth, and it answered, 'I am not
He;' . . . I asked the sea and the deeps and
the living creeping things, and they answered:
'We are not thy God; seek above us.' I asked
the moving air and the whole air with its inhabitants answered: 'Anaximenes was deceived;
I am not God.' I asked the heavens, the sun,
moon, stars; 'nor', said they, 'are we the God
whom thou seekest.' And I replied unto all
these: . . . 'since you are not God, tell me
something concerning Him.' And they cried out
with a loud voice: 'He made us'."

(Confessions)

Augustine was convinced that no rational creature that
"makes use of its reason" can be completely devoid of
an awareness of God. Except for "a few in whom
nature has become outrageously depraved, the whole race
of man acknowledges God as the maker of this world."

And, as for himself, the existence of God was a fundamental postulate of his thought.

"I ever believed . . . that Thou wert . . . though I was ignorant as to what was to be thought of Thy substance and what way led or led back to Thee." And, none of the "blasphemous questionings . . . which I read in the self-contradicting philosophers, could wrest this belief from me 'That Thou art' whatsoever Thou wert (what I knew not) . . . " Only those who are degraded and depraved beyond measure, thinks Augustine, could doubt that God exists. In all other men the light of reason still shines, despite the general depravity and corruption of human nature, to which his own nature amply testified.

To prove this, Augustine gave the world his remarkable "Confessions", the most candid book of its kind ever written. These confessions are addressed not only to his God, "in a secret *exultation with trembling*, and a secret sorrow with hope; but to the ears of the believing . . . sharers of my joy, and partners in my mortality, my fellow-citizens, and fellow-pilgrims, who are gone before, or are to follow, companions on my way."

After a life of dissoluteness and dissipation, sin and error, he at last came upon the light of Truth opening wide the gates of eternal Beauty before him. And his reason was not the least among the instruments that helped him attain this supernal vision.

Augustine was a product of Platonic rationalism and Plotinian mysticism, to which he added his Christian indoctrination. His entire mental life was a perpetual struggle with the problem of the nature of God and the Christian triune God: the three persons in the One God. So that, both as rationalist and Christian mystic, Augustine's chief task was to make clear the nature of God — to himself and to the world.

When still a young man, he came under the influence of neo-Platonism. This turned out to be of immense significance in his life; and it was an epoch-making event in the Western world, the first important contact between Christian religious belief and Greek philosophic thought.

Augustine had already embraced Christianity when he came across the *Enneads* of Plotinus. What did he find there, in Plotinus and neo-Platonism, that so entranced him? The "Idea of the Good", of Plato, had been transformed by Plotinus into the principle of the *One*. Plato himself must have had an inkling of this important change from the Idea of the Good to the Principle of the One, when he said: "If the one is not, nothing is." The One is that without which nothing else could be. The existence of everything depends upon this eternally subsisting Unity.

This *One*, however, must not be confused with the numerical one. It is not just another number! It is that *Unity* from which all multiplicity flows.

From this One, ever-creative and ever-creating, a second principle arises. And the name of this second principle? "The Intellect" — begotten of the One and its only offspring; closer, therefore, to the One than anything else in all creation, and the cause of all the diversity of created things. Plotinus called this, *Nous*, Mind or Intellect.

Augustine could find no rest until he would achieve the great transformation: *from Plotinus to Christianity*. How, he asked himself, could the God of Christianity be expressed in terms of the Plotinian philosophy?

For many years he labored on this problem. The clue came at last: the three persons of the Christian Trinity *were* all contained herein: the Christian God with all His essential attributes — God, the Father, (the One), the Word (the Intellect), and God, the author of all creation!

Plotinus had expressed the perennial way in which reason grapples with the problem of divinity, or the being of God. Augustine's task was now clearly mapped out before him: *to give this Plotinian theology Christian form.*

———

Any intellectual attempt to comprehend Augustine will fail to do justice to this unique individual unless another factor closely related to all his endeavors is first acknowledged: his attachment to humanity and to human problems; for, here is a saint in whom the flame of Life glows with an inextinguishable ardor, and in whom even the most philosophic utterances bear witness to the pulse-beat of our common humanity; the same volcanic, human passion, therefore, that drove him to taste the fruits of the most sensuous delights, to error and sin, now manifests itself in the sublime emotions which permeate his thought.

Thus, it may be truly said of Augustine, as indeed it has been said, that "he infused philosophy with passion; and learned to put wise order into his emotions

even when he lost none of them. His sermons range
from the sublimest mysticism to the proper heating of
churches", but, "whatever Augustine says, sooner or later
you will realize it is your fellow-man who is saying it."
(C.C. Martindale)

It is this man, thus constituted, so essentially human,
who now feels that he must "hand himself over to what
man's life really aches for — the supernatural love of
God." *(Ibid)* For, says Augustine, in one of his sublime
moments:

> "He always is, nor has been and is not, nor
> is but has not been; but as He never will not
> be, so He never was not. And He is whole
> everywhere." *(De Trin.)*

And the soul of man, says Augustine, "lives, and
moves, and is in Him, and therefore can remember
Him."

"It is of no little knowledge if, before we can know
what God is, we can know what He is not. For certainly He is neither heaven nor earth! nor, as it were,
heaven and earth; nor any of the things that we see
in the heavens; nor any such thing as we do not see, but
which perhaps is in the heavens. Again, if you were to
magnify in imagination the light of the sun as much
as you can, making it greater or brighter, a thousand
times, or times without number, this too is not
God. And if we think of the Angels as pure spirits
animating celestial bodies . . . brought together into one,
and become one, no such thing as this is God. And
the same would be true if you were to think of these
spirits without bodies — a thing indeed most difficult

for carnal thought to conceive. Behold and see, O soul bowed down by the corruptible body, and weighed down by the multitude and variety of earthly thoughts; behold and see, if thou canst, that God is truth . . . Ask not what is truth; for immediately the mists of corporeal images and the clouds of phantasms will intervene and will disturb the calm which at the first moment shone forth to thee, when I said Truth; see what there remaineth, if thou canst, in that first moment in which thou wert dazzled as by a flash, when there was said, Truth. But thou canst not; thou wilt fall back into those familiar, earthly things." *(De Trin.)*

No wonder that the faithful flocked to hear him while the faithless were convinced and converted! And yet, this man was human, all-too human. How human? Even in his relationship with his mother we find the human pattern: he loved her dearly, but refused her counsels, disregarded her wishes, was deaf to her pleas, and shortened her life.

"She commanded me", Augustine tells us, *(Confessions)* "and with much earnestness forewarned me, that I should not commit fornication, and especially that I should never defile any man's wife. These seemed to me no better than women's counsels, which it would be a shame for me to follow ... I was embarrassed among my equals to be guilty of less impudency than they were who bragged mightily of their mischief; yea, and boasted the more the more beastly they had been; and I took pleasure to do it, not for the pleasure of the

act only, but for the praise of it also; . . .
and when I lacked opportunity to commit a
wickedness that should make me as bad as the
lost, I would feign to have done what I never
did."

When only eighteen years of age, Augustine found
that he was the father of a son, "Adeodatus" (gift of God)
—"son of my sin" Augustine called him, and he loved
him with a tenderness rarely recorded in the love of a
father for his child. This boy was the offspring of
Augustine's attachment to a concubine to whom he was
devoted for fourteen years. It was at this stage of his
life that, as he says, he was willing to pray: "God, grant
me chastity — but not yet"; for his sensuous nature all
but possessed him; yet, his desire for truth was equally
as strong, for there had awakened in him a burning
desire for spiritual and intellectual stimulation and
comfort.

Augustine was blessed with an inquiring mind: "my
unquiet mind was altogether intent to seek for learning"
(Confessions) especially in matters philosophical;
so much so that he called Plato a "demigod" *(City of
God),* and even after he became a Christian, Augustine still revered his Platonic lineage; in fact, to the
end of his days he remained a Platonist. Most important,
however, for later generations, was the fact that the
subtleties of Platonism, Aristotelianism and neo-Platonism so sharpened his mind that he could defend his
Christian faith with a sublime logical eloquence. His
classical Greek training thus made it possible for him
to become the most convincing as well as the most subtle

apologist for the Christian religion. Augustine died in 430 A.D. For a thousand years thereafter the energies of the best minds in the Western world were devoted to the construction of logical edifices to prove the existence of God.

But all of the subsequent proofs for God's being find expression in this first great Christian philosopher. They are strewn throughout his vast literary empire, comprising more than a thousand items — books, letters, sermons, dialogues. Seven of these proofs have been listed, though they are not all of equal value and not entirely independent of one another.

Augustine the Rationalist

God, Augustine says, in a revealing phrase, is He "Whom it is permitted to no one to know as He is but whom no one is permitted not to know." In other words, we must acknowledge the Being of God; for, normally, some knowledge of God is a common and universal experience.

"Rare is the man who says in his heart, 'There is no God'."

The fool may say it, but this is really due to a corruption of his soul; since error of this sort, which makes the soul so blind through a love of the world as to find no room for a love of God, — such error is only the folly of fools, whereby "God gave them over to a false power of perceiving."

In short, no man who makes proper use of his

reason, that is, no man who is not either a fool or insane, can deny that there is a God.

Secondly, according to Augustine, we have the testimony of the Bible. This is the argument from Holy Scriptures or authority. Genesis tells us: "In the beginning God created the heavens and the earth." In addition, we have in the *New Testament* the testimony of men who saw certain deeds performed "which could never have been done if there were no God." And, in the *Old Testament*, we have utterances by the prophets regarding events the fulfillment of which "we now read and which indeed we behold." These predictions are proofs of God, who alone could have inspired these men with such prophetic sight.

Then, there is the famous ontological argument for the existence of God, which finds its first formulation in Augustine. By this argument Augustine seeks to prove God's existence from the very idea of God. All the elements of Anselm's later ontological argument for the existence of God may be found here in Augustine. The ontological proof proceeds from idea to reality, from the idea of God's Being to proof of his existence. So, God can only be described properly "as having supreme and original existence" for "that exists in the highest sense of the word, which is throughout like itself, which cannot in any part be corrupted or changed, which is not subject to time, and which admits of no variation in its present state as compared with its former condition. This is existence in its true sense." *(De Moribus Man.)* Of God alone is all this true; therefore the idea of God involves true existence; he cannot be conceived unless as existing, and he cannot be conceived as not existing.

The moment we think of God we think of such a nature "than which nothing more excellent or more exalted exists . . . above all visible and bodily natures . . . above all intelligent and spiritual natures that are subject to change . . . nor could anyone be found to believe that any being to whom there exists a superior is God. And so all agree that God is that Being who excels in dignity all other subjects." . . . Furthermore, God is "the supreme Good, . . . than which nothing can be conceived better . . . the good of all good." Here, supreme being and supreme goodness coincide; because in either case there is no corruption possible. The more of goodness, the more of being; the highest good, the most real being: God.

We proceed thus from the idea of God to His necessary being, from thought to existence; and this is the beginning of medieval metaphysical realism which was to dominate Scholastic thought for a thousand years.

The ontological proof, then, seeks to demonstrate that God, and the existence of God, may be deduced from the idea of existence itself, if existence is taken in its highest and supreme sense: perfect, true and original existence.

Now, all of the rational proofs for the existence of God involve a transition from thought to reality, from idea to object; and, as if to forestall the modern arguments against such a derivation of the *being* of God from the *idea* of God, Augustine warns us that in all rational proofs for God's existence faith is an essential prerequisite.

Reason alone is insufficient; and proofs by reason alone are inadequate. Reason can only demonstrate what faith has already accepted. Rational demonstration can only induce conviction when faith has already embraced as true what the demonstration seeks to substantiate.

In short, knowledge of God through reason must always be incomplete. Faith alone is sufficient; faith is sure; the way of faith is direct. Reason, by itself, may lead one astray; faith should precede reason, for, there is always the danger, in the case of reason, of distorted vision, through sin; but there is no conflict between the two, reason and faith. In fact, whoever has not found the way of faith *must* resort to reason; but it is a poor substitute for faith, thinks Augustine. On the other hand, when one first *believes* that God exists, then the rationality of that belief can be easily *demonstrated*.

But the rational proofs for the existence of God do not end with the ontological one. This ontological proof attempts, as we have seen, to demonstrate that God exists by an analysis of the *idea* of God; as such it is actually a proof by an examination of what is present *in the idea*. God's existence, however, may also be proven through his creations. All creation proclaims God's existence; but *knowledge* of God is given to man alone, through his mind or soul.

And this leads us to another proof for the existence of God. It is proof by inner vision or the testimony of the eye of the soul which can lead us to a knowledge of the divine being as the Unchangeable Light. This sight of the divine light is in reality the same as the contemplation of divine wisdom. But we must be prepared for this by a graduated ascension toward the Eternal Light.

The soul must pass from motion to sensation, thence to knowledge, to morality, to tranquillity, until it arrives at the contemplative life, and thereby, finally, to the contemplation of the divine.

This last stage is accessible to those only who have been cleansed and purified through the other ascending stages leading to this final stage of the soul — the contemplative stage.

No one can see or contemplate God himself — the contemplation therefore, as Augustine describes it, is " . . . a light, a melody, a fragrance . . . an embracement" *(Confessions)* which *comes from* God and testifies to his Being. This is the light of Truth, above the senses, above memory, the pure light of Truth. In the contemplation of Truth we discover God.

And this is Augustine's great discovery: "Where I found Truth there found I my God, the Truth itself; which since I learned, I have not forgotten." *(Confessions)* This is the final goal of the pilgrimage of the soul, for it is then that the voice of God speaks to us. No one who has once been privileged thus to hear the voice of God in his heart and to behold the Truth through the inner eye of the soul can ever again doubt God's existence. "It is easier to doubt that I live than to believe that Truth is not." *(Confessions)*

But, there are those of *inadequate spiritual perception.* For those whose inner light flickers dimly there is yet

another proof by which they, too, may easily discover
God's existence; namely, through what they see with
their *physical* eyes: in other words, the created world,
a world which bespeaks a creator, for "we may detect,
as it were, His footprints . . . even in those things that
are beneath us. They could not so much as exist, or be
embodied in any shape, or observe any law, had they
not been made by Him who supremely is, and is
supremely good and supremely wise." *(The City of God)*

> "Ask the loveliness of the earth, the loveli-
> ness of the sea, the loveliness of the wide airy
> spaces, the loveliness of the sky, the order of
> the stars, the sun making the day light with its
> rays; ask the moon tempering the darkness of
> the night that follows, the living things which
> move in the waters, which tarry on land, which
> fly in the air; ask the souls that are hidden,
> the bodies that are perceptible; the visible
> things which must be governed, the invisible
> things which govern — ask all these things, and
> they will all answer thee, See, we are lovely.
> Their loveliness is their confession. And these
> lovely but mutable things, who has made them,
> save Beauty immutable?" *(Serm.)*

The order of created things is only the effect, the
derivative (created existence) — from an original *uncreated* existence, the uncaused first cause of the world.
Thus are we led, even through our senses, to arrive at
a *first cause* from which the effect, the contingent, i.e.
created things, follow.

All things in heaven and earth declare: "We are not God, but He made us."

The world that is subject to change, dissolution and decay, is contingent, unstable, unreal.

Eternal being alone is real being — unchanged being.

"I beheld all other things that are beneath Thee, and I saw that they had neither any absolute being, nor had they absolutely no being at all. They have being because they are of Thee; and they have no being, because they are not that which Thou art!" *(Conf.)* Thus is *our reason* led to a first cause, the cause of the world of created things, which is *God.*

Furthermore, the universe is well-ordered — another evidence for the being of God. Everything, from seed to sun, reveals a preconceived plan:

"As in the seed there are invisibly and at one time all that which in time will grow into a tree, so the universe must be conceived — since God created all things at the same time — as having had within it all the things which were made when the day of creation came . . ."

And, there is purpose and design in nature: See how each animal "puts forth the senses, the eyes to see, the ears to hear, the nostrils to smell, the taste to discern flavors, — all the organs, in short, to execute their respective functions."

Everywhere we observe form, order, measure, — all of which implies *supreme* order, *supreme* measure, *supreme* form. But God himself is *transcendent* to all measure, form, or order; for He is "above every measure . . .

above every form, above every order" — "ineffable and singular potency."

And then, how much *beauty* is revealed in the created world! This beauty must be derived from a Beauty transcendent and immutable. It could not have created itself!

Did not Plotinus notice this too? this unmistakable proof of God in the world, evidenced everywhere, in the beauty of flowers and foliage, which proves "that from the supreme God, whose beauty is unseen and ineffable, providence reaches down even to these earthly things here below . . . all these frail and perishing things could not have so exquisite and elaborate a beauty, had they not been fashioned by Him whose unseen and unchangeable beauty continually pervades all things." *(The City of God)*

Lastly, Augustine foreshadows Descartes' argument (Cogito ergo sum: I think, therefore I am), by pointing out that the very fact of error implies the existence of him who errs. Our own existence we cannot doubt, no matter what else we may doubt: "If a man doubts, he lives."

But we not only exist; we also have life and a mind or soul. There are, according to Augustine, three grades of being: that which has only existence, such as a stone; living existences, such as animals; and man, who has existence, life, *and a mind or soul.* Augustine then argues that, if there is a higher being still, which is above the highest that we know of (the soul or mind of man) then this being, superior to reason, is Truth, and this Being also is God! Mathematical truths which deal with unchanging realities, and wisdom "in which the supreme Truth is discerned and known," find their source in this higher Being which is God.

There are certain truths comprising wisdom that are common to all rational men, and which are as clear and certain as are the propositions of mathematics: that the incorruptible is superior to the corruptible, the eternal to the temporal. These are immutable truths, says Augustine.

They lead us to believe in an eternal Truth, above the soul or reason which discovers it. And this eternal, immutable Truth is *God*.

Furthermore, our minds must behold perfection before we can even judge whether things are perfect or not; we must have the *idea of perfect beauty* before we can judge of beautiful things, the *idea of goodness* before we can know what is good in the world of created things — these are all eternal elements through which our imperfect world manifests the *idea of perfection*. God shines through by way of these eternal things, and only because there exists a Being in whom perfection, goodness, beauty, eternity are absolutely, immutably real, are perfection, beauty, eternity, conceivable at all in the imperfect world of created things. To know these absolute things we must know *Truth* or *God*. This is *the* good of the soul. "For me to cling to God is good."

If this anticipates Spinoza's doctrine of the knowledge of God as the highest good or virtue of the mind, by twelve hundred years, we may find other of Augustine's thoughts expressed in almost Spinozistic words:

"All substance that is not a created thing is God."

"Other things that are called essences or substances admit of accidents, whereby a change, whether great or small, is produced in them. But there can be no accident of this kind in respect of God; and therefore He who is God is the only immutable substance or essence, to whom Being certainly . . . most especially and most truly belongs."

"For God is more truly thought than expressed; and He exists more truly than He is thought."

"The striving after God is therefore the desire of beatitude, the attainment of God is beatitude itself . . . we attain Him, not by becoming entirely what He is, but in nearness to Him . . . and in being inwardly illumined and occupied by His truth and holiness. He is light itself; it is given to us to be illumined by that light."

"Evil is that which falls away from essence and tends to non-being . . . It tends to make that which is, cease to be."

Augustine the Mystic

Augustine's devotion to the idea of God's existence does not end with the rational note. There are, in addition, numerous and abundant instances of his close personal relationship to God which ring true to his nature and which find expression in melodious mystical effusions. Here all is forsaken except his love of the eternal God who is now an ineffable but intimate confidant:

"But yet when I love Thee, what is it that I love? Not the beauty of any body, not the order of time, not the clearness of this light

that so gladdens our eyes, nor the harmony of
sweet songs, the fragrancy of flowers, or spices
of aromatical odours, not manna, nor honey,
nor limbs delightful to the embrace of flesh
and blood. None of these things do I love, in
loving my God. Yet do I love a kind of light,
a kind of voice, a kind of odour, a kind of
food, a kind of embrace, when I love my God,
Who is the light, the voice, the odour, the
food, the embracing of my inward man. When
that light shineth into my soul which is not
confined to place, when that voice soundeth
which is not snatched away by time, when that
odour pours forth which is not scattered by
the air, when that food excites a taste which
is unconsumed by eating, when that embrace is
enjoyed which is not torn asunder by satiety:
this it is which I love when I love my God."
(Conf.)

Nor does he reserve these experiences solely for himself; he fain would share them:

"If thou dost love to see thy God, if in this
exile thou sighest with that love; behold the
Lord thy God maketh trial of thee, saying, 'do
what thou wilt, fulfill thy desires, prolong
wickedness, augment luxuriousness, think whatever pleaseth lawful. I will not punish thee
for this, I will not send thee to hell, I will
only deny thee My face'. If thou hast been
horrorstruck, thou hast loved! If at this that
was said to thee, 'Thy God will deny thee His

face,' if at these words thy whole heart hath trembled, if in the not seeing thy God thou hast imagined a great punishment — thou hast loved truly." *(Serm.)*

Perhaps the best of Augustine is to be found here, in these touching deliverances of his mystical nature, abounding in genuine experiences and ecstatic insight. For God is not any "ordinary light which all flesh may look upon." He is the unchangeable Light beheld only "with the eye of my soul . . . He that knows the Truth, knows what that Light is; and he that knows It, knows Eternity." *(Conf.)*

"All things can be said of God, yet is nothing worthily said of God. Nothing is wider than this utter want." *(Joan. Evang.)*

"With a hidden goad Thou didst urge me, that I might be restless until such time as the sight of my mind might discern Thee for certain." *(Conf.)*

There is a passage in Augustine describing a scene after his conversion, of which it has been said that it has the massiveness of Milton, and, we might add, the simple beauty of Dante.

Augustine and his mother are sitting one day by a window overlooking a garden in the courtyard; they talk of God and the love of God and, for a moment, Augustine thinks that they actually rose to an understanding of God.

Here are his words: "And while we were thus talking of His wisdom and panting for it with all our heart, we *did*, for one instant, attain to touch it; then, sighing, and leaving the first fruits of our spirit bound to it, we returned to the sound of our own tongue . . ."

Reason and Revelation

Despite Augustine's mystical tendencies however, we must never underestimate his trust in reason; for even as he extolled faith he also confided in reason. In fact, his analysis of reason and faith in matters of religion is one of the master creations of Augustine's fertile mind.

He observes that it is by our reason that we are led to see even the fact that faith must precede reason. In every instance our reason must tell us what we are to believe before we can believe it. Belief is thinking to which our acquiescence has been added.

"Who does not see that thinking is prior to believing? For no one believes anything until he has first *thought* that it ought to be believed. For . . . it is necessary that everything which is believed should be believed after thought has preceded it; even belief itself is nothing else than thinking with assent. Not everyone who thinks believes, since indeed, many think in order that they may not believe; but everyone who believes, thinks . . . thinks in believing and believes in thinking." *(De praedest. sanct.)*

There is no conflict between reason and revelation, since God is the source of both. Hence it is right and proper for one to seek to understand what one believes. "Far from us the thought that God detests that whereby he has made us superior to other animals; far from us an assent of pure faith which should relieve us from accepting or demanding proof."

But faith is the crowning phase of our spiritual activity; it is the result of God's grace: in this sense it is the beginning and end of knowledge — the eternal quest of which understanding is the reward.

"Understanding is the reward of faith. Therefore seek not to understand in order that you may believe, but believe that you may understand." *(Joan. Evang.)*

As a young man, Manichaeism attracted Augustine. Here, he thought, was the possibility offered "by pure and simple reason" to be led to God. But he soon discovered that this was not as he had expected. Man's short life and the limitations of human reason demand a solution to perennial problems by authority — "lest life be finished by us in unbelief." "One of those who in former days were held wise among the Greeks said that the truth bears the same relation to faith as eternity does to that which has only begun to be."

To the Platonists belongs the credit of being among those philosophers who sought God and "the cause by which the universe has been constituted, the light by which truth is to be discovered and the fountain by which felicity is to be drunk." *(City of God)*

The Platonists, according to Augustine, foremost among the philosophers, realized that God is the highest Good and the true philosopher one who loves God.

There are two types of knowledge: a knowledge of things temporal and a knowledge of things eternal. For the first, our reason will suffice; here we may know adequately through our natural reason alone; but the second is the gift of God's grace — it is God Himself who becomes our teacher in this knowledge of grace;

and He does it through faith or revelation. For this knowledge, therefore, our reason will not suffice, because "valid conclusions may be drawn not only from true but from false propositions." *(De doctr. christ.)*

Furthermore, reason is never had by us pure and undefiled. "The minds of men are obscured by familiarity with darkness, which covers them in the night of sins and evil habits, so that they cannot perceive in a way suitable to the clearness and purity of reason." *(de moribus eccl. cath.)*

"If anyone supposes that man, living, as he still does, in this mortal life, could dispel and clear away every obscurity induced by corporeal and carnal thoughts, and attain to the serene light of immutable truth, and cleave constantly and unswervingly to this with a mind wholly divorced from the course of this present life, that man understands neither what he asks, nor who he is that is putting forth such a supposition." *(De cons. Evang.)*

Therefore it is necessary that we be led "into the light of truth under the congenial shade of authority."

Only God's grace can lead us to Truth by making possible, first, the act of faith; then, when the mind is purified by faith, may it accept the divine illumination.

Philosophy may prove God's existence; indeed it can and does. And at first, Augustine believed that this knowledge of God's existence provided by philosophy could be completely satisfactory. But the more he became immersed in the Church and its doctrines, the more he doubted the sufficiency of secular philosophy for salvation. Belief in Christ must supplement the rational proofs for the existence of God.

ST. AUGUSTINE

"True and genuine philosophy has no other task than to teach us what is the original or uncaused cause of things, and how great is the intelligence abiding in it" but "Christ did not die in vain, and therefore human nature cannot by any means be justified and redeemed . . . except by faith and the mystery of the blood of Christ." *(De nat.et gratis)*

Therefore the true philosophy must involve one in a complete understanding of Christian dogma and belief; for all true philosophy is given over to the exposition of Christianity: the only true philosophy is the Christian.

The Triune God

Augustine's main aim is to find a rational justification for the triune God of Christianity. The mysteries of divine Being cannot be revealed through any corporeal or anthropomorphic notions. We can only know God as he *really* is through faith in the revealed doctrines of Christianity, and it is the Bible that contains these. The authority of the Scriptures therefore would suffice for a proper appreciation of the divine nature; but we find in the Bible many anthropomorphic expressions and corporeal figures of speech, such as: "I the Lord thy God, am a jealous God". These anthropomorphic expressions are to be understood symbolically, not literally. From the material and human we must rise to the spiritual and divine. We must so purge our minds as "to be able to see ineffably that which is ineffable." To this state we can be "nourished by faith . . . that we may be rendered apt and able to comprehend it." *(De trin.)*

And so it is also with the divine Substance, which can only be understood by a transcendental leap beyond the letter of the Biblical account. The Bible tells us that God is a trinity of Father, Son and Holy Spirit; these are three persons who are one and the same substance or essence. These are not three Gods, but One, since the three persons have "a divine unity of one and the same substance in an indivisible equality." *(Ibid)*.

But the unity must not be so understood as to destroy the distinctions within the Godhead; "the Father is not the Son; and the Son . . . is not the Father; and the Holy Spirit is neither the Father nor the Son but only the Spirit of the Father and the Son."

Augustine's interpretation of the trinity insists on *three* persons, each of whom may be distinguished from the others, but all of whom are inseparable because they have but one nature or essence. Thus we may call the trinity one essence or substance and three persons, or one essence and three metaphysical substrates — so long as the reality of the distinctions within the divine Being is expressed, while their unity, equality and inseparability is also acknowledged; so long, says Augustine, as it is realized that these names "did not intend diversity to be meant, but singleness to be denied." *(De trin.)*

And Augustine's metaphysical leanings now assert themselves in a remarkable way. He anticipates the Kantian position by pointing out that the gap between the finite and the infinite, the world and God, is so immeasurably great that any knowledge which may be gained by us of the transcendent being of God will necessarily be uncertain and incomplete.

But God made man in his own image. And Augustine searches in man for traces of this image of God — this Trinity. It is in the spiritual nature of man, in his rational soul that Augustine finds this image of God, a duplication of the original by reflection. He finds it in the unity of the rational soul which truly evidences the triune nature of God; for the soul is an indivisible trinity of mind, the Father, knowledge, the Son, and love of this knowledge which is the Spirit of the Father and Son. These, like the trinity of God's Being, may be distinguished from each other but they are, like the original divine Trinity, equal and inseparable. Thus, if God made man in his own image, the divine Trinity is reflected in the unity of man's rational soul . . . But even in the outer man, Augustine finds the Trinity: in man's vision, wherein we may distinguish the object seen (the Father), the act of vision or image (the Son) and "that which keeps the sense of the eye in the object seen, — viz. the attention of the mind" or the will to see (the Holy Spirit). This is a trinity, according to Augustine, by which the three — the object, the image and the will uniting the object with the image, Father and Son, requisite for the act "are tempered into a kind of unity; that is, the form of the body which is seen, and the image of it impressed on the sense, which is vision or sense informed, and the will of the mind which applies the sense to the sensible thing, and retains the vision itself in it." *(Ibid)*.

But this trinity of the sense of *perception* is immeasurably surpassed by the trinity found in *conception*. In this trinity of the conceptual we find memory, internal vision and the will uniting them *without a diversity of substance* such as was introduced in the case of the external sense of sight.

These trinities are the traces of divinity witnessing the being of God in the world of created things. There is here, in the mundane sphere, a reflection of the divine trinity — the three persons in the Godhead; primarily in the soul and mind of man. But we must always be cognizant of the fact that God's mind can in no way be likened to our own, and the memory, understanding and will of God must not be confused with the memory, understanding and will of man.

Nonetheless, there is here a reflection of the three persons in the Godhead. It is the image of God "in this very point . . . so great a good is only made possible by its being His image."

The very highest trinity in the image of God, however, is reached in the mind remembering, the mind understanding, and the mind loving itself — a true reflection of the deity "because the mind remembers itself and understands and loves itself only because it can also remember, understand and love Him by whom it was made." *(De trin.)*

This is the highest state of human happiness, according to Augustine, and it is possible only because of the sustaining power of the Father, through which man's existence is made possible, the illumination of the Son, through which man's wisdom becomes possible, and the grace of the Holy Spirit, through which goodness becomes possible. In so remembering, understanding, and loving God, is human life perfected. For man to be-

lieve that God exists, is for him to see how all existence
is possible; to have a knowledge of God is the key to
wisdom; and to love God is for man to become himself
good. The contemplation of this eternal Trinity — of the
existence, the knowledge, and the love of God, constitutes man's true happiness.

Thus did Augustine solve the mystery of the three
persons in the Godhead: the equality and indivisibility
of the three persons in the Christian Trinity.

God exists and He is man's highest good. For man to
know this is for him to be blessed. Augustine devoted
all the energies of his powerful mind to the elucidation
of the triune God. But this necessitated his advance from
anthropomorphic notions of God to his final interpretation of *the triune God as Truth, Wisdom and Goodness
in One.*

Evolution of Augustine's Thought

Augustine's great problem was to arrive at the conception of God as Spirit. To this conception he struggled
for the greater part of his life; and the progression to
this elevated standpoint constitutes the most exacting
and the most moving experience of his life.

Beginning with an anthropomorphic notion of the
deity which he had gained from his mother's simple
faith, his first idea of the divine Being is as of "some
Great One, who while concealed from our senses, could
hear and help us."

From this first and naive notion of God he rose to
the idea of divine Being as identical with Truth and
Wisdom. This gave him that universal desire, as he says

in his *Confessions,* "to love, seek, obtain, hold, and embrace, not this or that sect, but wisdom itself whatever it were."

This desire for universal truth and wisdom he obtained through pagan philosophy, especially the "Hortensius" of Cicero.

The Manichees, who seemed very learned and claimed to lead man to God by reason alone, now engaged Augustine's thought. And he was led to the conception of God as of one who, as he says, "has parts . . . whose being is bulk."

Augustine strove for a higher view of the divine which lay hidden in all of these views but which had not yet appeared to him with sufficient clearness. The Manichean conception of God no longer satisfied him and he now struggled against their ideas.

"Thou didst not," he says, *(Conf.)* "in them taste to me as Thou art; for Thou wast not these emptinesses, nor was I nourished by them, but exhausted rather."

He was getting further and further away from the idea of God as "any solid substantial thing." But the idea of God as pure Spirit he had not yet attained. "Thou wert not Thyself, but were phantom, and my error was my God." *(Conf.)*

Struggling still with the problem of divesting the divine Being of human characteristics, he says: "It seemed to me very unseemly to believe Thee to have the shape of human flesh and to be bound by . . . bodily lineaments . . ."

Finally, he reached the conclusion that God's nature must be unchangeable and incorruptible "because, though not knowing whence or how, yet I saw plainly and was sure, that that which may be corrupted must be inferior to that which cannot be corrupted."

But it was still a spatial God whom he had adopted — "as being in space, whether infused into the world or diffused." *(Conf.)*

God was somehow in the world; he was "vast, through infinite spaces, on every side penetrating the whole substance of the universe, and beyond it, every way, through immeasurable boundless spaces; so that the earth should have Thee, the heavens have Thee, all things have Thee, and they be bounded in Thee, and thou bounded nowhere." *(Conf.)*

But now he made another stride forward. He was ready to give up the notion of God as a vast corporeal substance — rather must He be, he thought, an immutable and incorruptible *Being*. And the problem of evil also interposed itself between him and his God in an irreconcilable manner. God must be good. Only a good God could have created this world. But there is also evil, *real* evil in the world. Then either God is good but not omnipotent, or omnipotent but not good.

It was at this stage that Augustine fell upon the writings of the Neo-Platonists in Latin translation. The neo-Platonic philosophers had their own profound notion of evil; evil was, for them, a *privation* of good rather than something opposed to goodness. All that exists is good; evil is no substance "for were it a substance it should be good." Hence God could be both omnipotent and good. In God there is no evil. In reality there are only grades of goodness: "either . . . an incorruptible substance and so a chief good; or a corruptible substance; which unless it were good, could not be corruptible." In God, therefore, there "is nothing whatsoever evil." All evil in the world is the result of the appearance of lack of harmony; actually, and from the standpoint of the whole of creation, all things are in harmony with the whole of creation and therefore *good*.

Furthermore, the notion of Spirit, an incorporeal reality, more real than anything material or spatial, was now made clear to him through these neo-Platonic philosophers. Having read the Platonists and been taught to search for incorporeal truth . . . I perceived "that Thou wert, and wert infinite, and yet not diffused in space, finite or infinite."

If this be so, then the doctrine of Christ as the Word and Wisdom of God, the Christian doctrine which his mother so desired him to embrace, was philosophically acceptable: indeed, "had I not sought Thy way in Christ, our Saviour, I had proved to be . . . killed."

The way was now clear for Augustine to adopt his final position: God created and sustains a world which is essentially and thoroughly good. He is everywhere, but his Being must not be confused with the matter or space of the world.

He is the *Truth* of things — not their matter. And all things *are* true — insofar as they exist. Falsehood is only *our thought* about what does *not exist*, even as *it belongs to the essence of Truth that it exists*. Augustine's idea of God as Spirit was now complete. All he had to do was to bring this into harmony with Christianity: to add belief in the incarnation and the redeeming power of

Christ, as well as the equality and indivisibility of the three persons in the Christian Trinity.

God and Christ now became, for Augustine, inseparable: Christ the Word and Wisdom of God — and, according to his neo-Platonic training, a philosophically acceptable notion. Augustine the Theologian and Augustine the Philosopher were now at peace. So closely did Augustine fuse the two: the Platonic-Plotinian, and the Christian, or model the latter after the former, that ultimately, it may be said that he only read the gospel of St. John into the *Enneads* of Plotinus: "the Word of God, being God, is that true light that lighteth every man that cometh into the world." That is why the controversy still exists as to whether Augustine was actually converted to Christianity, or to neo-Platonism. Alfaric asserts that "morally as well as intellectually it was to neo-Platonism rather than to the Gospels" that Augustine was converted.

But Augustine's own constant and unmitigated references to Christ, the Trinity, and Christian authority, bespeak his concern as equally, if not chiefly, with the substantiation and defense of Christian dogma and belief.

Perhaps it is truer to say that because of differences in emphases and tone in the writings of Augustine "we are in the presence of two different conversions and two different men." Perhaps the dualism in Augustine's nature was never completely overcome and the Theologian and the Philosopher never quite reconciled; and the Christian Augustine and Augustine the Platonist *never* at peace. All his work was merely the reflection of his restless soul, seeking ever for the immutable and divine.

WHAT THE GREAT PHILOSOPHERS THOUGHT

The Penitent Sinner

No account of Augustine's thoughts on God can be complete unless we note the intimate experiences of his contrite soul, shaken to the depths of his being as he was by the realization of vain and wasted years, unillumined by the presence of God and not given over to the service of God:

> "My evil and abominable youth . . . the more defiled by vain things as I grew in years and could not imagine any substance but such as is wont to be seen with these eyes." *(Conf.)*

Nor can we divorce the visions of his contrite heart from the heart of Augustine's thought. His life as a thinker is intimately bound up with his conversion, and his renunciation of the errors which clouded the vision of his mind. His passionate revolt against his own passionate nature is part of the catharsis which made possible not only his conversion but his philosophy of the divine. In short, Augustine the thinker must be viewed in the light of his direct experiences as a man. In his own words:

> "Wretched I was; and wretched is every soul bound by the friendship of perishable things; he is torn asunder when he loses them, and then he feels the wrechedness, which he had, ere yet he lost them. So was it then with me. I fretted, sighed, wept, was distracted; had neither rest nor counsel. For I bore about a shattered and bleeding soul, impatient of being borne by me; yet where to repose it I found

not. Not in calm groves, not in games and music, nor in fragrant spots, nor in curious banquettings, or in the pleasures of the bed and the couch; nor, finally, in books or poesy, found it repose. All things looked ghastly, yea, the very light; whatsoever was not what He was, was revolting and hateful, except moaning and tears. In those alone found I a little relief.

"Times lose no time; nor do they roll idly by; through our senses they work strange effects on the mind. Behold, they went and came day by day, and by coming and going, introduced into my mind other imaginings, and other remembrances; and little by little patched me up again with my old kind of delights, unto which my sorrows gave way. What restored and refreshed me chiefly, was the solace of other friends, whom I did love, that instead of Thee I loved: and this was a great fable, and a protracted lie." *(Conf.)*

"There sang all around me in my ears a cauldron of unholy loves. To love and be loved was sweet to me; but more, when I obtained to enjoy the person I loved. I defiled, therefore, the well of friendship with the filth of concupiscence, and I beclouded its brightness with the hell of lustfulness; and thus foul and unseemly, I would fain, through exceeding conceit, be fine and courtly, and I then fell headlong into the love, wherein I longed to be ensnared." . . . "and I swelled with pride . . . until

"I fell upon a certain book of Cicero. . . This book of his contains an exhortation to philosophy, and is called '*Hortensius*'. It altered my affections, and turned my prayers to Thyself, O Lord; and made me have other intentions and desires. Every vain hope at once became worthless to me; and I longed with an incredible and burning desire for an immortality of wisdom, and began now to arise, that I might return to Thee. For with Thee is wisdom. But the love of wisdom is, in Greek, called 'philosophy', with which that book inflamed me." *(Conf.)*

Two opposed strains find ground for conflict in the life and thought of Augustine. He lived, tasted all the fruits of the senses and the flesh; yet the quest of happiness he recognized as paramount in the life of man, while the senses and the flesh did not yield him happiness.

His life, spent in satisfaction of the will, gave him a key by which to understand all human life as primarily the act of willing. The inmost motivating energy of human nature lay in the will to be and in man's quest for happiness. The search for happiness is the impelling force behind all the functions of man. That is the first strain in Augustine's thought, the modern strain — his stress upon the will, and happiness through satisfaction of the will.

But he was equally convinced that all the urging, all

human willing and striving is vain and futile, unless it leads to its opposite: contemplation, and the beholding of divine Truth. In this, and in this alone, is there true joy, happiness, blessedness for man.

All the promptings, urgings, and restless strivings of the will are of value only in being stones upon the path to that state of eternal peace — wherein the very urge to be ceases to be!

The grace of divine revelation, the vision of divine truth, stemming from above, infuses the will and silences it. And this is the joy which passeth all understanding. The ideal of mystical contemplation, which he discovered in neo-Platonism, thus led Augustine to the absolute bliss, the divine grace of Christianity; filled and illumined by the highest truth, man can reach the will-less contemplation of the eternal being of God: this is the reward of divine grace to which the endless striving of the will must surrender for that which infinitely surpasses it in worth, namely, the heavenly rest and eternal joys of the contemplative life. For Augustine, God was first and foremost a being with whom it was possible for man to have close personal relationship, and in this alone was man's true good to be found. To give this relationship proper rational support, Augustine, as philosopher, turns to neo-Platonism and henceforth defines God as the One, — simple absolute Being, transcendent to all created things, the ground and source of all true reality; in terms of Christianity expressed thus: "Father, Son, and Holy Spirit, one God, alone, great, omnipotent, good, just, merciful, creator of all things visible and invisible." *(The Trinity)*

As Windelband says:

"For the temporal life, Augustine demands the full and never-resting exertion of the struggling and acting soul; *for eternity* he offers the prospect of the peace of becoming absorbed in divine truth . . . in the eternal blessedness where the resistance of the world and of the sinful will is no longer to be overcome. Where love has no longer any want that must be satisfied, there this love is no longer anything other than a God-intoxicated contemplation." *(History of Philosophy)*

But, ultimately, the secret of Augustine's influence lay in his mystical piety. His whole later life is a classic example of genuine religious experience. In his own words:

"Thou hast created us for Thyself, and our hearts know no rest until they repose in Thee."

"Thou art the Lord my God, since Thou standest not in need of my goodness."

"My whole hope is only in Thy exceeding great mercy. Give what Thou commandest; and command what Thou wilt."

"I will love Thee, Oh Lord, and thank Thee and confess unto Thy name, because Thou hast put away from me these so wicked and nefarious acts of mine. To Thy grace I attribute it and to Thy mercy, that Thou hast melted away my sin as though it were ice."

Here is a note of personal devotion, deeper and perhaps more truly heartfelt than any that had been sounded within the Christian Church since St. Paul; and religion as a vital intercourse with a living God was henceforth to be a permanent characteristic in the lives of many a future saint and sinner.

Augustine was hard at work upon his thousand and one literary ventures when the Vandals descended upon Africa and swept the Roman Legions out of their way. He was in Hippo when that city was besieged by the conquering hordes, — an old man, ill, and unhappy because of the turn of events. Stoically, he accepted the inevitable and prayed:

"I ask God to deliver this city from its enemies; or, if that may not be, that He give us strength to bear His will; or, at least, that He take me from this world and receive me in His bosom." His wish was granted.

And Augustine's City of God was triumphant even while the worldly city was suffering the agonies of mortal defeat.

SHANKARA

SHANKARA

I.

One must search the centuries with unusual dilligence in order to find men of undisputed superiority in the field of philosophy. Many of the great teachers of India belong in the company of such individuals of unquestionable philosophic genius, from among whom I choose, as representative, Shankara — philosopher, poet, savant, saint, mystic and religious reformer, who flourished in India in the seventh or eighth century A.D.

Sir Charles Eliot in his book *Hinduism and Buddhism* (Vol ii p.208) says that the philosophy of Shankara "in consistency, thoroughness and profundity, holds the first place in Indian philosophy."

Radhakrishnan quotes Thibaud to the effect that "The doctrine advocated by Shankara is, from a purely philosophical point of view, and apart from all theological considerations, the most important and interesting one which has arisen on Indian soil." . . .

Radhakrishnan himself says: "It is impossible to read Shankara's writings, packed as they are with serious and subtle thinking, without being conscious that one is in contact with a mind of a very fine penetration and profound spirituality . . . Shankara stands out as a heroic figure of the first rank in the somewhat motley crowd of the religious thinkers of medieval India." *(Indian Philosophy)*

Authorities differ as to the precise date of Shankara's life; some say that he lived as early as the middle or the end of the 6th Century A.D. Max Muller sets the date of his birth at 788 A.D. and of his death at 820 A.D. Shankara belonged to the simple, hard-laboring class of Brahmins, the Nambrudi. He attended a Vedic school as a youth and was the pupil of Govinda, who first taught him the principles of the Advaita System. Shankara's philosophy therefore is known as the Advaita-Vedanta System.

Already as a boy of eight, Shankara is said to have devoured with delight all the Vedas. He was a child prodigy of Vedic learning. The mystery of life enchanted the imagination of the child and he very early became enamoured of the beauty of holiness. Thus even "before he learned the ways of the world, he rejected them." *(Radhakrishnan: Indian Philosophy)*.

With youthful ardor Shankara became a wandering teacher, travelling from place to place and engaging in endless discussions with leaders of other schools of thought. He established four monasteries, and died at the age of 32 at Kedarmath in the Himalayas.

Like Socrates, Shankara felt impelled to lead men on the path of virtue, and this entailed, on his part, a life of complete detachment from the world. His own philosophy came naturally as a result of his commentaries on the ancient texts: the most important among the Upanishads, the Bhagavad Gita and the Vedanta Sutra. Shankara aimed at a spiritual reform based upon Brahmanism; and his speculations on the Upanishads led him to the discovery of mystic truth.

He tried to redirect the trend of his age through a philosophy that would satisfy the spiritual needs of men more so than that afforded by the Buddhistic or other religions of his day. He came to the conclusion that through *thought* alone can man triumph over the evils, trials and tribulations of life; for Thought could lead to the realization of the identity of the individual soul with Brahman, the world-soul. This is the purpose of life and this, too, is true liberation.

Shankara enumerates four specific qualifications in order to make of philosophy the exalted intellectual discipline which it rightfully can be:

1. "Discrimination between things eternal and non-eternal." This involves the ability to distinguish between the world that changes and a changeless reality. Those who possess this power will be drawn to metaphysics, inevitably and irresistibly.

2. "Renunciation of the enjoyment of rewards here and in the other world." There is little in ordinary life to satisfy the demands of the spirit. Philosophy flourishes and finds justification when this is once realized.

3. Moral preparation. He who seeks truth cannot long allow himself to be enslaved by existing things. Detachment from the world and liberation from desires are marks of superiority.

4. Longing for liberation. One must desire freedom before one can attain it.

II.

What strikes a Westerner as surprising in the philosophic speculations of Shankara is the logical keenness of his argumentation. Though his main premise is that logical reasoning is the road to appearance and unreality rather than to reality and truth, he nonetheless employs strict, logical and deductive reasoning in order to establish his main thesis, which is that deductive reasoning alone will not suffice. And he thereby anticipates the position of Descartes and Kant of later Western philosophy, while in other respects the Advaita Philosophy of Shankara closely resembles Hegelianism.

To understand the philosophy of Shankara we must first take note of his specific contribution to Indian Philosophy. There are many ancient Indian systems of philosophy, but we may distinguish three major developments of Indian philosophic thought: The Vedic (from approx. 1500 B.C. to 600 B.C.), the Epic (from approx. 600 B.C. to 200 A.D.), and the Six Systems (dating from about the year 200 A.D.).

Buddhism and Jainism, through their critical attitude toward the older religions, initiated a great movement of philosophic thought and a series of philosophic speculations which are known as the Six Systems; namely, 1. the Nyaya (primarily epistemological, dealing with the problem of knowledge, and the various ways through which we gain knowledge: intuition, inference, comparison and hearsay); 2. the Vaisesika (dealing primarily with particular objects and individuals, souls and atoms, and employing the categories of substance, quality, movement, generality, particularity, and inherence); 3. the Samkhya (which is relatively materialistic. It adopts the view of the reality of matter, and the reality also of an infinity of individual souls which are independent of the world-soul. It is naturalistic, in so far as it posits a substance and a process of development, cause and effect being the undeveloped and developed states of the one substance); 4. the Yoga (which, in contrast to the Samkhya, extols the mental over the material, stressing especially the importance of mental discipline, and which also has theistic leanings); the Purva Mimamsa (which deals primarily with duties and observances, stressing especially the relationship of act (as cause) to result (as effect); 5. The Vedanta Sutra (which attempts to explicate the teachings of the Upanishads in the concluding parts of the Vedic literature.)

6. The short aphorisms of the Vedanta Sutra are by themselves quite unintelligible and many attempts were made to interpret and clarify their meaning. This resulted in various systems of philosophy. Among these interpretations of the Vedanta Sutra is the Advaita System of Shankara.

———————

In a remarkable anticipation of Descartes, Shankara begins by asking wherein certainty may be found. Experience is the foundational reality. But there are many varieties of experience. The experience of the senses may be deceptive. Memory too may lead to error and not to truth. The entire world of wakefulness may be no more real than the dream world, for the experiences of the dream world are as real in their own realm as are those of the waking consciousness in its realm.

Yet, though we may doubt everything that we experience *we cannot doubt the existence of the self that doubts*. One cannot think "I am not": it is a contradiction in terms. To think, is to be. We cannot deny the existence of the self for "it is the essential nature of him who denies it." And yet, we cannot know the self by thought. The self is rather an immediate experience of something distinct from the senses, from the body and from the understanding. It is the object or idea behind "selfhood," the notion behind consciousness, and it is not affected by the death of the body or the extinction of the mind. Even if the whole world were a void, the void would presuppose a self that knew it as a void.

If the self or soul cannot be doubted or denied, neither can the universal soul be doubted. For, the empirical self or "I" can only be conceived in relation to the permanent I, the Atman, because every single aspect of my self, serves a purpose beyond its immediate end. A deeper ground of being is thus presupposed in every act of the self. And Brahman, the universal soul or self, is therefore as real as the permanent self, the Atman.

God, or the divine, must be real if we are real. If I cannot deny the being of my self I cannot deny God. Such is the meaning of this doctrine as translated into Western terminology.

SHANKARA

The basic tenet of Advaitaism — of which the Advaita-Vedanta of Shankara is an offspring — is, what in terms of Western philosophy may be called Absolute Idealism, since the various levels through which the Atman is made manifest may be likened, as Radhakrishnan says, to "the Hegelian Idea that the successive steps by which the human mind gradually passes from less adequate to more adequate conceptions of reality correspond to the stages of the process by which reality itself is manifested with ever-increasing adequacy in an ascending order of phenomena." *(Indian Philosophy, vol.ii, p.459 f.n.)*

To understand the system of Shankara it is necessary for us to see him in the framework of the school of philosophic and religious thought of which he is one among several exponents. The Advaita Vedanta boasts of two other great founders, one of whom is Govinda, Shankara's teacher, and the other the teacher of Govinda, Gaudapada.

Gaudapada is the first true exponent of the Advaita Vedanta System. There are certain doctrines foundational to Advaitism which find expression in Gaudapada's works; and Shankara's own primary principles rest upon these, for without them there can be no Advaita philosophy. Some of these are: the doctrine of degrees to reality; the identification of the Atman with the Brahman; the doctrine of Maya; the important realization that cause and effect reasoning cannot apply to the nature of the ultimate reality; that the only true road to freedom is wisdom, etc. All of these are primary insights of the Advaita System which already find full expression in Gaudapada's thought.

Some of the basic doctrines of Gaudapada have not only the unmistakable touch of philosophic truth but also, in addition, a peculiarly modern ring. Thus, Gaudapada argues that, in view of the various grades of consciousness, we have no reason to attribute less of reality to the dream-world than to the world of the waking consciousness. There is a coherence to the occurrences within the dream-world even as there is to the waking world, which makes it necessary for us to attribute to the dream world an equal measure of reality as what we attribute to the phenomenal world of the waking consciousness. We must not expect of the dream-world that it conform to our experiences of the world when we are awake. It is of a different order or grade of reality, but, though different, it is not for that reason any the less real. Radhakrishnan explains: "The water in the dream can quench the thirst in the dream, and to say that it does not quench the real thirst is irrelevant." Fully a thousand years later, Descartes, the father of modern philosophy, was to attack the same problem for the Western World, and with much the same results:

"When I consider the matter carefully, I do not find a single characteristic by means of which I can certainly determine whether I am awake or whether I dream. The visions of a dream and the experiences of my waking state are so much alike that I am completely puzzled, and I do not really know that I am not dreaming at this moment." *(Meditations, p.1)*

The fact that the objects and experiences of the waking consciousness are common to all conscious men while the dream experiences belong to the dreamer alone makes no difference; because, for Gaudapada, *life itself is only a waking dream! Both* the world of the consciousness that is awake and that of the dreamer, are, for Gaudapada, equally *unreal!* "As in dream, so in waking, the objects seen are unreal." *Only the subject, the self, is real. All that is object is unreal.* Whatever presents itself as an *object* to consciousness is *unreal.* This is an ancient thought common to the Upanishads and to Buddhism, which Gaudapada develops with Kantian acuteness. The only reason for our believing in the objective reality of the common waking world is because we have the testimony of other people to the same experiences as ours; actually we do not experience what they do; all we experience is our own conscious awareness of objectivity. And we believe them when they tell us that it is the same for them. This involves us in the space and time relations, and in the causal relations, of our common sense world of experienced "facts". But, for Gaudapada, these relations — spatial, temporal, and causal — do not constitute anything ultimate in the nature of things.

"By the nature of a thing is understood that which is complete in itself, that which is its very condition, that which is inborn, that which is not accidental, or that which does not cease to be itself." This definition gives us a new test by which to judge of whether anything be real or unreal. And it reveals to us the important truth that all the things of the world, and all the souls in the world, are by themselves — nothing; only as *Atman* are they real.

For Gaudapada, cause and effect reasoning is inadequate. Causality, according to Guadapada, even as for Kant, is only a category of thought, a condition of knowledge, but it is impossible to explain reality by means of it. In fact, for Gaudapada "nothing is produced either by itself or by another, nor is anything in fact produced, whether it be being, or non-being, or either." Nothing is created, nothing produced or destroyed; all of these — creation, production, destruction, are mere appearances, as unreal as the phenomena which they are supposed to account for. In fact, all individual things, all individual souls, and the world, are unreal. It is only by the category or principle of causality that they attain a semblance of reality. But we must give up the causal principle and transcend the phenomenal world to reach the nature of the real. It is for this reason that we cannot make of God *the cause* of the world — causality is an impossible fiction; nor is the waking state *the cause* of the dream world — here too causality does not really explain anything. For the Advaita philosophy the mental world is as unreal as the material world; the only reality resides in the pure subject, the Atman.

In short, for Gaudapada the entire world is an appearance for a mind that perceives it; *the world exists only for the mind.* All reality is mental and nothing objective is real. There are no objects apart from ideas of them. All things are relative to the perceiving mind and even the true and the false have no basis in the nature of the Absolute, for all objectivity is equally false.* Even the distinction between the knower and the

* "The perception of the rope as rope is as vicious as the perception of the rope as snake." (Radhakrishnan: Indian Philosophy, p.457, vol.ii)

known is unreal. Everything is relative to our experience of it. The dream is real so long as we dream; waking experiences are real so long as we do not dream; and the third possibility, dreamless sleep, is equally unreal. They all reveal their equal relativity and unreality, however, only when one awakes "from the sleep of delusion" and when one then "realizes the unborn, ever awake, dreamless, one . . ." Gaudapada musters another argument for the unreality of everything, namely, that since things have a beginning and an end *they must be unreal,* for "anything which is naught in the beginning and is naught at the end, necessarily does not exist in the middle." In other words, anything that exists in time cannot, for Gaudapada, be said to be; only that is real which excludes all temporality, which is beyond time; this alone has absolute self-existence.

But if "all that we see or seem is but a dream within a dream" (Edgar Allen Poe), there is for Gaudapada a true and absolute reality which transcends all relativity. In fact Gaudapada holds, even as Hegel did, more than a thousand years later, that the relative implies the absolute and the finite the infinite. For Gaudapada *Atman alone is real;* even as in the Upanishads, beyond the world of the waking consciousness, beyond the dream world, and beyond the state that is neither awake nor a dream, there is the Atman, basic to them all, one and indivisible, the only reality: "That which is cannot not be, even as that which is not cannot also be." In fact being and thought are identical, if thought is understood in a sense transcending human cognition, involving no relations, no object set over against a subject, no dualism and no multiplicity. This is absolute Thought. "The ever unborn, awake, dreamless, illumines itself of itself. It is ever illumined by its very nature."

Indeed, the Advaita Philosophy has such contempt for objectivity that it holds even the objectivity of the mental world to be unreal. Only Atman, which is pure subject, the only subject, is real. But if the Atman, the pure subject, is neither material nor mental, it is not for that reason nothing. Atman is identical with the pure knowledge or cognition of the Brahman. The unconditioned Atman and the infinite Brahman are one.

The extreme subjectivism of Gaudapada's philosophic position brings him dangerously near to solipsism and nihilism, in fact more so to the latter than to anything else. All reality, all objectivity, all becoming, all change, is unreal. Nothing, in truth, is: "There is no destruction, no creation, none in bondage, none endeavoring (for release), none desirous of liberation, none liberated; this is the absolute truth." Knowledge implies distinctions, of knower and known; it refers to something to be known of which we must predicate existence, or non-existence, but neither existence nor non-existence may properly be applied to the highest reality which truly *is*. All objective existence leads only to relative knowledge, error and illusion. Nothing really is, except what cannot be known through the predicates of knowledge, and what cannot be said to either exist or not exist. In short, nothing is except Atman and Brahman.

But if Atman is the true self, the only unconditioned reality, how is it that so much that is not real, so much of the not-self, appears to be? How does the indivisible

Atman become the multiple unrealities of the visible world? How does the self become the not-self? How explain the many, since the one, Atman, cannot be divided? There is a confusion here which drives us to seek an explanation for the world of existences, an explanation to account for creation.

The explanations regarding creation that are usually offered are confusing enough in themselves. Gaudapada says: "Some regard creation as the manifestation of God, while others regard it as of the nature of a dream or illusion; others maintain that it is the will of God, while those who believe in time declare that everything proceeds from time. Some say that creation is for the sake of enjoyment, while others hold that it is for sport."

Gaudapada adopts the view that the world and all created things are the result of God's infinite power, the manifestation of the very nature of the divine being: "it is the inherent nature of the shining one." "The Atman imagines himself by himself through the power of his maya. He alone cognizes the objects so set forth."

But whatever may be the explanation for creation, it is certain, for Gaudapada, that the way of liberation from bondage to the world of illusion, is for man to realize the Atman in his, and in every man's, individual soul. Thus are the barriers between man and his true, permanent self broken down. Once the soul is set free it can no longer be born again. A freed soul "is never born, being beyond the range of causality."

There is room, also, for the ethical ideal in Gaudapada's system. Right knowledge must be supplemented by the pursuit of the highest good for complete liberation; and religion, too, can help in the attainment of the highest good. The particular form of religion falls in the realm of relativity. The infinite may be worshipped in any way one chooses, for the finite soul can represent the infinite to itself in an infinity of finite ways, but all forms of worship ultimately depend upon one absolute. As for himself, Gaudapada adopts the Yogic method which yields for him a knowledge whose object is Brahman — beyond conception, beyond duality and multiplicity, his soul centering in the Atman.

"When the mind ceases from imagining, by a knowledge of the truth of the Atman, it becomes naught, and remains at rest for want of things to cognize." This, for Gaudapada, is the highest state, for it has Brahman as the object of knowledge, and it is the path to ultimate and eternal bliss.

III.

Such is the trend and such the thoughts of the great Indian predecessors of Shankara. The pendulum of philosophic thought swings uneasily between extreme Scepticism, Subjective Idealism, Objective Idealism, and Criticism, to use Western terminology for Eastern thought; while systems of naturalistic and materialistic philosophy also find their exponents and defenders, anticipating by over a thousand years the schools of Western philosophic thought that harbor the same tendencies: those of Descartes, Berkeley, Hume, Kant and Hegel.

Basing themselves upon the Upanishads, the Baghavad

SHANKARA

Gita, and the Vedanta Sutra, all of which are replete with germs of philosophic speculation on religious subjects, these great commentators and systematizers of a later date, during the Middle Ages in India, constructed imposing systems of philosophic speculation and religious thought, purifying and clarifying the meanings of those ancient texts.

And they played, as it were, with notions of great philosophic import: the reality or unreality of the world, the phenomenal and the noumenal, the mysteries of consciousness — its dream state and waking state, the nature of knowledge and the ways of knowing, the origin of the world, and the being of God.

Philosophy and religion here merge in a single stupendous effort to explain the nature of reality, the meaning of life and the way to liberation and redemption for man.

The Vedanta is the "end of the Veda." The Upanishads comprise "the final end of the Veda" and the principles and doctrines of its final chapter. Hence the Upanishads express the essential message of the Vedas. The Vedanta Sutra is also called the Brahma Sutra, because it deals primarily with Brahman or the unconditioned self and its relation to the conditioned self.

The Upanishads, the Vedanta Sutra, as well as the Bhagavad Gita, are repositories of ancient Indian wisdom, and it is upon these and their religious and philosophic doctrines that the later commentators, too numerous to mention by name, based themselves. Shankara is one of the greatest among them.

One wades through the thoughts of these Indian mystics as through a perilous sea of philosophic currents and cross currents, in quest of their concept of divinity. It appears that God is not the same for these Indian thinkers as he is for the Westerner; nor does He bear the same relation to the world as in Western thought. God is not the creator of the universe. Creation itself is inexplicable. God is rather, for these mystics, a great spiritual essence diffused throughout creation and uniting with itself the permanent self or soul of man, to instruct, guide, and lead man to liberation from illusion and error. He is an Absolute in the Hegelian sense; but Hegel's Absolute is a far more highly developed notion of the Absolute as Idea, the result of the categories of the universal Notion.

In the Indian philosophies we have a wealth of theological speculation based upon various interpretations of the Upanishads. The many hundreds of Sutras (each of which consists of barely a few words) yield a wealth of intimations regarding the nature of God, the world, the soul, its bondage and deliverance. The commentators labor incessantly at these vague premonitions of later systematic philosophic speculation. They establish a variety of traditions which soon crystallize into different schools at variance with one another and entailing numerous and conflicting interpretations of the original Sutra. This basic text, itself the result of many independent authors, deals with the nature of Brahman and His relation to the individual soul and to the world; with the problem of how the world gradually evolved from the divine source and its reabsorption into Brahman; also, with the nature of the soul, and its relation to the body, of its attributes and its relation to God, of its dependence on its own deeds; and many other discussions and accounts, theological and psychological, including that of the condition of the soul after death, rebirth, and of the final release, after which there is no further return.

Even as in the later Western philosophy of Spinozism there is but one infinite Substance, Brahman, and this is the highest reality; all other substances are not independent substances at all but modifications of the single divine Substance, the infinite Brahman. Brahman, in the Vedanta Sutra, is the beginning and end of all things, the efficient and material cause of the world, pure, true, omniscient, omnipotent. He is described as the cosmic light, cosmic space, cosmic breath, and the light that burns eternally in the soul. He dwells in the heart of man. All things have their ultimate being in Him, the Supreme Spirit, source of all being and the only object worthy of adoration and worship. Brahman, uncreated and eternal, creates every particle of the universe and bestows upon the world the power to evolve. Indeed, evolution is only possible because Brahman, who dwells in all things, informs the world and the elements of the material universe with the urge to produce, to grow and to evolve. Thus, because of the presence of Brahman in all aspects of creation, is there the development of ever higher levels of existence in all things. Brahman, the cause of the world, infuses its innermost essence into every part and particle of it; so that everything is, in essence, Brahman, and thus the infinite cause and the finite effect are, for these Indian mystics, interchangeable. The essence of anything has within it the divine spark because Brahman is in all; the world differs from Brahman only as the clay pot differs from the clay, and evolution may be likened to a piece of cloth which at first, when rolled up, does not show its entire nature, but when spread out, reveals all that is present in both instances — when the cloth is rolled up and when it is unrolled. Cause and effect are interchangeable, though they appear as different.

Shankara, along with other commentators on these important philosophical issues, attacks this problem of the identity of Brahman and the world. He is too critical of the appearances, of the world of phenomena, to equate this world with the divine Brahman. Indeed, the world exists, he explains, only for those who are under the influence of erroneous perception. To the inadequate understanding of man alone does Brahman appear as identical with the world, or as transformed into it. In truth, only Brahman *is;* only an unconditioned ultimate spiritual reality may truly be said to be. The world as known, the knower, and knowledge itself, are all real and true only in Brahman. So argues Shankara.

But even in the *Sutra,* reality is granted only to the absolute; all symbols are instruments for the meager intelligence of man. True, absolute reality is unmanifested. And religion, which is not mere idol worship, true religion, is the attribute of him who possesses an adequate vision of God. This is intuition, the highest function of spirit. The attainment of self, the realization of the ultimate universal essence in each individual, is the goal and purpose of human existence. Liberation is attained through the knowledge of Brahman, because it is this ultimate knowledge that puts an end to all the karmas (destinies of each individual) which have not yet begun to function. The body itself will last until those karmas which *have* begun to unfold are completely exhausted, but when the soul of an individual reaches Brahman there no longer is any return. The commentators differ as to the chief attributes of the soul that is released, but essentially these are spiritual, thought-full and of an almost infinite power, due to unlimited knowledge. Nonetheless, the soul, thus released, cannot be likened to God, for He alone is omnipotent with the unlimited power to create, rule and dissolve the universe. There is an eternal distinction between the soul of man and God. Brahman, though evolving into the universe, is, after all, eternally transcendent to it. He is the change-less source of the ever-changing world, the infinite and eternal amidst the finite and temporal.

For Shankara, *the world is the result of a change which produces in Brahman no change.* The world, as we experience it, neither *is* nor *is not.* It hovers inde-terminately in an intermediate region wherein existence and non-existence have equal significance. Hence Shan-kara distinguishes between the absolute and the empirical, the truth of the one (the Absolute) remaining untouched by the truth of the other (the empirical). For Shankara there is an infinite spirit in the bosom of phenomena, at the heart of reality, in which all ideal values reside. He distinguishes also two types of happiness: first, the hap-piness which is the result of our conduct here on earth and can only be transitory; but the glory of the Vedanta lies in the fact that it helps us to a vision of reality, infinite and eternal, of the Brahman, whose end is not a happiness attainable either on earth, or in heaven, but ultimate, true happiness — namely, freedom from rebirth. It does not look to the future; it does not depend on the past; it is absolute, ultimate release from bondage.

Like Descartes, Shankara discovers that while we may doubt the reality of all other things in the world, we cannot doubt the existence of the self that doubts. The self is basic to all conscious experience, including doubt. No conscious experience is possible for us without the self. We can therefore think away everything else but we cannot think of the self as non-existent. And yet, we cannot know the self through thought, since thought itself belongs to the realm of not-self. Therefore, the self is real and yet it cannot be proven. It is the basis of all proof, a logical necessity prior to all proofs but itself lies beyond the realm of rational proof. The true self is not the empirical self; only the permanent self, the Atman, is undeniable. The true self involves us in the notion of self-existence and this brings with it immediately the concepts of eternity and immutability. The permanent self therefore, or Atman, necessarily arouses in us the affirmation of the Brahman, the eternal and infinite Being. Hence the true self is, for Shankara, neither states of awareness, a continuum of such awareness, or a stream of consciousness. These all belong to the empirical self, with its feeling, mental states, and conscious experiences, which vary with time. Indeed, nothing in the world of nature could *be* without the presupposition of the self which itself is out of time but which orders events in a temporal series to create the "natural" world.

Actually we can only get at the true notion of the permanent self, or the Atman, if we empty it of all experience, bodily and mental. It is then that, for our understanding, it is reduced to nothing. Actually, however, it is this pure consciousness, devoid of parts, qualities or attributes that comes nearest to the true, permanent self, or Atman.

Thus we are led to a reversal of the common-sense notion as to what consciousness is.

It is not the product of sense, nerve processes or brain functions. Atman, which is eternal self, the ultimate consciousness, is the true cause, the ground of all finite consciousness, and indeed of all objects and events in the world which exist for that consciousness. This ultimate, foundational, divine consciousness, basic to all reality, is entirely different from the consciousness that experiences in humans, the consciousness which is the outgrowth of a long process of evolutionary development in man. Atman is *pure* consciousness, *pure* awareness, "the supreme principle in which there is no differentiation of knower, knowledge and known; infinite, transcendent, the essence of absolute knowledge." It is an absolute knowledge that creates its object in the act of thinking it, the pure intelligence which cannot be without existence; and it is bliss, for bliss is freedom from suffering. And Atman, without desire, and without regrets, is such existence, free from suffering. Indeed, all activity is motivated by desire and presupposes pain, nor can it attain to truth. For the Atman, however,

WHAT THE GREAT PHILOSOPHERS THOUGHT

activity and limitation are equally unreal; it is one, self-dependent, infinite, absolute and the permanent self in all selves. Yet the Atman is not a person, since personality involves the distinction between it and other existences. It is for this reason that, from the standpoint of the empirical self, the Atman, the pure self, appears as unreal, and the empirical self the only self that is real. But this is only as it appears from the standpoint of empirical logic. Beyond this lies *intuition*, wherein the truth of the ultimate universal consciousness appears, certain and indisputable. In the light of the absolute of intuitive truth, the self knows itself because it knows the absolutely real, without dimensions, extension or division, everywhere and eternally the same, equally in the part as in the whole, without plurality or diversity. Only insofar as we partake of this infinite universal life and share through our consiousness in the Universal Consciousness and through our thought in Universal Thought, —to that extent are we real; *only because Atman is, are we.* "Our experience is possible because of the universal Atman in us."

From the universal in man to the universal in the world it is but a step, but from Atman to Brahman there is no step, for Atman and Brahman are one! Both are the ultimate in being, both involve unconditioned consciousness, all-pervasive presence, truth, freedom and blessedness. Atman and Brahman are one and the same infinite being; the distinction which we have established between them, namely that the Atman is the subjective in selfhood while the Brahman is the objective, universal self, is not a real distinction, for in ultimate being even the distinction between objective and subjective loses all meaning; indeed the subjectivity of the Atman may be said to be a universal objectification, and the objectivity of Brahman the deepest inward subjectivity. Only to the eye of the intellect is this duality cognizable or real. Actually, duality is here out of the question. Indeed, "advaitam" means non-dual.

Furthermore, none of the attributes by which intellect can describe the infinite nature of the one, Atman or Brahman, can ever be adequate to its true and absolute nature. Shankara tells us that even the bare characteristic of its being one, is still a falsification; it is one in the sense only of having no other or second to itself. It, Brahman, is unlike anything we can think or imagine in any sense. There is nothing existing to which we may liken it. Being at the opposite pole to all finite existences, we can only characterize it negatively; only of the finite can we speak or think positively. To determine Brahman positively is to limit and condition his limitless being. No distinctions of any kind can be applied to the infinite and eternal. Whatever is similar or different is so only in the field of the empirically real. Ultimate, absolute reality knows no distinctions or differentiations. It is "wholly other" but not therefore not real; it is non-dual but not for that reason one; it is wholly negative for our intellectual apprehension, but the most positive of all being nonetheless. To know Brahman we must think away space, and time, sense qualities, phenomenal characteristics and all material or mental attributes. Are we then left with nothing? On the contrary. Only if our understanding were infinite could we know Brahman; or, if Brahman were finite! But neither of these is so. Thus Brahman is not nothingness nor emptiness; it is our human way of comprehending His infinite nature that forces us to deprive Brahman of all the attributes which we attach to the real, while Brahman is, in truth, the fullest reality. To lose Brahman in the human way is in reality to find him. The mystic knows Brahman as total reality; he only loses what is irrelevant, inessential, inconsequential, by denying of him as infinite what only in the finite makes sense. The highest affirmation of the divine is possible only when one has achieved a transcendence of finitude. We may think of God as great, vast, unimaginably powerful and omniscient, but all of these attributes, though they may arouse worship of God, do not comprehend His infinite nature. Like Plotinus and the neo-Platonists, Shankara concludes that the supremely real could better be defined in terms of what it is not, than by any positive designations of what it is. Indeed, *any* attributes only tend to limit the limitless being of the infinitely real, the supremely true. Existence itself does not apply to God in the same sense in which it applies to anything which is not God, since God does not depend on anything else in order to be. Hence the authenticity of His being precludes the attribute of existence. Being beyond time, temporal duration, which is what we mean by existence, cannot be applied to the divine. We can only hope to comprehend God by negating of Him all the characteristics of His own otherness. The highest possible designations of the divine are infinite being, unconditioned consciousness, and bliss. This excludes all the lower forms of knowledge involving the categories of relation, causality, and creation of the universe. But beyond this knowledge of the analytic intellect, there is a higher experience wherein essence and existence unite and issue in the conception of the true Infinite and the unconditioned Absolute. And this is not a mere striving or yearning of spirit after Spirit alone; it is the most actual of realities; it transcends logical intellectualizing.

As Plotinus says with reference to the same experience: "We form a conception of its Authentic Being from its image playing upon the Intellectual Principle. This image of itself it has communicated to the Intellect that contemplates it; thus all the striving is on the side of the Intellect, which is the eternal striver and eternally the attainer; (while) the Being beyond, neither strives since it feels no lack, nor attains, since it has no striving." *(Enneads)*.

Perhaps the best modern summation of the semi-mystical, semi-rational views of Shankara in this regard is the one of F. H. Bradley in his *Appearance and Reality:* "Fully to realize the existence of the Absolute is for finite beings impossible . . . But to gain an idea of its main features — an idea true so far as it goes, though abstract and incomplete — is a different endeavor . . . And surely no more than this is wanted for a knowledge of the Absolute. It is a knowledge which of course differs enormously from the fact. But it is true for all that, while it respects its own limits; and it seems fully attainable by the finite intellect."

IV.

Shankara, however, does not end with this universal and divine Absolute. There is, according to him, a determinate personality, which is Brahman as Ishvara. It is this God (Ishvara) who is the cause of the world. For Shankara, as for Kant, the rational proofs for the existence of God are all inadequate because the whole question of existence as applied to God is absurd. For God to exist, He would have to take on the determinations and characteristics of objects, i.e. He would have to cease to be infinite and become a finite manifestation in the world of phenomena, an object among objects. But God is pure subject, absolute Being, the totality of all reality.

To this infinite Being other categories than those of our logical reasoning must be applied, and these are primarily intuitional in character. Nonetheless, like the medieval scholastics of the Christian world, Shankara labors to reconcile reason with scripture. It is possible to prove, as the scriptures contend, that Ishvara, or God, is the cause of the world. God is pure Being, First Cause of all existence, unproduced yet productive of all else. But He is a divine force who also draws all His effects back into Himself; and the return issues in another round of existence, the new forms depending upon former lives which require atonement. So long as false and inadequate knowledge, attachment to error and illusion continues, rebirth is inevitable. Those who are liberated, no longer return; rebirth is for them unnecessary, for they have attained the truth and achieved adequate understanding. God, then, eternally creates and destroys, only

SHANKARA

according to the law of karma. The good that men do
in one lifetime lives after them in the next. Hence God
himself must suit His purposes according to the deeds
of men. He cannot arbitrarily choose for any man a life
that is not in conformity with that individual's attainments in prior existences. Each new life is determined
solely by the moral qualities of its preceding ones. Even
as rain, says Shankara, helps the plants to grow, while
what they grow into depends in the last resort not on
the rain but on the seed which is watered, so does God
help men to attain their true nature and to bring out
their essential self, but these selves are, for good or ill,
themselves their own determining factors. Hence, though
God is all-powerful, the life of every man depends,
ultimately and primarily, upon his own prior deeds and
aspirations. Hence it is, also, that from the one God, who
creates all things from the fullness of His joy and His
infinite life and power, an endless variety of souls and
an infinite diversity of lives follow.

The life of God (Ishvara) combines and contains all
parts of the living universe. In this sense God and the
world are identical. All is Brahman. Everything that
exists is the manifestation in the realm of space and
time of what always was and exists in God. But there
are cyclic periods of extinction and renewal when Ishvara
demands a return of all things into His infinite Being.
During these periods the material world loses itself in
a vague and indistinct suspension, while souls, freed for
the moment from bondage to life, sleep unconsciously.
They must, however, soon again resume an embodied
existence, when Ishvara creates the material world anew,

that is, when the consequences of all their deeds have not yet been completely fulfilled. Then the wheel of birth and death begins to turn anew.

Individual souls are parts of God. Ishvara contains them all, though they remain, through their deeds, independent and distinguishable even after death. The materially-embodied individual soul is the Jiva. The Jivas form a collective unity in a cosmic self; this is Viraj or Vaisvanara. It is the cosmic self awake. But these Jivas in dreams are each the lingin or the taijasa, All taijasas combined form the super subtle self, the Hiranyagarbah or Sutratman. And the union of all individuals (prajnas) is Ishvara. There are progressive stages of materialization as Ishvara, from being in the state of withdrawal, being Brahman encased in pure buddhi, which is the spring of all thought and willing, unfolds from dreamless sleep and pure transparent body to waking consciousness or creation; and there is a progressive idealization when the process is reversed. The world thus, for Shankara, is a phenomenalization or appearance in relation to Brahman — it is a mixture of Brahman, the infinitely real, and Maya (illusion and appearance). But other Advaita philosophers hold that any relation is necessarily excluded from Brahman, and therefore refer to Ishvara or God the Creator as the seat of Maya, and hence that Brahman, through Ishvara, is the material cause of the world. Maya serves to conceal the real and to make manifest the unreal. Thus Brahman appears as the world, and the world, in appearing, has no effect upon the nature of Brahman, for here the cause produces its effect without itself undergoing any change. God is the cause of the world but remains eternally and unalterably the same and divine in His essence. There is a knowledge of Him which is adequate and complete, the intuition of His essence; and a knowledge which represents our mental weakness and ignorance (avidya); the latter is the knowledge which is ours because we must understand the divine Ishvara as maya — since we know the divine only by way of space, time, causality, expressing the finite and negative in ourselves which obscures the Infinite and Absolute in the universe. The chief aim and purpose in life is to avoid avidya (ignorance and darkness) and to attain the liberation which comes from a supreme knowledge of the eternal illumination which is God.

———

Shankara, then, has given the world the philosophy known as Advaita (the philosophy of monism or non-dualism, expressing the infinite nature of the one divine Brahman) in the most complete form to which the great systems of Indian philosophy during the Middle Ages have attained. It is a monument to his genius and a masterpiece of intellectual and spiritual ingenuity. His God is the Absolute, and may at times appear far removed from the personalistic notions of the divine Being current in Western thought. But that is only one side, the intellectual, dialectical side to Shankara's conception of God. There is also the moral nature of the divine and the attribute of Holiness, which are prominent features of Shankara's notion of the divine Being; for God is represented also, by Shankara, as the essence of life itself, and religion arises from the sense of infinity which is innate in the soul and which ends by the soul becoming itself infinite. Shankara's God can not only be adored, as the Creator and Governor of the universe, with His infinite power, justice, mercy and righteousness; He is the object, also, of genuine worship. God, despite his metaphysical transcendence in conception, bears for Shankara, the same relation to man as the lover to the beloved, as master to servant, as father to son. The highest worship, for man, is achieved by obliterating the distinction between the individual and the Supreme Being. Hence religion as ordinarily understood is imperfect, its experience is fragmentary as compared with that of the true religion which is an apprehension of infinite reality and which transcends the external symbolism of the ordinary worshipper.

When the ideal goal of the religious consciousness is reached, the very distinction between the Absolute as known and a personal God vanishes, even as the distinction between the human and the divine is obliterated in that transcendent experience. The true worship of God consists in the complete identification of creature and Creator. As Shankara says, quoting the great religious seers of mankind who proclaimed the identity of the individual soul with Atman, the universal soul: "verily I am Thou, O holy Godhead, and Thou art I."

Perhaps Schopenhauer summarized it best when he said: "Whoever is able to say this to himself ('That art Thou') with regard to every being with whom he comes in contact, is certain of all virtue and blessedness, and is on the direct road to salvation."

SHANKARA

The message is perennially the same: whether Christian, Hebrew or Indian: God is infinite and eternal Being, to be worshipped adequately only through a transcendence of the limitations of human reason and through a grasp of His supreme Being by the Mind and Spirit in the soul of man which is itself divine.

————

MAIMONIDES

MAIMONIDES

(1135-1204)

I

The story of the Jews in the Middle Ages forms a fascinating, though sordid chapter in the history of European thought. Forced into isolated communities and driven in most countries into Ghettos by their intolerant hosts, the Jews utilized their physical retreat as a means to spiritual advancement; fashioning their own secret doctrines to supplement, and, at times, to supplant their sacred teachings. Thus did the Kabbalah, Jewish occult and mystical lore, come into existence; thus the semi-rationalistic, semi-mystical proofs for the existence of God, for the eternity of the world, for the immortality of the soul, and many other, and now basic, tenets of the Jewish faith.

Grounded in a sublime religiosity which found expression in a philosophico-mystical literature, in part inherited from their own ancient sources, Biblical and Talmudical, in part transmitted to them from the ancients by the Arabs or by their own Jewish metaphysicians, there arose a great body of philosophico-ethical-religious doctrine among them. This they jealously hoarded and guarded, from generation to generation, with reverent care.

The summit of this transmission of Jewish lore and law, was reached in Moses the son of Maimon, the "Rambam" of the Jews, the "Rabbi Moyses" or "Moyses Aegyptius" (because of his long residence in Egypt) as he was known to the Scholastics — the "Maimonides" of the modern world.

Maimonides had, not the Christians, but the Moslems to contend with. He was born in Cordova, principal city of then Moslem Spain, on the eve of Passover, March 30, 1135. The Jews had settled in Spain prior to the Moslems, but with the Moslems there came a freedom of thought and general liberty and prosperity that ushered in a renaissance of learning and culture to which the Arab world itself had largely contributed through its revival of Greek philosophy and science — especially by way of Aristotle. Moses Ben Maimon had imbibed this ancient Greek culture and had fused it with the great traditional learning of his own people. But, as in the case of most great geniuses, life was not easy, and the road to truth paved with innumerable thorny impediments. To begin with, the freedom and precious liberties of the Moslem conquerors was destined to be of short duration. For there soon came the fanatical Berbers from the African desert who seized power and ruled with dreadful intolerance. All non-Moslems were offered the alternative of death or the adoption of Mohammedanism. Maimonides, then thirteen years of age, left Cordova with his father and family in search of a new home. After some twelve years of aimless wandering in South Spain they found a temporary resting place (1160-1163) in Fez, North Africa; but religious persecution prevailed there too and the family was forced to move on to Palestine. They stayed there only a few months and then settled in Egypt. There, Maimonides lost his brother, a business man with scholarly interests who had supported the entire family. Maimonides now turned to the practice of medicine, for he remembered the old Rabbinical injunction against accepting money for teaching. He became court physician to the Sultan Saladin and later to Saladin's son Al-Afdahl. But Moses Maimonides was also a philosopher, and the official leader of the Jewish community in Cairo. He loved philosophic speculation and longed to devote himself completely to this fascinating study of the mysteries of the universe, God and Man, reason and revelation, and the rational and divine ways to ethical perfection. But his duties as a physician were burdensome to a degree far beyond the conception of the medical man of modern times, and his numerous literary efforts in philosophy were penned under the most difficult conditions.

To his close friend Judah Ibn Tibbon, who wanted a little of his time, he writes:

> "My duties to the Sultan are very heavy. I am obliged to visit him every day, early in the morning. When he or any of his children or any inmates of his harem, are indisposed, I dare not quit Cairo, but must stay during the greater part of the day in the palace. It also frequently happens that one or

two of the royal officers become ill, and I must then attend to their healing. Hence, as a rule . . . even if nothing unusual happens, I do not return to Fostat (his home about 1½ miles distant) until the afternoon. By then I am almost dying of hunger. I find the ante-chambers filled with people, both Jews and Gentiles, nobles and common folk, theologians and bailiffs, friends and foes — a mixed multitude, who await my return.

"I dismount from my animal, wash my hands, go forth to my patients, and beg them to bear with me while I partake of some refreshments, the only meal I take in 24 hours. Then I attend to my patients, and write prescriptions for their ailments. They go in and out until nightfall, and sometimes, even until two hours and more into the night. I converse and prescribe while lying down from sheer fatigue, and when night falls, I am so exhausted that I can scarcely speak.

"Therefore, no Israelite can have a private interview with me except on the Sabbath. On that day the whole Congregation, or at least the majority of its members, come to me after the morning service, when I instruct them . . . we study together until noon; then they depart. Some of them return, and read with me after the afternoon service until the evening prayers. In this manner I spend that day."

But this is not all. To be born a Jew was already a great impediment and involved a precarious existence; but for one to be a Jew in high office, with all the intrigues of court life in those religiously turbulent days, was doubly difficult. The Jew of exceptional talents such as Maimonides, who had high moral standards in addition, had his hands full. So, in another of his letters we read:

> "The high offices to which Jews attain these days are not, in my opinion, an unmitigated good fortune worthy to be striven after. As the Lord liveth, they are actually evils of no small proportions. For the man who enjoys true bliss is one who attends to perfecting the religious life and the performance of his obligations, and who shuns all the evils of men and all ugly human traits. But he who holds public office is subject to many afflictions, for he may lose favor with the Gentiles and be degraded by them, or he may fall into the power of the state and suffer harsh treatment and bodily harm. And if, on the other hand, he makes his conduct conform to the desires of the people, he places himself against the Torah of the Lord."

To understand Maimonides we must first understand the medieval mind, Christian as well as Jewish. For medieval man the ideal of knowledge was knowledge in the light of the whole, the universal, the cosmic, the perennial. He has no patience with piecemeal knowledge. Science was either universal or no science at all.

And he had only one single source from which all scientific knowledge could be drawn: the writings of Aristotle which had been rediscovered by Arabs, Jews and Christians. For medieval man Aristotle was "the master of those who know" and Aristotle's thought represented all there was to be known.

It was therefore natural to seek in Aristotle for the bases of correct "scientific" reasoning about any and all subjects, physical, metaphysical and theological. Maimonides is no exception. But the critical faculty is not altogether silenced because of this; indeed, in many respects the conclusions of men like Maimonides, who lived in the 12th and 13th centuries, are more advanced and more rational than what passes for knowledge even in our own day. Two notable instances may be cited in this regard: 1. his attitude towards Astrology, wherein Maimonides refuses to abide even by certain isolated Biblical and Talmudical endorsements of it. Maimonides rejects astrological beliefs on the grounds of intrinsic absurdity and, what is just as important, the fact that belief in astrology is incompatible with freedom of the will and free choice, upon which all moral conduct depends. It is contrary to reason to believe in astrology and hence, no matter what the texts, Biblical or Talmudical, say on the subject, Maimonides pleads for independent individual judgment, saying: "man must never throw his understanding behind him . . . the eyes are directed forward and not back." 2. Another instance in this respect, as regards Maimonides' advanced point of view, is his recognition of the importance of diet for health, a subject on which few medical men have, even to this day, seen the light, and which 800 years ago engaged the attention of Moses Maimonides.

II.

Two great rivers feed the ocean of Medieval Jewish thought: mysticism and rationalism, and these in indisoluble union; or, to vary the metaphor, the mantle that hangs over Medieval Jewish thought is loomed by two distinct but indistinguishable threads — mystical exaltation and rational explanation. So adroitly are these two threads interwoven as to make it impossible of unravelling them into separate strands, even by the acutest analytical scrutiny.

The greatest among the Jews *could* not, *would* not follow either of these two threads alone. There was always room for the other one too; nay, an inward necessity demanded always the one to complement the other. Reason *had* to become ecstatic and revealing, and ecstasy *had* to find a rational source to be completely satisfying. Therein lay, perhaps, the secret of Medieval Jewish philosophical and theological speculation.

Ecstasy involves poetry — that is why every lover is a potential poet; and religious inspiration often issues in imaginative verse. Only two Jews escaped this inevitable poetic externalization; these were Maimonides and Spinoza. But, internally, they too reached down into the wells of poetic, religious and mystical inspiration for their rationalistic effusions. There is nothing prosaic about Spinoza's geometry; nothing purely rational about Maimonides' logical deductions. Because of this ingrained mystico-rational inspiration, there arose, among the Jews of the Middle Ages, an occult wisdom, inaccessible to the multitude, but open to the higher reason of the intellectually superior, those who sensed the mysteries of eternity, divinity and infinite perfection, and who could learn to "understand" the deepest meaning and signif- ication of these. No Jew was exempt or excluded as unworthy or undeserving of this illumination. Rich and poor, young and old, scholar and pious believer mingled in the waters of transcendental deliberations regarding the mysteries of creation, the meaning of the Torah and the Talmud, and the divine evidences of Biblical revela- tion in the minutest aspects of the created world. As old as the Jews themselves are these ancient longings of the Hebrew spirit, this mystic intensity combined with rational deliberation.

All mysticism — Hebrew, Christian, Moslem, Hindu — may be said to be *essentially* the same. And yet, they are not quite the same. Into Jewish mysticism the Hebrew mystics of the Middle Ages poured the painful sense of immediate danger and momentary despair, the pangs of the persecuted and despised, and an undercurrent of disillusionment with the world; all of this charged their transcendent religion with an intimacy born of suffering such as the Christian mystic of the Middle Ages could not experience. Added to this was the prospect of econ- omic insecurity induced by isolation and the heavy de- mands made upon them by King and State, and the possibility of torture at the hands of degenerate mobs.

The extent of this persecution, which is widely recorded and well authenticated, is sufficiently attested to by an edict of Pope Innocent IV (1247) who protested these excesses perpetrated against the Jews and pleaded for a cessation of them, forbidding their recurrence, as follows:

> "Certain of the clergy and princes, nobles and great lords . . . have falsely devised godless plans against the Jews, unjustly depriving them of their property by force, and appropriating it to themselves; . . . In fact, in their malice, they ascribe to Jews every murder, wherever it chances to occur. And on the ground of these and other fabrications, they are filled with rage against them, rob them . . . oppress by starvation, imprisonment, torture, and other sufferings, sometimes even condemning them to death; so that the Jews, though living under Christian princes, are in worse plight than were their ancestors under the Pharaohs. They are driven to leave in despair the land in which their fathers had dwelled since the memory of man. Since it is our pleasure that they shall not be distressed, we ordain that you behave toward them in a friendly and kind manner. Whenever any unjust attacks upon them come to your notice, redress their injuries, and do not suffer them to be visited in the future by similar tribulations."

But this plea was ignored and we find other humane Popes repeatedly denouncing the injustices, persecutions and excesses perpetrated against the Jews. To the eternal glory of the Catholic Church it must be noted that while it was customary for state after state to issue orders expelling the Jews from their territories, they were never expelled from the Papal States of Rome or Avignon. In fact, it was the Catholic Church that made possible a barely tolerable existence for the Jews in the Middle Ages.

"Had it not been for the Catholic Church," writes the great Jewish historian Graetz, "the Jews would not have survived the Middle Ages in Christian Europe."

At any rate, the very mysticism of the Jews of the Middle Ages bears the impress of their sufferings; and this constitutes the thesis upon which their faith was to thrive. The antithesis was a sense of security in the being of their Lord — far greater than all worldly power, far surer than all mundane risks, washing away the ills of this world and drowning them in the vast sea of the universal power and goodness of their God, who stood ever ready to protect them from injustice and to shield them from evil men bent upon their destruction.

Creed and ritual helped too. Ancient ceremonies and festivals kindled the smoldering flames of religious intoxication, often self-induced through willful deceptions. It was an almost naive, a child-like faith that these people had in the being of their God; and they loved to dwell on proofs for His existence and means of establishing, determining, and describing His infinite nature. They were determined to leave no stone unturned, no path unexplored, leading to a revelation of the glory of the Creator, the Lord, their God. Thus pantheistic and emanantistic doctrines mingled with rationalistic and mystical ones. From Pythagoreanism, Platonism, neo-Platonism, Aristotelianism, and the Bible, they culled the building-blocks for their great metaphysical edifice whose superstructure was theology and whose crowning glory was the Being of God.

And now they saw — or there were those among them who saw — that these infinite mysteries could not too readily be revealed indiscriminately to every passerby; and that therefore the Bible too had been deliberately planned in order to make these eternal truths acceptable and understandable to the multitude who would not otherwise know their God and His divine significations.

Thus there came into being the Kabbalah and all the other secret doctrines attesting to the spiritual intimations of the Jew, torn between a super-sensuous religious feeling presided over by the authority of traditional beliefs and the rational convictions of his inquiring mind; and thus there ensued in the Jewish soul the conflict between revelation and reason.

This conflict Maimonides tried to resolve.

"Our sages tell us," he says, "that it is impossible to give a full account of the creation to man . . . it has been treated metaphorically in order that the uneducated may comprehend it according to the measure of their faculties and the feebleness of their apprehension, while educated persons may take it in a different sense." Thus he begins his approach to the nature of the deity.

A Supreme Intelligence exists and governs the universe. Only *because* God, the source of being and life exists, does anything exist: "if it could be supposed that He does not exist, it would follow that nothing else could possibly exist." (A self-existing divine Substance in place of Maimonides' God is the very essence of Spinozism).

"A thing which has in itself the necessity of existence, cannot have for its existence any cause whatsoever."

Actually, all we can know about God is the fact that He exists. When we say, beyond that, that He is intelligent, omnipotent, merciful, One, these have totally different meanings when applied to God than when applied to man. In fact, we can never know *what* they mean when applied to God.

Above all, God must be incorporeal — hence all physical attributes by which the Bible describes Him must be interpreted figuratively only.

To define God at all, by any positive attributes, qualities or qualifications, is already to misinterpret His nature. Perhaps that is the reason also for the difficulties involved in the problem of creation, i.e. the problem as to whether God created the world in time or whether, on the other hand, the world is eternal — a dilemma impossible of solution, for either alternative baffles the reason of man.

It is only from the human point of view, again, that evils are evil; the *whole* requires what we call evil; from the standpoint of the cosmos even the evil in the world may be good; furthermore, most human misfortunes are evils of man's own doing.

To be a man, man must have free will — but this freedom makes him sometimes choose evil. God will not interfere though he knows the choice that man will make.

As to immortality — the "active intellect" which existed before the body and is not a mere function of it, will survive the body; but the "potential intellect" *is* such a bodily function and dies with it.

As he states it in the *Guide for the Perplexed:* "the soul that remains after death is not the soul that lives in a man when he is born." The implication here is (and Maimonides in fact makes it clear through the expression "acquired" soul for the immortal soul) that, like Aristotle and Spinoza, he believed that man becomes immortal by acquiring immortal thoughts. Elsewhere, and for the same reason, he quotes with approval the rabbinical saying that "a bastard who is a scholar takes precedence over an ignorant high priest" *(mishne Torah).*

Actually, this view of immortality is the same as that of Averroes, the great Arabian commentator on Aristotle, and it constitutes a denial of individual immortality. This radical view of immortality created perhaps the greatest storm of all against Maimonides by Jews, Christians and Moslems alike.

His main philosophic work, the *Guide for the Perplexed*, comes to the following important conclusions: that human reason must be re-enforced by revelation; that the God of the Scriptures is a spiritual being so that the anthropomorphic expressions regarding God in the Bible have only a figurative meaning and were to be understood thus; that no attributes of a positive nature could be applied to God, only negative ones; that God, as Aristotle had proven, must exist as the Unmoved Mover of the World and as the *necessary* source of all *possible* being; that the eternity of the world, as Aristotle conceived it, which conflicts with the story of creation of the Scriptures, must be abandoned for the Biblical view but that the Biblical account of Creation must be taken allegorically; it is then, in fact, the more satisfying of the two since it makes a purposeful intelligence the cause of the world instead of assuming a purely mechanical causality, and it is not contrary to reason; that evil is only a privation of good and the result of the fact that man has free will; that prophecy is "an emanation of the Divine Being" . . . but "prophecy consists in the most perfect development of the imaginative faculty"; that nature everywhere manifests design and hence a directing designer; and this too in the Law and in the Biblical narrative. Finally, Maimonides grapples with morality and ends with a list of important moral precepts.

The *Guide* was attacked by the Mohammedans as "undermining the principles of all faiths" (Abd-al-Latif), and by the Rabbis as "selling the Scriptures to the Greeks", denying the immortality of the soul, replacing the Talmud with philosophy, and as substituting for the living God of the Bible an unknowable God, the result of Maimonide's own metaphor-loving mind, a God who could never induce prayer or piety; while the orthodox Christians who were already, for reasons of their own, banning the works of Aristotle and Averroes from the universities, now turned to burning the works of Maimonides in public (1224) in Montpellier and in Paris (1238-1242). This was after Rabbi Solomon ben Abraham of Montpellier, to defend the Jews against charges of harboring rationalists in their Congregations, anathematized the philosophic works of Maimonides, and excommunicated all Jews who studied profane science or literature as well as those who treated the Bible allegorically. Not to be outdone by their adversaries, the liberal rationalist Jews of Montpellier who sprang to Maimonides' defence, replied by excommunicating any Jew who debarred his son from the study of science.

The Jewish communities were torn by Rabbinical bans on all study of the profane sciences as proposed by some, and, in fact, ending in a decree issued by the head of the Barcelona Congregation, excommunicating any Jew who should teach, or before the age of 25 study, any secular science except medicine, or any non-Jewish philosopher.

Denunciations of the works of Maimonides poured in from Spain, France, Palestine, from Jews everywhere, and an uncompromising war ensued in the Jewish communities between the accusers and the defenders of Maimonides and his liberal views. With all this there came, in addition, new persecutions of the Jews and fears of reprisals by the now powerful Inquisition. Gradually, the Jews retired again into their age-old isolation, the uncompromising views of the orthodox Rabbis had won the day, the Hebrew schools reverted to a more or less literal interpretation of the Scriptures; in fact all of Europe was soon again blanketed with irrational beliefs and superstitious fears for the next two or three centuries, until the dawn of the Renaissance would usher in the light of day.

But Moses Maimonides had had his say and the world was never to forget the lessons of his inquiring mind.

WHAT THE GREAT PHILOSOPHERS THOUGHT

III.

When we try to determine what precisely makes the contribution of Maimonides so enduring, we find the reason for his persistent appeal and survival through the centuries, to lie, above all, in the fact that he endeavored, as a Jew, to reconcile the teachings of his revealed religion, including its commandments and prohibitions, all its metaphysics, theology and ethics, with the dictates of his sovereign reason. As such, and perhaps without his knowing it, he was voicing something not peculiar to the Jews alone but to the Christians and Moslems as well, for all of them were struggling, in this age, that is, in the 12th and 13th centuries, with the same difficult task; reason, which for many centuries had given up its authority to revelation, was now beginning to awaken to its own sovereign rights and was claiming for itself more than mere subservience to theological dogma and belief.

This awakening of reason was a little premature; the time was not yet ripe, but in the exceptional spirits among Jews, Christians and Moslems, among those, that is, who are the pathfinders of the race, the dawn of reason was making itself felt in no uncertain terms. The struggle for this expression of the will of reason was a severe one, within the individual himself and between him and the external world. Maimonides, completely convinced of the divine source and origin of the Bible and the Torah, and also of the divine mission of the Jews and their God-given prerogatives through their sacred books and prophets, was nonetheless equally aware of the need for a rational justification for all of man's thoughts, beliefs and actions. The two strains were just about of equal force in his soul and the inevitable result was a severe conflict which it was not easy for him to conceal from the eyes of those who were critical of his chances of success to reconcile revelation and reason, or those who were not willing to accept any compromise with reason because of their undivided devotion to the beliefs of their fathers.

Maimonides had somehow managed to effect a more or less permanent peaceful solution within himself of the warfare between luminous reason and blind faith. We have it in his own metaphorical expression in a letter to the Jews of Provence wherein he states very frankly that though the Torah was his chief love, philosophy and science often succeeded in enticing him with their own delightful charms: "Although from my birth the Torah was betrothed to me, and continues to be loved by me as the wife of my youth, in whose love I find a constant delight, strange women whom I at first took into my house as her handmaids have become her rivals and absorb a portion of my time."

But it was not only his time but his heart that philosophy and rational science had appropriated. Of Aristotle, the dominant rational spirit of that age, he writes: "He (Aristotle) had indeed reached the highest summit of knowledge to which man can ascend unless the emanation of the Divine Spirit be vouchsafed to him, so that he attains the stage of Prophecy, above which there is no higher stage." He thus makes it clear that we must never surrender our intellectual powers.

Nonetheless, Maimonides considered himself first and

primarily as a Jew, with an intellectual mission of universal significance for his people. He set himself up, by an inner command, as the spiritual leader of the Jews the world over and interpreter of their laws and doctrines. He was intent upon preserving the heritage of the Jewish people, to codify their laws, explain their beliefs, insisting upon the divine origin of their doctrines and exhorting every Jew on the face of the globe to attend strictly to the teachings of the Torah, the precepts of the sages, and the daily habits and actions enjoined upon them as Jews, the chosen people. Hence he formulated thirteen articles of faith as fundamental tenets, basic to one's being a Jew. These articles every Jew had to firmly believe in:

1. Belief in the existence of a Creator, the cause of all other creations.

2. Belief in the Unity of God.

3. Belief in the incorporeality of God.

4. The belief that God is without beginning and eternal.

5. The belief in His being our master whom alone we must worship.

6. That there is such a thing as prophecy.

7. That of all the Prophets there was none like Moses nor would there ever be another like him.

8. The belief that the divine Law which was given to Moses on Mt. Sinai came in its totality from God.

9. The belief that this Law is eternal and immutable.

10. That God knows the acts and ways of men.

11. That somehow God will reward the righteous and punish the evil-doers.

12. Belief in the coming of the Messiah.

13. Belief in the resurrection of the dead.

His aim was to simplify the Talmud (the great body of Jewish commentary on the Bible and the Law) and make it comprehensible to every intelligent Jew; and thus to prevent the divine significance of Jewish thought from degenerating into the doctrines of misguided literalists.

It is for this reason that Maimonides became the center of that fierce warfare which divided the Jewish people into two hostile camps for centuries to come. For the orthodox literalists his interpretations were too liberal and his expressed views too radical. For the more liberally minded among the Jews the literalists failed to recognize the immense significance of the very fact that Maimonides refused to comply by any literal interpretation of the Bible or the Talmud. The real significance of Maimonides' new approach to religion and the Bible was first to appear, however, when the rationalistic thinkers of the Renaissance, in complete independence of all dogma and creed, based religion solely on the natural light of reason and what *it* could reveal of the workings of the divine in the universe and in man. Thus, from the point of view of modern thought, Maimonides in his very attempt to rescue the precious ore of the

Jewish faith had, through his stress upon the importance of a rationalistically satisfying approach, made the first advance from blind belief to rational substantiation and thus had brought to the consciousness of Western man the importance of reason for the explication of his innermost faith.

The far-seeing Christians, headed by St. Thomas, as well as the advanced among the Moslems, were subconsciously aware of this fact and recognized in Maimonides their own similar need: for reason to substantiate their faith. It is because of this that, despite his concern with what was purely Jewish in religion and theology, he could become a source of profound influence upon the thought of the later Christian Scholastics, so that Alexander of Hales (who died in 1245) known as "the master and father" of the Franciscan School, frequently quotes Maimonides, Albertus Magnus (Albert the Great, 1193-1280) as well as John the Scot (Johannes Scotus, 1266-1308) refer to him with obvious reverence, and St. Thomas Aquinas (1225-1274), the greatest of all medieval theologians, turns to the *Guide for the Perplexed* of "Rabbi Moyses" as his guide in his attempt to reconcile religion with reason and Christianity with Aristotelianism. Leibnitz (1646-1716), centuries later, expresses admiration for Maimonides, and Spinoza, despite his far more strictly rationalistic approach and severe criticisms of Maimonides, obviously, in frequent instances, treads in the very footsteps of Maimonides' initial rationalistic interpretation of God, man and the universe.

Indeed we find whole sections of Maimonides' *Guide for the Perplexed* devoted to an almost Spinozistic eulogy of the intellect and of "the obligation . . . of exercising one's independent power of thinking on the subject of God after having obtained the knowledge of Him"; for "this is the form of service to God which is reserved for those who have apprehended Truth. The more they think about God and let their minds dwell upon Him, the more intensive their service to Him.

> "Those, however, who think of God and mention Him frequently without any knowledge, but just following some imagination of a belief taken over on the authority of others, are in my opinion not only outside the palace (of God) but far removed from it . . . since that idea which is in their imagination and which they mention with their lips does not correspond to any reality whatsoever."

Chapter LI of Book III of Maimonides' *Guide for the Perplexed* gives us a good description of his aims and purposes as regards understanding and worship of the divine Being "which is the highest purpose of mankind":

> "I shall open this chapter with a simile. A prince is in his castle; his subjects are partly dwelling in the city and partly outside of it. Of those in the city, some have turned their backs towards the prince's palace, and face the other way. Others are making for the house of the prince and are directed towards it, seeking to obtain entry in order to have audience with the prince; but to this moment they have not yet seen the walls of the palace. Some of those

who are going towards it have reached the palace and are wandering round it in search of the gate. A few have entered through the gate and are passing through the forecourt. Others again have got so far as to enter the inner courtyard of the palace and thus are in the same locality as the prince, i.e. in the palace itself. Penetrating as far as the inside of the palace does not yet mean that they see the prince or speak to him. Far from it. After entering the palace further efforts are required; then only does one reach the presence of the prince and sees him from afar or near, hears him speak, or is allowed to address him.

"I shall now explain this simile to you which I have invented: those who are outside the city are all those human beings who possess no religious belief whatsoever, be it of a speculative or of a traditional kind . . . These are like animals devoid of reason; in my view they are not to be classed as human beings, but among the beings below the humans, but above the apes, since they do possess human form and outline and higher intelligence than the ape.

"Those who are in the city but turn their backs to the prince's palace are men of thought and speculation who have arrived at false opinions, be this due to some major error that crept into their reasoning or because of their acceptance of the erroneous ideas of others.

Because of these opinions they are in such a position that with every step they become further removed from the palace. These are much worse off than the first group. It is they whose elimination and the utter extermination of whose ideas is at times a necessity, lest they cause others to go astray.

"Those who are making for the palace and aim at entering it, but have never as yet seen the palace, are the great mass of those who obey the Law, or in other words the 'men without learning who occupy themselves with religious duties.'

"Those who have arrived at the palace and are walking around it, are those possessed of religious learning, who accept the right opinions as to traditional beliefs and study the detailed ordinances of the works demanded in the service of God, but have never made an attempt to speculate on the principles of their faith or inquired in any way into the justification of any item of faith.

"Those who have embarked on speculation concerning the principles of religion have entered the forecourts. These are, no doubt, people of varying ranks.

"Those finally, who have succeeded in obtaining demonstrative proof of everything that can be demonstratively proven, and have reached certainty with regard to all those metaphysical matters on which certainty can be reached, and have almost reached certainty wherever no more than this was possible, those, I say, have penetrated to the presence of the prince in the inner parts of the palace.

"Know, my dear son, that as long as you are occupied with the mathematical sciences and the technique of logic, you belong to those who walk around the palace in search of the gate . . . As soon as you learn the natural sciences you enter the palace and pass through its forecourts. When you complete your study of the natural sciences and get a grasp of metaphysics, you enter *into the inner courtyard* of the prince (Ezekiel 44, 21, 27) and have achieved to be in the same house as he. This is the rank of the learned, though they are of different degrees of perfection.

"But as for the man who after having reached full perfection in metaphysics, exercises his mind independently and inclines with his whole being to God, leaving aside everything else, and devotes all the activities of his intellect to contemplation of the universe in order to find in it guidance towards God, so as to learn how God governs it — such men are those who have obtained admission to the audience-chamber of the prince . . . One among these, through the high degree of his perception and his complete abstraction from everything else, got so far that it was said of him *and he was there with God (Exodus 33, 28)*".

MAIMONIDES

In another part of the *Guide,* Maimonides extols the power and importance of man's intellect, again in almost Spinozistic terms:

> "This intellect which has come to us as an emanation from God is the bond that exists between us and Him. . . . if you wish you can strengthen and broaden this bond, or you can weaken it and make it gradually thinner until you cut it off altogether. This bond is strengthened by exercising the intellect in the love of God . . . Its weakening and thinning is the result of employing your powers of thinking on other things. Even if you were the most learned of all men in the truths of metaphysics, the moment that you empty your mind of God and are with your entire being engaged in some unavoidable . . . or . . . necessary business, you thereby cut off the bond between yourself and God. You are at that moment not with Him, nor is He with you. The relationship which exists between you and God is at that time actually severed. For this reason the people of virtue begrudge the times during which they are occupied with other things and warn us against this mistake: 'do not remove God from your thoughts' (Shabbath 149a)". *(Excursus Chapter LI, Guide)*

A little later on, Maimonides gives us the following explanation as to the levels of perfection attainable by man:

"Ancient and modern philosophers have shown that four types of perfection are attainable for man:

"The first and lowest is the one for which the inhabitants of the earth destroy each other, i.e. the perfection of wealth. It comprises the property, clothes, instruments, slaves, lands and such like which a man owns . . . This is a perfection which has no real connection of any kind with that person, but only a relation. The pleasure derived from it is in any event for the most part purely imaginary, i.e. the pleasure of saying: this is my house, this is my slave, or this property is mine, this is my army. If he were to look at himself he would discover that all this is outside his own self and that every single one of these possessions exists on its own account. Therefore, as soon as the relation ceases, that individual, who was a powerful king, may one bright morning find that there is no difference between him and the lowliest of mankind, though no change has occurred in any of those things that had stood in a relation to him. The philosopher shows that he who devotes his energy and efforts to the acquisition of this kind of perfection strives for something purely imaginary, for it is a thing which has no permanence. Even if the wealth remains in his possession throughout his life, no perfection in his own self will ever result from it.

MAIMONIDES

"The second kind of perfection is more closely connected with man's own self. This is the perfection of physique and appearance, as when a man's constitution is perfectly balanced and his limbs and organs are in proper proportion and of the requisite strength. This kind of perfection is also not considered to be a final purpose, because it is physical perfection which is given to man not insofar as he is human, but insofar as he is animal, and he shares it with the lowest beasts. Moreover, if a man were to reach the utmost degree of strength possible for him, it would not be equal to that of a strong mule, not to speak of that of a lion or an elephant . . .

"The third kind of perfection affects the substance of the person more deeply than the second. It is the perfection of ethical virtues, . . . Most religious prescriptions are designed for the attainment of this kind of perfection. This kind of perfection is, however, merely a prerequisite to something else, not a purpose in itself, because all ethical qualities refer to relations between a person and others. In a way this perfection in a man's ethical qualities is nothing but a prerequisite for the benefit of society. It thus becomes an instrument for something else. Just suppose that a man is all alone and has no business with anyone: in that case all his ethical qualities will be found to be vain and void. There would in such a case be no need of them and they would in no way contribute to his personal perfection. It is only with regard to others that man needs them and receives any benefit from them.

"The fourth kind of perfection is true human perfection; that is, the attainment of rational virtues. By this I mean, of course, the conception of ideas which lead to correct opinions on metaphysical matters. This is the ultimate purpose, and this is the one which bestows upon man true perfection, being peculiar to him alone. It brings him eternal life, and by it man is man. Consider each one of the preceding types of perfection, and you will discover that they belong to others, not to yourself — or if you must needs have it according to the conventional view, they belong to you and others at the same time. This last perfection, however, belongs to yourself exclusively, and no one else has any share in it."

For this reason, i.e. because of his unbounded admiration for the powers of the mind, Maimonides held that Gentiles who attained the knowledge of the Creator and admitted the Unity of God, that is, the scholarly Gentiles, would positively share in *Olam Haba*, the world to come or Paradise. And in this he was in agreement with the sages in the Talmud who had said that a Gentile who studies the Laws of Moses may be likened to a High Priest. The Jews were, in this respect, more tolerant and advanced than the Christians and Mohammedans for whom infidels (i.e. non-Christians or non-Moslems) could take no part in the future bliss of their Paradise to come.

The stress of Maimonides upon the superiority of intellectual over material and physical or even moral excellence is an instance wherein he surpasses Aristotle himself in elevating the intellectual qualities far and beyond any other human attainments.

Despite this high regard for human reason, Maimonides does not shrink from the conclusion that God's mind and knowledge are infinitely different from and superior to man's. This must necessarily be so in view of the fact that "God's knowledge is not a thing superadded to His essence" hence "between His knowledge and ours there exists the same difference of substance as between the substance of heaven and earth . . . The sum total of the idea I am trying here briefly to explain is the following: we cannot apprehend the true nature of God's essence; yet we know that His existence is the most perfect, without any admixture of imperfection or change or affection in any way. Similarly, though we do not know the true nature of God's knowledge, because it is His substance, yet we know that He does not sometimes apprehend and at other times remain unaware, i.e. that He never acquires new knowledge; also, that His knowledge is not of a multiple nature, nor finite; that nothing of all existing things is hidden from Him, and that His knowledge of them does not change their nature, but the possible retains its nature as a possibility. Anything in this enumeration that appears contradictory, is so only owing to the structure of our knowledge, which has nothing in common with His knowledge except the name."

Maimonides explains that "the entire law with its commands and prohibitions is based upon the principle that God's knowledge of what is going to happen does not change the contingency from its nature", meaning thereby that if man's conduct were determined by the fact that God has knowledge of what it will be, then all moral laws and commands would be worthless. Hence we must assume that, on the one hand, God has a knowledge of future events, including man's future conduct, and, on the other hand, that this does not affect in any way man's responsibility for what he is going to do. "This", says Maimonides, "is very difficult for our imperfect minds to grasp."

How could it be otherwise in view of the fact that "whatever we know, we know from observation of reality. Therefore our knowledge does not extend to what will be or that which is infinite, and we constantly acquire new . . . knowledge according to the things from which we derive them. It is otherwise with God: He does not derive His knowledge of things from the things, so that His knowledge would be multiple and ever new, but those things themselves are a consequence of His knowledge, which precedes them and establishes them as they are, whether this be as an incorporeal being, as a perpetually existing individual composed of matter, or as a thing possessing matter passing through various individuals according to some consistent law.

"This is the reason why in the case of God there is neither a multiplicity of items of knowledge, nor acquisition of any new or different knowledge. Through knowing the true nature of His own unchangeable essence, He knows everything that results from all His works. For us to desire to understand how this takes place, is the same as to desire that we were He and that our perception were the same as His. The proper belief for a person who seeks truth and justice, is to hold that nothing whatsoever is hidden from God, but everything is accessible to His knowledge, which is identical with His substance; further, that it is out of the question for us to know anything of this type of perception. If we knew how it works, then we should ourselves be possessed of that intelligence with which that type of perception is achieved. This, however, is not possessed by anyone in the universe except God alone, whose essence it is."

One final word regarding a profound but relatively unknown aspect to the thought of Maimonides, namely, that he denies any and every independent value to moral perfection, recognizing only theoretical knowledge as true perfection, while, subsequently, he sees the highest end of knowledge of God to lie *in our knowing His love and justice and imitating these* as far as this is possible for man. Through this, Maimonides in fact distinguishes between two types of moral perfection: 1. such as does not rest upon philosophical knowledge and 2. that sort of moral conduct which is produced by reason of the very knowledge of God. It is this latter type of moral perfection which Maimonides finds as included in, and that it is in fact an expression of, the knowledge of God — its value lies precisely in that *it is the sort of moral conduct whose very being is an expression of the knowledge of God.*

It is doubtful if human reason has ever reached a higher or more elevated point of view.

————

Moses Maimonides died at the age of 69 in the year 1204. His remains were taken to Palestine. Years later his enemies inscribed on his tombstone: "Here is buried Moses, the son of Maimon, who was excommunicated and was a heretic." But the world knows him as *the* "Rambam", greatest among the Jews and among the noblest of mankind.

ST. THOMAS AQUINAS

ST. THOMAS AQUINAS

(1225-1274)

Thomas Aquinas does not stand alone, nor is his philosophy, commonly known as "Thomism", an isolated phenomenon in thirteenth century Europe. For many years, reason had been knocking at the gates of Christian thought, seeking, through devious ways, admittance to the inner sanctuary of its theological structure. The newly established universities at Paris, Oxford and Cambridge, the broadening of the intellectual horizon brought about by contacts with the East through the Crusades, the influence of education in the twelfth century, and, above all, the revival of Aristotle's metaphysical writings through translations and commentaries —all led to a gigantic effort, in the 13th century, to gain entrance for reason into the theological foundations of the Christian faith.

St. Thomas was in the forefront of this great wave and he marks the culmination of a widespread movement throughout the Western world — Arabian, Jewish and Christian — for a rational approach to religious beliefs.

WHAT THE GREAT PHILOSOPHERS THOUGHT

For seven centuries, since Augustine attempted to reconcile the Christian faith with Platonism, the Platonic tradition reigned wherever philosophy had gained a foothold or had seeped through the crevices of dogma and creed in the Middle Ages. Then, the revival of Aristotle's works through translations and commentaries slowly transformed Arabian and Hebraic theology into synthetic products, fusing the Greek with the Moslem or Jewish.

In the 8th century, Aristotle's influence was most keenly felt in the Moslem world. In the 12th century, there came the impact of Aristotelianism on the Jews and the attempt at harmonizing Judaic doctrine with the philosophy of Aristotle; Maimonides was the apex of this movement.

Finally, with Latinized versions of Aristotle's works gaining currency in the Christian world, from 1150 on, Catholic theology was in the throes of the Aristotelian revolution; and attempts at incorporating Aristotle's metaphysics into Christian doctrine steadily increased in number and intensity. St. Thomas finally accomplished this by opening wide the gates of Christian theology to reason; thus the great intellectual edifice of the Middle Ages known as Scholasticism found its consummation in the monumental work of Thomas Aquinas. Others among the Scholastics had also labored for a synthesis of Aristotelianism with Christianity, but St. Thomas succeeded in infusing new life into the pagan Aristotle. He was convinced that Aristotle's logic, metaphysics and theology could serve as a support to the Catholic faith and to Catholic dogma; in Aristotle he found a rationalistic foundation for the Christian belief.

ST. THOMAS AQUINAS

It has been said of him therefore that he succeeded not only in raising Aristotle from the dead but also in baptizing him. For, instead of the fear of Aristotle which obsessed the authorities of the Church in the 13th century, St. Thomas made of him an ally in the struggle of the Church for vindication of its faith. It was through Aristotle that he enlisted reason in the cause of faith.

The confidence of St. Thomas in this great philosopher was due primarily to his conviction that the light of Reason and the light of Faith come from the same source — God — and that therefore the most rational of philosophies (Aristotle's) *must* be in accord with the truest and surest of faiths (the Christian).

Thomas thus marks the culmination of the age of Scholasticism. The undercurrent of mysticism which had permeated all previous medieval thought had almost spent its force; and there is now only rational deliberation on the problems of life, God, and the meaning of existence, as well as on the nature of faith, divine grace and human salvation.

Some medieval thinkers tried to conceal the true nature of their heterodoxy. Thus, Siegr of Brabant says: "When we philosophize we seek the thoughts of the philosophers rather than the truth." For St. Thomas, however, philosophy was a means for comprehending the nature of reality. "The pursuit of philosophy", he writes, "is not in order to find out what men have thought, but what the truth . . . is." Aristotle's philosophy was, for him, a stepping stone to truth.

II.

For a time there seemed danger to the faith in the exhilaration and enthusiasm with which the discovery of pagan thought was received in the universities and monasteries of the medieval world. There was fear that important points of Catholic doctrine were contradicted through Arabian interpretations of Aristotle's thought. Hence efforts were instituted to make translations of Aristotle from the original Greek, with new commentaries, free from Arabian influence, and so to stem the flood of heretical Arabian *Averroism*. In 1263, Pope Urban IV did not stop with this prohibition however, for what was needed now, he realized, was a new interpretation of Aristotle's works so as to make possible a true Christian use of their contents. Aristotle's teachings had spread from one center of learning to another and the influence of his thought had too deeply penetrated the mind of Western man to be ignored. Pope Urban IV therefore summoned Thomas Aquinas to the Papal Court requesting a commentary by him on Aristotle. And he also summoned William of Moerbeck who, at Thomas' request, made a new translation of Aristotle's writings available in Latin, directly from the Greek original. The result of the collaboration of these two men under the patronage of Pope Urban IV was the monumental commentary upon Aristotle by St. Thomas, by which Aristotle was to become an ally of the Christian faith.

An understanding of Thomas' metaphysics and theology involves us at once in a consideration of his logical structure which, though Aristotelian in essence, is, at the same time, the creation of his own fertile mind. We must therefore explain as clearly as possible, within a relatively short analysis, the main premises of St. Thomas' thought.

Our age stands at the opposite pole to that of the Scholastics. Modern man concerns himself primarily with the mechanics of motion and the processes of evolution, both of which involve change. The modern conception of the world is based on the fact that everything moves and changes; and the philosophy of modern man, from Galileo to Einstein, is a philosophy of motion, change, and evolution. Mechanics and evolutionism dominate modern thought. Hence, the science of mechanics for the laws governing the movements of, and changes in, inanimate bodies; while the doctrine of evolution accounts for the processes and changes in living beings.

But medieval man concerned himself not with motion and change, but with the *being* that changes, from form to form and from species to species: the *being* that is man, the *being* of God, the *being* of anything.

What is it *to be?* That is St. Thomas' main question.

Thomas finds that the most important fact about any existing thing is that it *is;* we cannot question the fact that *it is.*

Upon this irreducible minimum of *being,* St. Thomas builds his metaphysics.

We begin with the datum that something *is;* and in this acknowledgement of the fact that anything *is,* there lies a fundamental recognition that *being* is foundational to reality.

It may sometimes *seem* that the contrary is true; that everything is constantly changing into something else.

Because of this, modern man is obsessed by the apparent reality of change, and he concludes therefore that *change* is fundamental to reality. But, for St. Thomas, as for the Scholastics in general, the fundamental reality is *being*, not change; *things change because they are not yet complete*, they change insofar as they *are not*; but their reality *is*, and is adequately understood not in the mixture with not being which is made manifest through change; on the contrary, their reality is only adequately comprehended as part of that which is *complete* and *unchanging* — God.

Six centuries later, Hegel, the great German philosopher, was to utter the self-same truth in somewhat more elaborate language when he said: "All *finite* things involve an untruth; they have a notion and an existence, but their existence does not meet the requirements of the notion. God alone is the thorough harmony of notion and reality." God is, for Hegel, absolute thought . . . All that *is*, is real only as a moment in this absolute Mind; hence as a manifestation of the divine, absolute Idea. Here too, in 19th century absolute idealist philosophy, there is a dependence of philosophy on religion, of metaphysics on theology. In the 13th century, however, it was St. Thomas who gave expression to this insight when he said that the being of anything can only be truly comprehended as part of the Being that *is complete:* God.

Hence, for St. Thomas, *being is,* but it is always changing; and there is an ultimate unchangeable being which includes all that into which things change. There is change from *one state of being to another:* not just change, but change of *states of being.* Everything that a being can be reveals itself as finite and *limited* being at each moment of its existence; hence the necessity of its changing into something else.

Now the medieval philosophers believed in the power of reason to fathom the nature of reality and to know it in the mind as it is in *fact* and in *truth!* It is because of this ingrained faith in reason that we find St. Thomas attempting a transformation of the Christian faith through the infusion into it of a rational factor. For this purpose he utilized Aristotelian notions such as being and non-being, matter and form, the actual and the potential, etc., as rational weapons. Reason ascends to a level higher than sense. It is reason that tells us that what we see, touch, taste, etc., *is;* and it tells us further that it is imperfect, *less actual* than it could be; in other words, that whatever we experience through sense reveals through its changing states something which is ultimate, complete and unchanging, hence that that which meets us in the world of sense is merely partially actual. It cannot reveal all that is itself; but the more we know about it, the less imperfect it becomes; and the less unknowable it becomes, the more actual and real it becomes. Upon this premise St. Thomas builds his immense superstructure.

To *be* or to exist was, for St. Thomas, a divine privilege since *God himself was the Infinite Act of Being or Existing*. It is perhaps in the interrelationship between these two aspects of the nature of Reality, the interrelationship between the divinity of all being and the Being of the Divine, that the uniqueness of Thomas' outlook resides. We shall revert to this a little later; let us now rather acquaint ourselves with the personality of this great man. Who was Thomas Aquinas?

III.

St. Thomas' works reveal a deep radiant peacefulness; and one finds it difficult to believe that the life of the man who composed these majestic and logical lines had, in great measure, consumed itself in strife. A fundamental quality of inner peace contrasts sharply in Thomas, with an outwardly turbulent life.

In his 45th year — five years before his death — writing "On the Perfection of the Spiritual Life" he ends with the following words:

> "If anyone wishes to write against this, I will welcome it. For true and false will in no better way be revealed and uncovered than in resistance to a contradiction, according to the saying: 'iron is sharpened by iron'. (Prov. 27:17) And between us and them may God judge, who is blessed in eternity. Amen."

The Count Lundulf of Aquino, father of St. Thomas, Lord of Loretto and Belcastro, was one of the most loyal vassals of the Emperor Frederick II. The Emperor and the Pope were then in a life and death struggle, and the Count, Thomas' father, was naturally involved in it.

But his youngest son, Thomas, he of the saintly spirit
and divine intellection — what cared he for these earthly
struggles? It seemed to him a waste of time to follow
the fortunes of his father's royal house. What he wanted
was peace and tranquillity for study and meditation.

Thomas was preparing himself for a function far removed from the conflicts of this world and superior to
all its aims and ideals. He had decided on preaching the
truth.

At fifteen, we find him studying at the Benedictine
Abbey of Monte Cassino which was situated between the
Papal and the King's respective territories, so that it
came directly into the zone of battle, and the more so
since Monte Cassino was also a castle of the King. In
the year 1239, the Pope announced the excommunication
of Frederick II. The Emperor countered by ordering the
fortification of the castle greatly expanded and its gar-
rison augmented. The monks had to leave their monastery. Thomas Aquinas, a lad of 15, went on to Naples. It must have been destiny itself that drove him
from the seclusion of the monastic life into the very
center of the intellectual battlefield of that day — the
University of Naples — a school which Frederick II himself had formed to combat the Church. Hence, the "Liberal Arts" departments, and — Aristotle. Here he also
found what his heart most desired, the mendicant orders:
for the young nobleman, Thomas, wanted to become a
mendicant monk; that was his greatest wish.

But at that time, the two newly established mendicant
orders, the Franciscan and the Dominican, were looked
upon with contempt by the respectable society of the

day, the lords, the middle class, and the secular clergy, all of whom called these mendicants the "demented" "poor men" — even "heretical" and "sons of the anti-Christ," for they were, most of them, "Aristotelians," a term of derision in those days.

Strange, that this Order of St. Dominic, which combines the two ideals of study and poverty, should have been the attractive force in the life of this young man of noble birth; so that, at the age of twenty, Thomas joined the Order. Other young noblemen of the time also entered these mendicant orders; but in the case of Thomas, his decision to become a mendicant Dominican friar aroused the ire of Frederick II, since Thomas was the son of one of his vassals. And Thomas' father was heartsick at the thought of his princely son becoming a disreputable mendicant, the more so since the brother of the Count of Aquino was the abbot of Monte Cassino to which office his son might no doubt have succeeded had he so desired. In fact, the whole family of the Count looked with something not unlike horror upon this radical step of Thomas, the youngest son of that noble house who had by this act disgraced it. But Thomas, like so many other inspired princes of history, had caught a glimpse of the invincible power of truth and its immeasurably higher worth than worldly power; and he disdained the opinions of lesser men who would never understand his clear perceptions because of the distorting media of their worldly minds. So he went on his way regardless of what others thought.

But the Emperor did not see it thus. To him it appeared as though the son of his most trusted vassal had joined, at least morally, with the opposing forces: those of the Pope. Indeed, all Franciscans and Dominicans were commonly regarded as allies of the Pope. Furthermore, because of his family attachments, the action of Thomas in joining the Dominicans could easily have been construed as treasonable. Therefore it was that the Friars Preachers forthwith dispatched Thomas to Paris. The news of his escape, however, reached certain members of his family and, on the way to Paris, Thomas was captured by his brothers and held prisoner, with the consent and assistance of the Emperor, as it appears from the fact that Pope Innocent IV vehemently protested to the Emperor against this action. Nonetheless, Thomas was imprisoned in his father's castle of San Giovanni for over a year until, with the aid of his sister, he succeeded in making his escape and resuming his journey to Paris. Once again, despite the turmoil of those turbulent days, during which the general council assembled at Lyons dethroned the Emperor, Thomas began his theological studies in this Metropolis of Theology, Paris. He was forthwith dubbed by his fellow students "the dumb ox", presumably because though only a little over twenty he was of huge proportions, strong but of slow movement and a silent bent of mind.

Life in the cloister was not as peaceful as one might suppose. The Dominicans, as well as the Franciscans, were being insulted and physically attacked on the streets of Paris and elsewhere because of their presumed "heretical" and "enlightened" views, due mainly to their Aristotelian leanings, until the King of France himself, Saint Luis, who was later to become a friend of St.

Thomas, sent a royal guard to the convent to protect it against assaults and vandalism.

It was here, in Paris, that Albertus Magnus taught, and Thomas became his pupil, out of which there developed a friendship between master and pupil which was to effect a change in the entire intellectual outlook of the Western world. Soon, Albert and Thomas were to be transferred to Cologne where Albert established a college for the Friars Preachers; Thomas spent several years in intellectual work, maturing rapidly here. From Cologne he was summoned back to Paris to teach at the university, but both he and the saintly Franciscan Bonaventure were refused permission to teach there because of their being "mendicants." The Pope, however, ordered that permission to teach be granted them, whereat the University boycotted Thomas' inaugural dissertation. But all these attempts to discredit him proved futile and Thomas was in the end to become one of the most beloved and renowned among the teachers at the University of Paris.

It was now that his first work of importance, *On Essence and Existence,* was conceived and written. And thereafter came his other writings, including the *Summa Contra Gentiles,* culminating in his main work, the *Summa Theologica,* on which he labored for seven years without completing it. At no time did Thomas stay in any one place more than two or three years. After teaching three years as full professor of theology at the University of Paris, he was summoned to the Papal Court where he taught under Urban IV, after which he went to Rome on an assignment to establish a college of his

Order there. After two years in Rome, a new Pope, Clement IV, summoned him again to the Papal Court at Viterbo. There Thomas wrote his treatise *On the Governance of Princes;* then he went back again to Paris where his presence at the University was urgently needed to combat Augustinianism and Latin Averroism with Aristotelianism.

It must be remembered that all of these journeys entailed traveling by mule or on foot since Thomas was a mendicant friar. Arriving in Paris, he plunged into the tumultuous issues which were shaking that religious world, and he did it with a majestic calm and deliberation. While there, in the short period of three years, he also composed his voluminous commentaries on nearly all the works of Aristotle, the Epistles of St. Paul, and the Gospel of St. John; also the great *Quaestiones Disputatae* as well as a short summary of the whole of theology which he named the *Compendium Theologiae.* These works were all intended to resolve the intellectual conflicts of his day, and, along with these, he wrote numerous treatises for his *Summa Theologica.* In 1272 he was again recalled to Paris, and a little later, was commissioned to found another college for his Order, this time in Naples.

Suddenly, one year later, the Pope summoned him to a new general council at Lyons. It was toward the end of the winter of 1273-74 that Thomas set out on his long journey for this purpose. While on the way, at the Cistercian Monastery of Fossanova, he took ill, worsened rapidly, and died a short time thereafter. He was not quite 50 years old.

WHAT THE GREAT PHILOSOPHERS THOUGHT

The most remarkable feature, perhaps, about the works of St. Thomas is the fact that such masterpieces of majestic, logical reasoning as well as the calm which permeates them, (causing them to be justly compared with the organ fugues of Johann Sebastian Bach) should have been composed by him amidst the noisy strife and storms of the reigning jealous princes, churchly and secular, of his day, and their wars for theological supremacy. Thomas Aquinas, whose sole aim was the quest of truth, remained undisturbed, and his mind unclouded, by these contentious factions. His biographers repeatedly mention his enormous powers of concentration. It is said, that while writing his chief works, it seemed as though his senses were completely numbed; engrossed in thought even at meal-time, his plate would be removed without his becoming aware of it. Once, as he was dictating at night, he failed to perceive that the candle which he was holding had burned to the bottom and was singeing his fingers. He was a model of composure, even under the most exacting demands, and his works are the most impersonal expressions of any human mind during that turbulent century. There is no trace of subjective characteristics or personal traits throughout his immense intellectual output; but it is true to say, nonetheless, that the grandeur of his personality is reflected in his monumental creations.

As early as 1210, fifteen years before Thomas was born, the authorities forbade the teachings of Aristotle's natural science in Paris. Later, the *Metaphysics* of Aristotle was banned; and throughout the century it seemed to those who ruled over the spiritual destiny of Western man that Aristotle's conclusions contradicted some of the most cherished of Christian dogmas; hence the bans against Aristotle were renewed, again and again, during the 13th Century.

Thomas, who championed Aristotle as a rational fortification of the Christian faith, fared no better during his lifetime. His works, too, were prohibited as being against the best interests of the Christian Church. And even after his death, in 1277, all attempts at reconciling Aristotelianism with Christianity were denounced at both Oxford and Paris. But the spirit of the "Angelic Doctor," the saintly and inspired Thomas, won out in the end. The tide soon turned: the first great body to accept Thomism was the Dominican Order itself which in 1278 officially adopted the philosophy of their brother Thomas; and a half century later, in 1323, Thomas was canonized. Then, in the 16th century, it was officially decreed by the Church that he rank equally with the four great Latin fathers — Ambrose, Augustine, Jerome, and Gregory. Finally, in 1879, Pope Leo XIII pronounced Thomism the basic philosophy of the Roman Catholic Church.

But, whatever the judgment of the Church and the vicissitudes of his worldly fortunes, St. Thomas stands to this day as the grand example of intellectual faith and spiritual honesty, by which he succeeded in turning the superstitious and bigotted religion of the Middle Ages into the enlightened philosophic and rational religion which Christianity always had within it the intrinsic power to be. For these, and for other reasons purely philosophical which we shall soon note, he may be said to rank with Plato and Aristotle through his power to bring reason to bear upon the great problems that relate to the life of man and the nature of the universe — always with an invincible faith in the divine in man and the world.

The Thomistic view, as we have seen, is closely associated with that of Aristotle. For Aristotle, the changing world of physical reality bears *within itself* something which is changeless. And this permanent and abiding factor is the object of true knowledge. The human mind need not turn to another world of pure ideas (in the Platonic sense) in order to find truth. It finds it in the nature of things themselves. Thomas maintained essentially the same position. The Augustinians of Thomas' day, following St. Augustine, had placed the certainty of human knowledge in the divine Mind through which our minds share in the light of the divine ideas.

But for Thomas, the Aristotelian, the human mind can know the truth by its own natural light. Its own perfection, which is part of the perfection of God who is its author, guarantees the truth of its pronouncements. St. Thomas recognizes that the natural object of our knowledge is to be found in the physical world of sense and that we are by nature adequately equipped to comprehend that world. Starting with the data of the senses we can rise to a knowledge of the source of our existence. This is the goal of human reason.

Now, for Thomas, the soul of man is the substantial form of the body. There is a union of soul and body which makes man man. He is a composite of soul and body, and these, when united, form the complete reality, *the substance — man*. And, for St. Thomas, that which thinks is the *substantial reality* — the *whole man*. The act of knowing is, for him, not an act of the intellect or soul alone, but of the entire man, *body and soul*. Man's interest rises to God, but knowledge in man begins with the senses; his intellect is turned *outward* to the material world, and the senses thus become the channels of all natural knowledge.

From the point of view of *essence*, the soul is only a part of the complete man. But from the point of view of *existence*, the human soul has a complete spiritual *act of existing* of its own; it communicates to the body that act of existing, so that there results but *one substantial existence* of the whole composite being — *man*. St. Thomas, therefore, finds the unity of man to consist in man's *act of existing*.

Again, God has no need of anything; He does not need the universe. If it exists, it is only because of God's supreme goodness, because He wishes a world to share in His perfection. From another point of view, however, the universe is a consequence of God's Infinite Act of Existing, so that the infinite freedom of God, the infinite goodness of God, and God's Infinite Act of Existing, are equally the cause of the being of the world.

If the universe expresses God's Will, that will is yet itself a manifestation of God's Intelligence. All creatures, coming as they do from God, have a divine end in view; namely, to achieve perfection and thus to resemble God. The intellect of man can lead him to the apprehension of the highest good; and the traces which man discovers of the divine in nature spurs him on to a desire for knowledge of God's essence. But His natural reason alone cannot lead man directly to God. No matter how advanced and how lofty his rational speculations may be they must fall short of this ultimate goal. It is to *supernatural powers* that man must turn for ultimate happiness and the satisfaction of his deepest cravings. Indeed, by our free will it is made possible for us to turn to God and He is ever ready to assist us with supernatural aid to attain that happiness which otherwise would lie completely beyond our grasp.

The order of *grace* or faith is the means by which God makes this supernatural attainment possible; the possibility of a union with Him is best proven by the Incarnation whereby God Himself became Man to relieve us of our fear of not being able to unite with Him. Grace completes the natural; there is no conflict between nature and grace; the supernatural merely elicits the deepest needs and aspirations of the natural; grace supplants, because it surpasses knowledge in the Christian, St. Thomas, as it could not in the pagan Aristotle.

———

The classical Greek ideal was one of pure intellectual activity. Aristotle's conceptions mark the apex of this ideal. It is to these conceptions that the later Middle Ages turned, with all their spiritual might, in order to harmonize Aristotle with the Christian longing for salvation; because these demands of man's higher nature resulted, for medieval man, in the most soul-stirring adventures and conquests.

St. Thomas brings these conflicts to a focal point through his analysis of the will and the intellect in the nature of man and in the being of God. Man's will is primarily determined by a knowledge of the good; but it is the intellect which in each individual instance judges as to what is good, and thus determines the will. The will can only strive for that which is *known* to be good; its ethical conduct follows necessarily from a prior *knowledge* of the good.

Man's free will, which is thus bound up with his intellect, gives us a cue to the relationship obtaining between *God's Will* and the *divine Intellection*. God, too, creates only that which His wisdom ordains to be good. Hence the divine Wisdom is also superior to the divine Will; the divine Will is determined by God's Wisdom. *God ordains that the good be because His Wisdom recognizes it as good.*

Man's final destiny, being a state of eternal blessedness, must rest ultimately, even as St. Augustine realized, upon a vision of God which is intuitive and transcendent. This eternal vision of God, results necessarily in the love of God by which the final consummation is achieved.

It was Dante, the poet of Scholasticism, who gave this supernal vision its most beautiful expression. In fact, Dante is *the* poet of the Thomistic philosophy. And his Beatrice is the embodiment of the Thomistic ideal; for Beatrice is that vision, the eternal vision of heavenly beauty, grace and truth which every human soul craves, *insofar as it is rational.* The poet of Scholasticism thus ennobled the intellectual vision of the philosopher, and Dante and St. Thomas join in the beatific vision.

THE HIERARCHY OF BEING:
FROM MATTER TO GOD

Theology is, for St. Thomas, the supreme science, the science of God. And since God is the supreme end which all things desire, all the other sciences have this science, theology, as their true end. The special sciences give us a knowledge about things which are relative. Theology, on the other hand, is the science of the Absolute, of the perfect and complete end.

All things involve a deficiency and seek completion and fulfillment. But their true and ultimate completion they can find only in God. Thomas evolves a hierarchy of substances, from the lowest in the material realm to the divine, and he posits an entire series of intermediate beings between man and God. These are the angels, occupying the upper regions immediately below God. St. Thomas gives us an exhaustive account of the nature and attributes of the angels; in fact, being so much closer to God, they were deserving of a more extended treatment than that which is merely physical; hence the disproportion between the large section in the *Summa Theologica* devoted to angelology and the relatively small part relegated to physics.

St. Thomas classifies three groups of angels, under each of which there are three subordinate orders; thus, nine in all: Seraphim, Cherubim, Thrones, Dominations, Virtues, Powers, Principalities, Archangels, and, to complete the list of nine, there are, finally, mere angels, themselves differentiated according to the degree of the adequacy of their knowledge of God.

Modern man has reversed the process. He is not interested in angels, and his devotion to the physical and material far surpasses the quest of the purely spiritual, angelic or otherwise. But St. Thomas tells us that species of angels "exist in exceeding great number far beyond all material multitude . . . The reason for this is that, since it is the perfection of the universe that God chiefly intends in the creation of things, the more perfect some things are, the greater the abundance in which they are created by God." *(Summa Theologica)*

The continuity of Being is an important part of Thomas' world view. There is an unbroken series of substances in the Thomistic hierarchy of being. Hence there must be beings to fill the gap between man and God: there must be angels.

Furthermore, there is only one angel to each species. This is so because it is matter that differentiates the various individuals of a species; but angels, being immaterial, cannot differ materially. They differ only *formally;* hence there must be innumerable species of angels, forming an angelic hierarchy, each species of which is represented by only *one* angel. Materially they do not differ, since they do not participate in matter — for the angels are bodiless creatures — but formally they do differ since it is their various forms or species that make them different one from another; but that is also what limits them to one of a kind, each to a single species or form. In short, it is matter that individualizes, and since angels are not material, there can be no individualization within each species; there is one angel to each species and as many species as there are angels.

The angels, being matterless forms, are each a species unto himself.

The intellects of the angels are different from the intellects of men; being independent of matter, bodiless, they are not bound to the bodily organs of sense, hence not dependent on sense-perception for their understanding; they can therefore know more adequately, truly and directly than sense-informed beings such as man is.

But, though the intellects of angels are, no doubt, because of this independence on matter, higher than man's, they do not approach God's intellection, since the angels are still only finite, not self-existent but created beings; hence their essence is not identical with their existence.

God is highest in the hierarchy of being: infinite, perfect, absolute, pure Actuality. But below God are all the other grades and orders of beings; and these it is the aim of science to know.

1. *Science* gives us a knowledge of things through their causes — it tells us of the cause or wherefore of anything, any phenomenon or event. Furthermore, these causes which science discovers are the underlying, permanent and unalterable principles *in the nature of things.* Hence, science leads us to a knowledge of universal and necessary laws to explain the fleeting and contingent world which we contact through the senses. Science thus yields real and true knowledge because universals are real and true.

Universals have a threefold being: in the mind of God (ante rem) as a perfect cause; in the human mind as an idea or image of concrete things; and in things themselves (in re). It is the business of science to discover these universals in things.

2. *Philosophy* has a dual function: it may concern itself with natural truths, which have little or no bearing on man's ultimate destiny or his relation to God; but it concerns itself also with truths of a higher order (such as the existence of God) which are common to both philosophy and theology. When these two, philosophy and theology, deal with a common subject-matter, they harmonize in revealing both the divine nature and man's destiny. For God is the source of both, reason and revelation, either of which, stemming from God, must be true. God does not contradict Himself, nor will He deceive us — hence science and philosophy, which are natural to reason, can aid faith which has the divine end in view.

3. *Theology* is the science which belongs to the domain of faith and is distinct from reason; faith is a continuation of reason; because human thought is limited it needs faith to complete it. There are certain truths which are peculiar to theology alone, truths which neither science nor philosophy can comprehend though they may help in substantiating and verifying them. These truths belong exclusively to faith — they are of the very mystery of faith, such as the Incarnation and the Trinity, both of which are beyond reason; and the human mind can neither demonstrate nor comprehend them; they belong solely to theology and can be comprehended only by the authority of God Who revealed them to man.

However, the existence of God is a subject which

belongs equally to philosophy and to theology. We have already pointed out that *being* is, for St. Thomas, a fundamental category, universal in extent. First we affirm that anything *is;* then we proceed to a *specific class* of being — man, animal, and we say "this man *is*", "this animal *is*", by eliciting specifically and explicitly what is implicit in the notion of Being in general.

Being is thus the most universal of notions, including all that is or can be, from the lowest, which is mere potency (materia prima) to the highest (God) Who is pure Actuality. And between these two extremes of the *merely potential and the purely actual there lies the* entire realm of created things. Everything that is, is a mixture of actuality and potency (actus et potentia), except pure matter (mere potency) and God (pure Actuality).

Even the angels, though they are immaterial, are what they are because of the union in them of their *essence and act of existing,* and, of *substance and accident.* In all other things (i.e. material things) the composition is threefold: *essence and existence, substance and acciden,* and *matter and form.*

God alone is not composite in nature. In God there is neither materiality nor potency of any kind. His essence is His existence. He is pure Actuality. His action *is* His Substance.

If we could comprehend what we mean when we say "God exists" we would see immediately that His existence is involved in His Being; that in the proposition "God exists" the subject God includes the predicate existence. But since we cannot adequately comprehend the subject God, we do not see how existence necessarily follows from His Being. Therefore, the proposition "God exists" is not, for man, a self-evident or analytical proposition, and we must go in quest of proofs for the existence of God. *We then strive to demonstrate the truth of that which would be self-evident could we but understand adequately.*

There are, then, according to St. Thomas, five ways by which human reasoning, which proceeds from effect to cause, may prove the existence of God:

1. *Everything that is moved must be moved by something other than itself;* for motion is nothing else than change from potentiality to actuality, but this change can only be accomplished by something which is in a state of actuality. The actual informs, moves and changes the potential. It is impossible for anything to move itself, for that would be for it to be both moved and mover, actuality and potentiality in the same respect, which is impossible. Therefore, whatever is moved must be moved by another, and this by another, and this other again by still another, until we arrive at a first mover, moved by no other: God. Otherwise, we should have to go on to another and another to infinity, which is impossible.

2. From the *relation of cause and effect* we arrive at the same inevitable conclusion; for here again, we cannot go on to infinity. We must rest in a first, ultimate efficient cause among all the efficient causes, or there can be no intermediate causes or effects. Hence we must admit a first efficient cause, which is God, on

Whom all the other causes and hence all finite being depends.

3. *The proof from the relation of the contingent to the necessary:* all things are merely *possible;* they may be or not be; but it would have been impossible for anything to begin to exist, and there would be nothing existing, if there were not something the existence of which is *necessary*. Therefore, we must admit the existence of a necessary being having in itself its own necessity and not receiving it from another, but rather causing in others their necessity; otherwise we would have, again, to assume an infinite number of necessary things which have their necessity caused by another, and this is impossible. *The* necessary being which has its own necessity in itself and receives it from no other is God.

4. This proof proceeds *from the gradation or degrees of perfection* to be found in things. We notice various stages of goodness, beauty and perfection in created things; but these grades of goodness, beauty, etc., can only be conceived by us because we at the same time conceive of a maximum of goodness, beauty, perfection, etc.; consequently, we conceive that which is most being, for the things that are of maximum truth, beauty, goodness, are also of maximum being, as Aristotle explains in his *Metaphysics* ii. But,the maximum in any genus is the cause of all that is contained in that genus; the maximum of heat which is fire being the cause of heat in all hot things.

Therefore, there must be also a maximum being which stands in the relation of cause to the being, the goodness, beauty, and every other perfection which is to be found in varying degrees in the world; and this maximum which stands in the relation of cause to the being, the goodness, the perfection, etc., in the world, is God.

5. *"From the governance of the world"*: the order and adaptation to be found in the universe. In those things, such as natural bodies, which though lacking knowledge act for an end, so as to obtain the best results, it is evident that they attain their ends designedly. They cannot move towards an end unless they be directed by some being endowed with knowledge and intelligence of which they possess neither by themselves. Therefore, there exists an intelligent being by whom all natural things are directed to their ends; and this being is God.

All of these arguments, it must be noted, are intended by St. Thomas to prove, not as Anselm tried to prove, that if we *think* of God at all we must think of Him as existing. With St. Thomas the reasoning proceeds realistically. He argues not from ideas but from empirical facts. We cannot doubt the facts: that there is motion in the world, that events have causes, that there is order, adaptation and design in the universe. For St. Thomas, the only way to explain these facts, and explain them adequately, is by the existence of a supreme Being, God, Who is the Cause of these effects, the source of the motion, the causality, the contingency, as well as the perfectability in the world. And, St. Thomas rests his case with an unbounded confidence in these rational proofs; for reason is, for him, God's gift to man by which we may arrive at truth. Faith leads man to the same end through revelation, but faith must never contradict reason. Hence the two fields, reason and revelation, philosophy and theology, overlap.

The existence of God may be demonstrated rationally (through philosophy) and apart from revelation (theology). Indeed, the most important part of philosophy deals with matters of theological import and forms what Aquinas called *natural theology* as distinct from the *revealed theology* of the faith.

St. Thomas, then, bases his case for the existence of God not on the ground that God exists because we have an idea of Him in our minds, for no finite creature can have any adequate idea of the infinite; nor must we argue for the existence of God on the principle that there must be a creator for the created universe. Aristotle's view that the universe and the matter in it are eternal is just as reasonable as the view that God created the world out of nothing; for in this case there is, for Aristotle, an *eternal creation* by which *God's existence* eternally "creates" the universe. Aristotle held that there is an endless actualization of potentiality in the world which constitutes all universal activity. And this perpetual actualization of the potential depends upon an uncreated, self-caused, completely Actualized Form, a Being whose sheer perfection makes the whole world move and behave as it does; this perfect Being, the cause of all motion and change in the world accounts for the necessity of things being as they are, and is the source of the harmony, beauty and orderliness in the universe. Our reason, then, at once tells us that God exists.

But we must conclude also that God's necessary being is *pure Actuality:* one, immutable, perfect and supremely good; also, that He is infinite, and hence that He must possess, to an infinite degree, knowledge, wisdom, benevolence, freedom, and power, and so much of these and to so superlative a degree as to dwarf any of these as found in finite creatures. Indeed, so inconceivably, supremely perfect is God's knowledge which is a knowledge only of Himself, that the whole formal structure of the universe constitutes a sublime, eternal plan or model in the divine mind according to which the world is created.

God, then, exists; but when we are asked *what* He is, we cannot tell. In the *Summa Theologica*, St. Thomas explains that while the supreme happiness of the blessed in heaven consists in their pure and unhindered vision of the divine Nature, even this pure sight of the human mind cannot fully or adequately embrace the nature of God.

We may, it is true, by analogy, infer much regarding the divine nature, sublimating and purifying infinitely the attributes which denote perfection in created things; we may also arrive at a closer notion of God by negating all that implies imperfection and finitude and thus come closer to God by understanding what He is *not.* Hence, even under the limitations of our finite human understanding, we may rise to some measure of comprehension of God's Being. Thus we conclude that God is infinite, one, immutable, perfect, eternal.

Furthermore, we may designate with certainty that God is the *Creator* and *Preserver* of His creatures; that according to God's divine plan in His infinite Mind He fashioned all things after a series of perfect ideas or eternal patterns which have existed in the divine Mind throughout eternity; that He preserves and governs the world, watches over all His creatures and sustains them in their being so that they lapse not into the nothingness from which they came; also, that God aids us in all our strivings, cooperates in our actions, sustains us in our judgments and helps us by all means, natural and supernatural. Last, but not the least of God's great goods, is His Being the ultimate end of our being, the divine goal for which all things were made and to attain which all rational creatures strive.

In Thomas' own words, he tries to make it clear to us: "that all things tend to be like unto God; . . . that the last end of all things is to become like . . . God; that things have a natural tendency to be like God for as much as He is a Cause" and things are "causes of other things; . . . that God is eternal . . . unchangeable . . . having neither beginning nor end . . . for only things which are moved are measured by time: because *time is the measure of movement,*" but "God is absolutely without movement . . . therefore we cannot mark *before* and *after* in Him . . . in Him there is not being after non-being, nor can He have non-being after being; also is it impossible to find any succession in His Being, because these things cannot be understood apart from time . . . but God has all His Being simultaneously, and in this consists the notion of eternity"; . . . "that in God there is no passive potentiality", for "in God there is no matter"; "that in God there is no composition . . . every composite is subsequent to its components. Therefore the first being, God, has no component parts; . . . that in God there is nothing outside His nature . . . for anything outside its nature has something added to itself . . . in God there is no necessity imposed by another, for He is necessary of Himself and the cause of necessity in other things . . .; that God is His own essence . . . for in everything that is not its own essence there must needs be some kind of composition" . . . but "in God there is no composition. Therefore God is His own essence."

"In God Existence and Essence are the same since He exists necessarily of Himself . . . there is no accident in God . . . nothing can accrue to God besides His essence nor can anything be accidentally in Him . . .; that God Who is not distinct from His own existence is universally perfect being . . .; that terms applied to God . . . and to creatures . . . terms that denote perfection, goodness, wisdom, cannot be said of God except by similitude and metaphor, etc., etc."

The main concern of this chapter on St. Thomas Aquinas is with his views regarding the nature and being of God. We have consequently perforce had to eliminate many of the abiding ¡contributions of St. Thomas to the cosmological, psychological, moral and political doctrines of his and of succeeding centuries. Among these may be mentioned his distinctions, in the realm of *psychology,* of the powers of the nutritive soul (in plants), of the appetitive soul (of animals) and of the human soul which contains both of the lower orders, the nutritive and the appetitive, yet transforms these through the relation which the powers of nutrition and appetition bears to the intelligence of man and the higher ends which these serve in man. In *jurisprudence*, we have his view of law as the extrinsic principle of morality, and therefore his conception of law as obligatory only if it is reasonable, if it is for the good of the community, and if it is issued by proper authority and is properly promulgated; also, his distinction between *eternal*, or *divine law* and *natural law* which is a participation in the divine law, and is, as he says, written "in the fleshly tables of the heart"; and finally, *positive law* derived from eternal law and divided into *divine, ecclesiastical,* and *civil law.* In *politics*, we may mention his advanced view of *the State*, which is a result, for him, of the fact that "man is naturally ordained for the society of his fellow-men" and that those in authority in any civil society must have in view the public good, and that if any State loses sight of this it becomes unjust and tyrannical, and that when this occurs, both the conscience of the individual and the church have the authority to absolve the subjects from obedience to the ruler or tyrants, with tyrannical power always being held in check also by the *popular will;* for the aim of the State, according to St. Thomas, is not only economical, but also moral; hence it must provide for the education of all its members and it is incumbent upon it to be certain that no citizen suffers want. Thomas has no special preference for the democratic, aristocratic or monarchical form of government, since it is not the particular form of government that matters but rather the fidelity with which government in power adheres to the main purpose for which governments are instituted, namely, to insure the happiness and prosperity of their subjects. Finally, his views on morality: that the end of all human actions is the attainment of happiness but that God alone can fill the void in the human heart, a void which no amount of satisfaction of desires can fill, because it belongs to the dignity of man to seek nothing short of final and ultimate happiness or the attainment of the infinite good, which is God; therefore, all rational human actions, conscious or unconscious, must be directed toward the consummation of that one final goal: *the attainment of the infinitely good.* The enjoyment of this infinitely good in its entirety, however, is beyond our reach in this life; we must therefore look for its fulfillment in the life to come. Here on earth, in the meantime, we can so direct and govern our lives as to issue in actions which will tend to promote the supreme end for which man was created; and, in a general way, we may say that when the *object* of an act, the *circumstances* surrounding the act, and the *intention* are *good,* then the action is *good;* and if any of these are *evil,* then the action is evil. Thomas holds that man is naturally endowed with the power of virtuous conduct, but that the natural virtues, whether intellectual or moral, are acquired by the performance of actions pertaining to these virtues, with the theological virtues — faith, hope and charity — crowning the rest. These are but a few of the building-blocks of Thomas' immense philosophical edifice, in addition to his monumental contribution to the problem of the nature of God and the relationship of the human to the divine.

WHAT THE GREAT PHILOSOPHERS THOUGHT

For centuries the scholastics of the Middle Ages had labored, slowly gathering materials from all available sources, to build the structure of Scholasticism. St. Thomas synthesized their findings and fulfilled their ideals. Some among the scholastics, the pure rationalists, had abused logic and dialectical reasoning, and the mystics among them had renounced reason. But Thomas now succeeded in putting dialectical thought to sublime uses, giving expression to his own philosophy which is Platonism, Aristotelianism and realism in one. He labored relentlessly at the age-old problem of the relation of faith to reason. It was he who gave it its final form and ultimate solution. He assimilated all that he could utilize from Greek, Arabian, and Jewish sources, freely acknowledging the borrowing and unmindful of the consequences, for he was sure of his aim and firm in his purpose to transform whatever was of value in previous thought to the service of his own supreme end, namely, *the construction of the edifice of a Christian philosophy along rational lines* — and he did this with a sublime faith in truth, and in the firm conviction that knowledge and truth must always harmonize.

He is the grand example of loyalty to ideals and, without doubt, the most influential figure in the whole era of medieval thought.

St. Thomas was no master in the art of literary expression and he has left us no book that can be compared with the *Confessions* of St. Augustine for literary eminence. The brilliant, passionate and suggestive style and the persuasive rhetoric of the earlier saint is not to be found in the later. But his precise, methodical reasoning, and the almost mathematical rigor of his exposition, is well suited to the subjects with which Thomas primarily concerns himself. He depicts on a vast canvas: the meaning and destiny of human life, the nature of God, the ways to salvation, the true and proper aims of philosophy, and the wisdom procurable by man through knowledge and love, natural and divine. These ideals are ever present before the mind of St. Thomas as he pens the immortal sermons, the ten volumes of his *Summa Theologica*, the hymns and prayers, revealing a genius for poetic expression unparalleled in philosophic literature. And his main object, always: to co-ordinate the various aspects of human life and of the order of Nature, so as to make the whole scheme of creation reasonable, intelligible. Hence his perennial desire to reach up from bare existence, nay from nothingness, to the most consummate being — God — the beginning and end of all existence; to discover the intrinsic laws of nature through science and the moral law in man. For St. Thomas, duty and virtue lead to man's perfection, ultimately realized only when man is made like unto God in wisdom and goodness, with reason always as a guide and revelation as the light. It was Thomas' unshakeable conviction that God, being pre-eminently real, cannot be completely unknowable, and man, being grounded in sense, cannot of himself reach the supersensible and the divine. Hence the need of both, reason *and* revelation — the mysteries of Christian Revelation supplementing the limitations of rational human speculation about "immortal things." Christ initiated a new life of union with God and the way to this union is by the imitation of Christ and the reception of his grace and his life in the sacraments of the Church; and the greatest of the Christian virtues: charity.

Thus, St. Thomas, "the master of those who know" of the middle ages, becomes "a flame of heavenly wisdom" for the ages to come, and the Angelic Doctor truly angelic and of immortal fame.

SPINOZA

SPINOZA

(1632-1677)

It is doubtful if anyone ever attempted a deeper knowledge of God, or to understand God's Being more adequately, than the great philosopher Baruch Spinoza.

"It was perhaps from here that God was seen most near", said Ernst Renan, speaking at the dedication of the Spinoza House.

Of all philosophic conceptions of God the most sublime, Spinoza's theological notions have been the most rejected, even as he himself became a "holy outcast" among men. Soaring on wings of thought to infinite regions, his mind encompassed the unknown with the ease of one who traverses familiar terrain, for the divine was not at all foreign to his spirit. However, just because of this, men spurned him and disdained his teachings.

But with the passing generations there came ever better understanding of Spinoza and his thought, so that from the early judgments regarding him, such as that of Carolus Tuinman, Preacher of Middelburg: "Here lies Spinoza.

Would that his words were buried with him . . . the
spiritual plague . . ." and Colerus, who, despite his
admiration for the man, referred to Spinoza's works as
"an abominable production . . . nothing but lies and
blasphemies . . . the most pernicious atheism that ever
was seen in the world", we come to the more moderate
judgment of Leibniz who said: "frankly, Spinoza's arguments do not satisfy me . . . although he explains himself most clearly"; until we reach Spinoza's admiring
worshippers in the 18th and 19th centuries, such as
Schleiermacher, who vehemently defended Spinoza with
the impassioned words: "rejected but holy Spinoza! the
great Spirit of the Universe filled his soul; the infinite
to him was the beginning and end; the Universe his only
eternal love"; and Victor Cousin, who journeyed to the
scenes of the philosopher's early life in Amsterdam, and
said of Spinoza: "he knew neither pleasure nor action
nor glory . . . Adoring the Eternal . . . he disdained the
passing world," and of Spinoza's *Ethics* that it was "a
mystical hymn, a rapture, a suspiration of the soul after
Him who alone can lawfully say: 'I am that I am';"
until, finally, we come upon the testimony of 19th Century
men of science, such as Thomas Huxley, who writes
(Evolution and Ethics): "The student of nature, if his
studies have not been barren of the best fruit of the
investigation of nature, will have enough sense to see
that when Spinoza says: 'By God I understand a being
absolutely infinite, that is, a substance consisting of infinite attributes,' the God so conceived is one that only
a very great fool would deny even in his heart."

Spinoza flashed like a meteor across the Western sky,

three hundred years ago, and the light of his luminous path is still visible to those who peer into the infinities of space, of the universe and God. Indeed, Einstein, in the twentieth century, said: "My God is the God of Spinoza."

––––––––––

Spinoza believed that man is a fleeting incident in an infinite and eternal universe; that an absolute necessity governs the things and events in the world; that good and evil are subjective notions of the mind; and that for supreme happiness man must so reconcile himself to his finitude as to triumph over it, and thus be free to take delight in the infinity of which he may know himself to be a part.

These theses were dear to Spinoza, and entered his philosophy, which was the fruit of a lifetime of meditation upon God, man and the universe, until he came to know them in their interrelatedness.

Man is part of the infinite universe, but he is unique, for he has three classes of proper desires:

"To understand things through their first causes; to govern the passions or acquire the habit of virtue; and *to live in safety and with a sound body."*

To know, to understand, to ascend to first causes — this is primary, for Spinoza; from this all else follows; therefore he calls it an original end of man, not something merely *permitted* but *necessary.*

To make his meaning more precisely clear, Spinoza elsewhere refers to that same knowledge which ascends to first causes as *intuitive science,* which, as he says, proceeds "from an adequate idea of the (formal) essence of certain attributes of God to the adequate knowledge of the essence of things."

In short, to gain an understanding of things through a knowledge of God's attributes: that was Spinoza's aim.

Once this high altitude has been reached, the only view possible is that which sees all reality as, in essence, divine; how else could anything *be?* Nothing really *is* but God and his attributes. The unique station of individual things is their divine station, determined solely through their divine attributes.

For Spinoza, everything is, anything is, because *God is.* Hence he was called an acosmist, since everything appeared to him to be secondary to the divinity through which alone things could be. He was called a pantheist, because he said: "without God nothing could be or be conceived." He was called an atheist, because everything that is, he said, is not by reason of God's *will* or *desire* but because of God's infinite plenitude and perfection. He was called a materialist, because he ¡said that in addition to God being a *thinking* Being he is also an *extended* Being — that extension as well as thought expresses the essence of the divine nature. But none of these designations aptly comprehend his aims, for while the basis of his philosophy is metaphysical, his main end is ethical. Plato long ago said: "God eternally geometrizes," but for Spinoza, the geometry of God's thought is also a means to man's perfection.

We have, in Spinoza, a unique philosophic phenomenon, a personality in whom thought and conduct merged into a single entity, a philosopher who dispensed with all externals for the sake of inner contentment, and one who so co-ordinated the outer and inner aspects of his life as to attain a spiritual equilibrium which he himself termed bliss.

Spinoza may truly be called a martyr for philosophy, though he was not actually put to death because of his intellectual ideals. He suffered for the principles of his philosophic vision, for which he was willing to sacrifice everything in the world — fame, honors, racial and family ties, even friendships. His ethical ideal was the resultant of a metaphysical insight, attainable, as he thought, by all men. The improvement of human understanding would enable it to grasp the essential rationality pervading all things, and so enable man to attain a union of his mind with the intellect of God. And this would serve, also, to emancipate man from bondage to passions, through the adequate ideas of his understanding.

"It is of the utmost service in life to perfect the understanding or reason, as far as we can; and in this one thing does man's highest felicity consist. Indeed, blessedness is nothing but that very satisfaction of the soul which arises from an intuitive knowledge of God . . . but to perfect the understanding is only to comprehend God, His attributes, and the actions which follow from the necessity of His nature. Wherefore, the ultimate aim of the man who is governed by reason, that is, the highest desire, with which he strives to restrain all other desires, is that which impels him to conceive adequately himself and everything that can fall within the scope of his understanding."

WHAT THE GREAT PHILOSOPHERS THOUGHT

The problems and conflicts which occupied Spinoza are still with us. He saw that despite the widespread religious beliefs of mankind, man did not attain a more ethical life, because there was something essential to the *idea of humanity* that had been lost sight of by the religions of his day. Spinoza felt that what was needed was a better understanding or a more adequate knowledge of God, of man's essential self, and his relation to God. This knowledge would make man immortal and, in a measure, divine.

It was genuine religion and true piety that engaged the interest of Spinoza. All the older religions, he felt, were based on fear, on promises of rewards and fear of punishment. People were afraid as to what would happen to them after death, so they believed, blindly, and sometimes irrationally. These, then, were religions based on ignorance, superstition, fear and hearsay. People were religious not because they knew God and understood the workings of divine nature. They were "religious" while being ignorant regarding the divine nature, and they were equally ignorant of their own essential relation to God.

Spinoza thought that if man could learn to love God because he *understood* divinity and what follows necessarily from the divine nature, then he (man) would by that knowledge come naturally upon the path of true religion, piety, and right actions or moral conduct.

As for himself, he felt that he had finally attained this power to view all nature as an eternal order, divine in its manifestations. And the urge to acquire the inner truth of the natural as intimately our own he called "intellectual love." In short, he wanted to show man the way to freedom through adequate understanding.

"A passion", said Spinoza, "ceases to be a passion once we have formed a clear and distinct idea of it." Similarly, man ceases to be an animal once he has formed a clear and distinct idea of himself. If knowledge was imperative, Spinoza did not, however, mean the knowledge obtainable through merely inductive generalizations, such as that of the empirical sciences; these could not lead to essential knowledge and so did not constitute true science, even as a mere adherence to the dogmas of a supernatural religion did not lead to true piety and so did not constitute true religion.

But those who understood him were rare and few. For the Christians he was a Jew! For the Jews he was a Christian! For the scientists he was an abstruse metaphysician! And by all he was despised as an atheist! He was excommunicated. His books were denounced and burned. An attempt was even made on his life, and the publication of any new book, even under an assumed name, entailed fear of the gravest consequences. Spinoza writes to Oldenberg:

"Distinguished and Illustrious Sir:
When I received your letter of the 22nd July, I had set out to Amsterdam for the purpose of publishing the book I had mentioned to you. While I was negotiating, a rumor gained currency that I had in the press a book concerning God, wherein I endeavored to show that there is no God. This report was believed

by many. Hence certain theologians, perhaps the authors of the rumor, took occasion to complain of me before the prince and the magistrates; moreover, the stupid Cartesians, being suspected of favoring me, endeavored to remove the aspersion by abusing everywhere my opinion and writings, a course which they still pursue. When I became aware of this, through trustworthy men, who also assured me that the theologians were everywhere lying in wait for me, I determined to put off publishing 'till I saw how things were going . . ."

The greatest of his works therefore, the *Ethics*, was not published until after his death.

Spinoza retired to a life of seclusion. He had long since given up the honors and rewards of the world as a matter of philosophic conviction. Now he was forced to deny himself the companionship of men as well. Only here and there was there a soul worthy of intercourse, and even these often failed him at the crucial moment of adequate understanding. He took to grinding lenses as a means of earning a livelihood rather than run the risk of impairing his philosophic vision; and he rejected offers from men and institutions that, he felt, were not able to understand him. He worked hard, conversed little, thought much. At the age of 45 he died, broken in body but contented in spirit. A century and a half after his death he was pronounced one of the most religious men that ever lived: "God-intoxicated"; and the judgment of Heine that all future philosophers looked through the glasses that Spinoza polished, is an indication of the immense influence of the man and his thought.

Nonetheless, even to this day much of the esesntial message of Spinoza's philosophy has not thoroughly penetrated the mind of Western man. We have not yet learned to understand, what Spinoza wished us to understand, that human life is a part of the divine drama of mathematical necessity. Few of us have freed ourselves from dogma and superstition. Many have only relinquished one set of dogmas to embrace another: from the dogmas of the established religions they have passed on to the dogmas of empirical science; while, for Spinoza, the paramount concern was man's universal *will to be and to be eternal*. He meditated upon these in his philosophy and strove to achieve eternity in this life. Because of this, he was subject to a great internal conflict that resolved itself into a peace and repose which was immeasurably greater — a calm of surpassing understanding which he succeeded in conveying in his very words to those who could understand him.

For himself, therefore, Josiah Royce says that when viewing the order of nature, Spinoza could exclaim: "While it is necessary, while it it rigid, while it is in one sense merciless, it is also divine, and the value of our knowledge of this order is that thereby we are led to a love of God, to a peace which the world cannot give or take away."

WHAT THE GREAT PHILOSOPHERS THOUGHT

II.

We now turn to a view of Spinoza's main works and his leading doctrines and ideas and then pass, in Part III, to a detailed examination of his conception of God, which is the main object of this chapter. However, that will more readily lend itself to understanding when we have taken note of his general outlook and purpose. The breadth and scope of Spinoza's thought is even at this late date engaging the attention of scholars who continue to unearth undiscovered treasures in Spinoza's spiritual dominions.

We have already seen that while for his contemporaries Spinoza was an atheist and an unbelieving free-thinker, later generations pronounced him the "great and saintly Benedictus" (Jacobi), and the "God-intoxicated" man (Novalis); and that his influence spread universally until Hegel, the great German philosopher, in the 19th Century, could exclaim that to be a philosopher at all, one had first to be a Spinozist. During his lifetime, he was persecuted and despised. Spinoza withdrew within himself and his profound meditations, and his early death marked the end of a life of sublime philosophic synthesis which conveyed peace and contentment to all who could understand him.

But it is precisely here, at the point of understanding, that our difficulties with Spinoza's thought begin; for Spinoza was a philosopher who was, first and essentially, religious and mystical, but one who, unlike other mystics, was at the same time a lover of clear and lucid, correct and precise reasoning. This attempt, to be both mystic and rationalist, is the key to his greatness but it is also the cause of the difficulties we encounter when we seek to comprehend Spinoza's meanings, or endeavor the steep descent from God to the modifications of His Being, the modes of substance or the finite things and ideas of our world; and then the difficult ascent from time to eternity and from finite thinghood to divine and infinite Being.

Other mystics before him had to traverse the same steep, downward path, from God to man and the world, and up again from the finite many to the infinite One; but they were satisfied with what Plotinus called "the flight of the alone to the Alone". But Spinoza's was a *universal* experience, valid for everyone, wherever men live and seek perfection. For, reality and perfection were, for Spinoza, synonymous: the more reality a thing expresses the more perfect it is, and the more perfect a thing is, the more reality it expresses. Man expresses the utmost of finite perfection, since he is, through his intellect, in a position to know and understand divine law; he is therefore the acme of universal centralization, embodying in an eminent degree the reason diffused throughout the universe. In addition, he is also a self-conscious being, and hence capable of reflecting upon his own divine essence, and, indeed, capable of being conscious of his perfectability. Spinoza's philosophy appealed to this rational core in man, for his was a *universal* illumination. Spinoza, too, could have stopped at the purely subjective mystical experience. But he preferred to labor on to universality. Hence his mysticism is rationalistic to a degree previously unknown.

WHAT THE GREAT PHILOSOPHERS THOUGHT

Pursuing his ideal with a calm determination and re-gardless of consequences, it has been pointed out that Spinoza died at an age when Plato had not yet written his *Republic*, Aristotle his *Metaphysics*, Kant his *Critique of Pure Reason*, or Hegel his *Logic*. The urgency to complete his task was with him compelling, and in the three short periods which comprise his life we find the concentrations of those components which constitute his contemplative life as well as his harrowing experiences.

The first of these periods in Spinoza's life dates from his birth in 1632 to the year 1656 in which he was expelled from the synagogue.

His ancestors came to Holland from the Spanish Peninsula. The Jews were fleeing the Spanish Inquisition during those days and among them were the Marranos, that is, such Jews who adopted Christianity for fear of the Inquisition but who, nonetheless, in secret adhered to their own faith. The Dutch were their tolerant hosts. These refugee Jews came to Holland from Portugal in 1593; in 1598 those who had settled in Amsterdam founded the first Jewish synagogue there.

Spinoza's father, who was a merchant, joined the synagogue, and had Spinoza instructed in Hebrew and the Bible. Spinoza, however, even as a very young man, looked elsewhere for ever wider knowledge. He acquainted himself with the Greco-Jewish philosophic tradition, Josephus, Philo, the Talmud, the Kabbalah, Maimonides, Ibn Ezra. Later, he chose, as a means of earning a livelihood, the preparation of lenses for the telescope, which had only recently been invented; and, he became, also, assistant teacher in the private school

of Francis van den Enden, who was a learned skeptic of
the Renaissance. What attracted him most in van den
Enden's library were the works of Giordano Bruno and
Descartes. The language of intercourse among the learned
throughout Europe was still Latin; and Spinoza perfected
his Latin in order to be conversant with the leading
minds of the time.

Then there came the year 1656. Spinoza was now 24
years old. He seldom attended synagogue, and avoided
the company of Rabbis and Doctors of Divinity, in order
not to become a participant in their discussions. Two
of his classmates, however, to whom he seems to have
confided some of his opinions regarding God, matter,
angels and immortality, informed the elders of the
Temple of Spinoza's "heresies"; to the Rabbis these
Spinozistic opinions were shocking in the extreme: that
angels were mere hallucinations of the mind, that the
soul was nothing but life itself, that God's being extended
throughout the world of matter, and that immortality was
only a Rabbinical innovation and not to be met with
in the Old Testament — these ideas seemed to under-
mine not only the Jewish but the Christian religion
as well. And to displease and antagonize their Christian
hosts endangered the moral as well as the physical safety
of the Jews in that happy land.

Spinoza was summoned before the elders of the synagogue, charged with heresy and "contempt for the Torah".
He refused to retract or recant. After numerous warn-
ings, the sentence of excommunication was finally pronounced upon him. To all of which Spinoza remarked,
simply: "it compels me to do nothing which I should

not have done in any case." He changed his name from the Hebrew Baruch ("blessed") to the Latin "Benedictus" which means the same; and retired from all public relations, leaving Amsterdam and settling in a country place not far from the city. Thus there came for Spinoza at 24, the separation from his kindred, his race and his religion. Had Menasseh ben Israel, the head of the Jewish community at Amsterdam, not been in England pleading with Cromwell for admittance of the Jews to that country, it is almost certain that a peaceful settlement between the obdurate young philosopher and the equally unyielding Rabbis of the Temple would have been effected by that wise and tolerant spiritual leader of the Jews. But, destiny decreed, as Will Durant says, "that Spinoza should belong to the world."

His life and his thought, shaken by this experience, were now devoted to a critical appraisal of the time in which he lived. All political institutions, he says, should have as their main aim to save man's freedom of thought from the frenzy of the religiuos institutions. Any religious institution, no matter what creed it serves, whether it be Synagogue, Mosque or Church, will persecute, if and when it gets the power and will inflict the same wrong which it had suffered when it was weak. Hence, Spinoza cautions, religion must be kept separate from the civil government. Religious institutions are all right in their place, but the limits of their authority in relation to the individual must be strictly defined. Reason and the exercise of reason, which is the prerogative of every individual, must remain free. Reason must never become subservient to Scripture, and Scripture need not conform to Reason, since, teaching, as it does, justice and charity, it is, in its own sphere, self-sufficient. The State, also, must not interfere with religion but religion must not determine the State. In this, Spinoza, completely ahead of his time, reaches far into the political and social doctrines of succeeding centuries. And he counsels obedience of the individual to both Church and State in his *outer conduct* while reserving free and unrestricted self-determination of the individual in both thought and speech.

These views found expression in the *Theologico-Political Treatise* published in 1670. The Age of Reason demanded, said Spinoza, an accounting of religion, of the Bible and the God of the Bible. The Holy Books, he said, both Jewish and Christian, were deliberately allegorical and metaphorical, and "adapted, as far as possible, to the understanding of the masses . . . Scripture . . . narrates in the order and style which has most power to move men, and especially uneducated men, to devotion . . . Its object is not to convince the reason, but to attract the imagination." Hence, the miracles of the Bible.

"The masses," writes Spinoza, "think that the power and providence of God are most clearly displayed by events that are extraordinary, and contrary to the conception which they have formed of nature . . . They suppose indeed that God is inactive so long as nature works in her accustomed order; and vice versa, that the power of nature, and natural causes, are idle so long as God is acting; thus they imagine two powers distinct from one another, the power of God and the power of nature." But the philosopher knows that *God and Nature are one and the same being,* acting in accordance with universal and inevitable laws; and it is these that form the object of his adoration. These universal laws he seeks to learn and obey, for he knows "that in reality God acts . . . by the necessity of His nature, and His decrees . . . are eternal truths." The rest of mankind are only too willing to believe that God breaks natural laws and the natural order of events for them. Therefore all the miracles in the Holy Books, which the founders of religions employed for purposes of effect, for these are only vivid metaphors, allegories and emotionally-charged stories — intended for the purpose of impressing the imagination of the multitude, and thus to promote belief. That is why, says Spinoza, religions have had so much more influence over men than philosophers.

Such is the trend of his first published work: *The Theologico-Political Treatise.*

The book, published and printed under an assumed name, was immediately denounced, burned, refuted, Indexed, prohibited by Church and State, Jew and Gentile. Why? Because the excommunicated Spinoza, alone in his quiet study, in the attic of his country retreat, speculating on the causes of his persecution, came to the conclusion that the world in which he lived was ill — spiritually diseased; and the cause of its disease: misguided religion.

The God of the Bible, old and new, was a transcendent Being to be feared and obeyed; what was needed was an understanding of the only true God, the immanent God of Nature who, when understood, could be adored and loved. Spinoza is under the influence of Descartes. Reason, said Descartes, must doubt. But Descartes did not go far enough. He doubted the previously accepted philosophies; but, for Spinoza, the doubt had to be extended so as to cover also the accepted religions. So, in the *Theologico-Political Treatise,* he summoned the Bible, and the religions which sponsored it, to give an account of themselves before the bar of reason.

Spinoza next turned to a more detailed study of Descartes, the resulting work being his *Principles of the Cartesian Philosophy* with an Appendix: *Cogitata Metaphysica,* in which he refashions many of Descartes' conceptions according to his own insights.

At about this same time, Spinoza was working on an important "Short Treatise on God, Man and his well-being" — a sort of prelude to and preview of his chief work, the *Ethics.* This work is dominated by neo-Platonic influences, but also by other philosophico-mystical tendencies of the Middle Ages, notably the Jewish philosophers: Maimonides, Gersonides, and Chasdai Crescas, who had themselves been influenced by Alexandrian Jewish Mysticism, especially the teachings of Philo. But, more than to any of these, Spinoza was indebted to Giordano Bruno who had foreshadowed Spinoza's thought by his doctrine of the identity of God and Nature. All of these influences are patently present in this small book which reveals Spinoza's mental and spiritual progress during the years of transition to his complete and mature philosophy as expressed in the "Ethics."

His next book, *On the Improvement of the Understanding,* was intended by Spinoza as an introduction to the "Ethics". And before propounding his method for the improvement of the human understanding intellectually, Spinoza makes it clear that what is necessary, before anything else, is a revision of the usual ways of life and its attachments to the fleeting and transient things of the world, until we arrive at a love of the things of *eternal and abiding value*. For this purpose he relates his own experiences in this regard and tells how he came to his supreme love of philosophy, for which he was willing to give up everything else.

"After experience had taught me that all things which frequently take place in ordinary life are vain and futile, and when I saw that all the things which I feared, and which feared me, had nothing good or bad in them save insofar as the mind was affected by them, I determined at last to inquire whether there was anything which might be truly good, and able to communicate its goodness, and by which the mind might be affected to the exclusion of all other things. I determined, I say, to inquire whether I might discover and attain the faculty of enjoying continued supreme happiness throughout eternity . . ." He renounces honor, riches, fame, and finds that "the love towards a thing eternal and infinite alone feeds the mind with joy and a pleasure secure from all pain . . . The greatest good therefore is the knowledge of the union which the mind has with the whole of nature . . . The more the mind knows, the better it understands its forces or strength, the better it will be able to direct itself and lay down the rules for itself; and the more it understands the order of nature, the more easily it will be able to liberate itself from useless things: this is the whole method."

In philosophic comprehension alone, then, for Spinoza, is true freedom to be found, and true happiness to be attained.

The chief glory of Spinoza's mind, however, is his *Ethics*.

Let us begin with the Appendix to Part I:

"Those who wish to seek out the causes of miracles, and to understand the things of nature as philosophers, and not to stare at them in astonishment like fools, are considered heretical and impious, and proclaimed as such by those whom the mob adores as the interpreters of nature and the gods. For these men know that once ignorance is put aside, that wonderment would be taken away which is the only means by which their authority is preserved."

"Once ignorance is put aside" — that was Spinoza's great aim: to put aside ignorance. And if ignorance is to be put aside, we might as well begin with what is, for most men, the chief source of their ignorance: God. The first part of the *Ethics*, therefore, treats "Of God". Spinoza was convinced that the concept of God needed re-definition, clarification, and to be divested of its anthropomorphic characteristics.

No one had dared to throw the light of reason on the principles of religion, on the meaning of piety, on the concept of divinity. What was needed was clarification, of the nature of human intellection and its place in the order of nature. For, the mind could understand! The law-abiding character of natural phenomena was the result of a subtle, timeless rationality, whose eternal decrees all material and mental manifestations necessarily obeyed, unavoidably and irrevocably, from the storm-tossed debris in the ocean to the turbulent sweep of the passions in the human soul. The howling wind, the volcanic eruption, and the frenzied cry for revenge had each their natural causes, which could perhaps be controlled, if sufficiently understood!

What is understanding? There is a divine understanding, an infinite understanding, and there is finite human understanding.

Could the human ever attain the divine?

Spinoza thought it could — but not through miracles and the supernatural; rather through natural events and the divine order of their manifestation by way of the attributes of God. For to understand correctly and adequately is to understand things through their divine attributes:

"The highest endeavor of the human mind, and its highest virtue, is to know things with that most perfect kind of knowledge which proceeds from the adequate idea of certain divine attributes to the adequate knowledge of the essence of things."

Now Spinoza could so comprehend extension as an attribute of God, that he could reduce reality to the modifications or "modes" of "extension", and he could so conceive thought as a divine attribute as to reduce reality to the modifications or modes of "thought". Through these two attributes he could view nature *sub specie aeternitatis (from the standpoint of eternity)*, in its essential being, as dwelling in these divine attributes; and that was for him the stage of adequate understanding which does justice to the nature of God, having dis-abused the idea of God of all those characteristics which fail to be commensurate with the nature of God. This is the level of adequate understanding wherein, in Spinoza's words, we no longer *"imagine* God as present but *understand that He is eternal."*

Any other concept of divinity is modelled after our narrow human selves. We must transcend ourselves in order to understand God.

"When you say, that if I do not allow in God the operation of seeing, hearing, observing, willing and the like . . . you do not know what sort of God mine is, I thence conjecture that you believe there is no greater perfection than such as can be explained by these afore-said attributes. I do not wonder at it: for I believe that a triangle, if it could speak, would in like manner say that God is eminently triangular, and a circle that the divine nature is eminently circular: and thus would every one ascribe his own attributes to God." (Epistle 60).

We must rise to a level transcending our finitude and ego-centricity. Then the proportionality of things and events to their divine source and essence will become apparent. For everything expresses the divine nature through the divine attributes. But a stone is not as divine as man. Divinity is, it is true, also of *its* essence but a stone is not conscious of its divine essence, such as it is. Man alone can, through his intellect, become aware of his essential self and his relation to the order of nature, and thereby discover also his eternal kinship with divinity by achieving, through his understanding, an "intellectual love" of God.

That is Spinoza's *positive, rational mysticism!* Not the negative mysticism of the neo-Platonists and "the flight of the alone to the Alone" of Plotinus! Not the absorption in "Nirvana" of the Buddhists where nothing is, including God! For Spinoza *everything is, eternally, in God,* and the conception we fashion of God must be commensurate with His Infinite and Eternal Being. Wherever there is being, there also is God, or nothing could *be!* But God is not *only* being: he is also infinite and eternal. "God is absolutely infinite Being, i.e. a Substance consisting of infinite attributes, each of which (attributes) expresses an eternal and infinite essence."

And since all the infinite attributes express the divine nature equally, it follows that of the two attributes known to man, extension and thought, there is a correspondence of the order of things with the order of ideas, or, as Spinoza puts it: "the order and connection of things is the same as the order and connection of ideas", "the idea of the circle and the actual circle are one and the same thing;" so that, as every object follows of necessity from the divine attribute of extension, so does every idea of the object, correspondingly, follow of necessity from and through the divine attribute of thought. Hence if we could follow the object (the mode) through the attribute of thought to the divine intellection, as an idea in the intellect of God, we would see why it is, why it *must* be what it is, why it cannot be any different.

For, "whatever is, is in God, and nothing can exist or be conceived without God," and, "all things which are made are made by the laws of the infinite nature of God, and necessarily follow from the necessity of His essence," and "things could not have been produced by God in any other manner or order than that in which they were produced."

This is philosophic monism, with a zeal which gained for Spinoza a new sense of the infinite grandeur and perfection of the divine, mystical in content but rational in form; and this rational quest of the mystical and intuitive led him always to the view of the world "sub specie aeternitatis", from the standpoint of eternity.

"I hold", he writes in a letter to a friend, "that God is the immanent, and not the extraneous cause of all things. I say, all is *in* God; all lives and moves in God . . . It is however a complete mistake on the part of those who say that my purpose . . . is to show that God and Nature, under which . . . they understand *a certain mass of corporeal matter*, are one and the same. I had no such intention."

On the other hand, "whenever anything in nature seems to us ridiculous, absurd or evil, it is because we have but a partial knowledge of things, and are in the main ignorant of the order and coherence of nature as a whole", for, "nothing happens in nature which can be attributed to any flaw of nature"; therefore, considered in themselves, even "the emotions of hatred, anger, envy, follow from the same necessity and excellence of nature as does everything else; they have their definite causes through which they are to be understood, and they have their definite properties which are just as worthy of our knowledge as are the properties of any other thing in the mere contemplation of which we find pleasure."

And Spinoza embarks upon a treatment of human emotions and passions as objectively as though he were dealing with geometrical figures, "just", he says, "as though I were dealing with lines, planes and bodies", in order to map out the way of freedom from bondage to the passions which, through the improvement of the understanding, may lead man, in the very act of understanding the universe, to be delivered from it. That is Spinoza's method of salvation: to release us from our narrow horizons, from the prison-house of private pleasures, pains and grievances, the result of a narrowness of outlook which is *ignorance*. The broader our view, the more universal our conceptions, the more cosmic our sympathies, the more enlightened our ideals, the closer are we to God.

III.

What is Spinoza's conception of God?

To understand the peculiar nature of Spinoza's conception of the divine, all-comprehending, all-embracing unity which is God, we must first consider Spinoza's spiritual heritage. Though excommunicated because of his philosophical views and for his abandonment of the customary beliefs, laws and ceremonies of his people, Spinoza nonetheless retained one essential principle of the Jewish faith which must have taken deep root in his soul, and that was: "the Lord, our God, is *one* God."

SPINOZA

But Spinoza subjected this principle to his sovereign reason, and then turned what was the foundation of a religious *monotheism* into a maxim of philosophic *monism*. Out of the cry: "the Lord, our God, is *one* God," Spinoza culled the basic principle of his philosophy: *God is One.*

God is One. Nature is One. Substance is One: eternal, infinite, inevitable, perfect, cause of itself, of all being and all manner and mode of existence.

This was the starting-point of Spinoza's conception of God. But there were other contributory factors which were also instrumental in shaping his view of the divine nature; and these were, first, the influence of medieval Jewish Theology, and second, the ever-widening view of the physical universe of contemporary science; also, third, the philosophy of Descartes with its stress upon the mathematical method of exposition and its faith in the certainty of mathematical reasoning.

Taking these influences in the order of their enumeration, we may say that the first, that of medieval Jewish Theology, left with him a sense of the infinite perfection, grandeur and power of the divine nature. The second, the rise of modern science, with its ever-widening view of the physical universe, helped Spinoza to clarify his attempts at divesting the divine nature of all anthropomorphic notions, while the mathematical method of the Cartesian philosophy served to combine the mystical in Jewish medievalism with the precision of mathematical thinking. Hence, Spinoza could refer to the one, ultimate reality as *God, Nature, or Substance*, depending on whether it was the religious, the scientific, or the metaphysical conception of the divine Being that he wished to lay stress on; and the fusion of the basic factors in these, the fusion of religious fervor, scientific realism and mathematical reasoning, resulted in Spinoza's "intellectual love", more subtle than belief and more certain than mathematics!

Hence, when Spinoza speaks of God, it is with unbounded zeal and veneration for the power and perfection of the divine nature that he does so; and, God being the one and only Substance, all things follow, and follow of necessity, from the essential nature of God and his attributes.

What, now, can we legitimately predicate of the nature of Absolutely Infinite and Eternal Substance or God from which, as Spinoza says: "infinite numbers of things in infinite ways must necessarily follow"?

In a veiled and mystical way the medieval Jewish Theologians had already supplied the answer to this question. God, these Hebrews had said, and the thought of God and the objects of his thought, are one and the same thing. But what these medieval Jewish philosophers expressed as a matter of religious conviction, Spinoza was to temper with a rational control. For, what do we mean by saying: "the thought of God"? God does not think in the same sense in which we understand thought; nor can we say that things are God: things are modifications, "modes", of God's Being, as thought is one out of an infinity of God's attributes; but to say that God thinks or that things constitute His nature is nonsense. "Thought" is an attribute of God by means of which we come to understand how *ideas* partake of His nature, as "Extension" is an attribute of God by which we come to understand how *things* partake of His nature; but God is, properly speaking, neither thought nor extension, not the sum total of things nor the totality of ideas; for these are modifications of God's attributes.

What, now, is God? God is Substance. God is "a Substance consisting of infinite attributes". The Jews had said: There is only one God. Spinoza says: God, or the Substance of all things, is *one*. What then is substance? "By Substance," says Spinoza, "I understand that which exists in itself and is conceived through itself, I mean, that which does not need the conception of any other thing in order to be conceived."

What follows from this definition of Substance? It follows that Substance is the cause of itself, because if it were produced, or capable of being produced by anything other than itself it would not be Substance. It follows, further, that Substance is *infinite*. It must be infinite, because it does not depend on anything else for its existence; hence nothing can limit or condition it. It follows further still that there is and there can be only *one* infinite Substance, because two or more Substances would necessarily limit each other. There cannot be more than one infinite. A plurality of Substances would assume a plurality of infinites, which is absurd. Therefore, God is the one and only infinite Substance, existing in and through itself and conceivable only as thus existing. He is the only self-subsisting Being on which all other beings depend for their existence, and the only absolute, unconditioned Substance without which nothing whatever can either be or be conceived. Everything else is only a modification of this Infinite Substance which contains all actual and possible existences within itself.

Further, Substance is eternal. What do we mean by saying that Substance is eternal? A thing is eternal when its essence implies existence, that is ,when its existence is not explained by duration but follows necessarily from its essence. "The existence of God and His essence, are one and the same thing." Again, since eternal Substance does not depend on anything extraneous to itself for its existence, it must be *free* because it is not determined by any other existent or being. Substance is free because it is not dependent upon or constrained by anything which is not itself. Its being *follows necessarily from its own nature.* Liberty, then, is identical, for Spinoza, with *inner necessity.* Substance is free because its essence involves its existence. Substance is *free* because it *necessarily is. Absolute freedom* and *absolute necessity* are one and the same thing! To be free is to be determined by nothing extraneous to one's being. To act freely is to act by the laws of one's own nature. God's freedom consists, then, in His following the laws of His Nature, the necessary laws of Eternal Substance, and not in His free will, desire or pleasure. For God to be the cause of the world, then, is for Him to exercise His freedom, or, for Him to realize or actualize His Being as Substance. God, as Substance, is the cause of the world because for God to *be* Substance is for Him *to carry out the necessary laws of eternal Substance* and thereby to give rise to the universe. In like manner, things are the effect of the divine activity, since they are the necessary modifications of divine Substance.

God, then, is the cause of the universe in much the same way as the circle is the cause of its equal radii, as the triangle is the cause of its three angles, and the universe is as much an effect of God's "will" as the equal radii are the effects of the will of the circle. Spinoza's conception of God excludes not only every personal sense of the divine Being but he even rejects the notion of God as a transcendent cause of the world. God, for Spinoza, is the *immanent cause* of the world. He is the innermost nature and order of things. He is the universe in the guise of Eternal Substance.

What follows from the nature of divine Substance?

While from the nature of a geometric figure there follows of necessity a *finite* number of properties, so there follows of necessity from the nature of infinite and eternal Substance, an *infinite* number of attributes. But these would require an infinite intelligence to comprehend. They are, no doubt, comprehended in the being of God or eternal Substance; but human intelligence knows only two of these divine attributes: *extension* and *thought*.

Extension and Thought are what the human "intellect perceives as constituting the essence of divine Substance." They are the two aspects under which our understanding subsumes reality. These are not two opposed Substances because there is only one Substance — God. Extension and Thought are two different ways by which we understand the one divine Substance.

Each of these attributes is infinite after its own kind; that is, each gives rise to an infinity of things of its own kind — extension to an infinite number of material things, and thought to an infinite number of minds and ideas. But these attributes, thus infinite in number, are still only *relatively infinite*, because neither extension nor thought exhausts reality. Only Substance is *absolutely* infinite, comprising all possible existences; but extension only comprises the infinity of material things, and thought, an infinity of minds and ideas. Each attribute excludes the other and both exclude all the other attributes that are unknown to man.

Each attribute comprises a world of its own; extension, the world of matter, and thought, the world of mind. But neither attribute gives us any inkling of what the other is like, nor do both — extension and thought — tell us anything of the unknown worlds subsumed under the other unknown attributes. Extension and Thought are two aspects of Eternal Substance, and independent of one another; hence matter and mind are two independent aspects of the divine nature. There can be no interaction between them. All things proceed from the nature of God or eternal Substance. Things, in themselves, are neither material nor mental, but *divine* — that is, they can assume an infinity of forms under an infinity of attributes. To us, however, they appear either under the attribute of extension as material, or under the attribute of thought, as spiritual or mental. But, "the idea of the circle and the actual circle are the same thing, now under the attribute of thought and again under that of extension." Each attribute, then, expresses the eternal and infinite essence of God; but each in its own manner, and both are proper and adequate guides for our understanding the nature of God or divine Substance.

Each attribute gives rise to an infinity of finite modifications or "modes"; and these are the particular individual things and ideas of our world — *things,* comprising the modifications of Substance under the attribute of Extension, and *ideas,* comprising the modifications of Substance under the attribute of Thought. These individual things and thoughts are not free for, they do not, like eternal Substance, follow the laws of their own nature, nor do they exist in their own right. They are subject to a causal chain involving all other individual things and ideas. But, if they are not free, neither are they accidental, for "in the nature of things nothing contingent is granted, but all things are determined by the necessity of the divine nature for existing and working in a certain way."

Thus, while God or Substance is infinite, eternal, and self-caused, the modifications or "modes" are finite, of limited duration, and they exist by cause of another; a mode, *a thing may or may not be,* its existence is merely possible, not necessary; but God *necessarily exists,* absolutely and eternally, and is the ground of all possible and actual reality or being.

———

Thus, while the veneration and awe of the divine Being remained with Spinoza, it was a God purged of all anthropomorphic elements that enticed him and whom he revered — a God who is the universe in its infinite existence. As Spinoza himself tells us in the Appendix to the first part of the *Ethics:* "In these propositions I have explained the nature and properties of God:

that he necessarily exists; that he is one alone; that he exists and acts merely from the necessity of his nature; that he is the free cause of all things and in what manner; that all things are in God, and so depend upon him that without him they could neither exist nor be conceived; and finally, that all things were pre-determined by God, not through his free or good will but through his absolute nature or infinite power."

God is thus, for Spinoza, infinite and eternal Nature comprising within itself all possible attributes and their modifications; he is the ground and source of all being. He is and acts as he necessarily must be and act by reason of his infinite and eternal being, his infinite power and perfection.

The attributes of God are infinite in their kind and infinite in number. Human reason can attain to a knowledge of only two of these attributes — Extension and Thought. The first, extension, gives us, in the end, the world of material things; the second, thought, gives us the mental world of intellection, ideas and volitions. The individual physical objects of our world, and the particular minds and ideas, have their being only in and through the eternal Substance or God; and they are also, as particular individual objects and ideas, parts of an order of nature which makes them determined in their activity according to external causes and influences emanating from other objects and ideas. But neither extension and thought (the attributes) nor matter and mind (in the world) can influence one another. The realm of Matter is not a product of Mind or conceivable in terms of Mind. And the realm of Mind is not a product of or conceivable in terms of Matter and Motion. Both are Substance itself viewed under two different aspects. Substance is the world of Matter *and* Mind viewed under the aspect of eternity. And Substance viewed thus, that is, Eternal Substance, is God.

Every object which has a formal existence as an extended thing must have a corresponding existence as an idea in thought *for which* it is an *object*. And, the totality of things which exist "formally" in our world have a corresponding existence "objectively" in the Intellect of God.

"If intellect", says Spinoza, "pertains to the divine nature, it cannot like our intellect, follow the things which are its object; . . . but, on the contrary, the truth and formal essence of things is what it is, because as such it exists objectively in God's Intellect . . ."

"I think I have shown with sufficient clearness that from the supreme power of God or from His infinite nature, infinite things, in infinite ways, that is to say, all things, have necessarily flowed, or continually flow by the same necessity, in the same way as it follows from the nature of a triangle, from eternity to eternity, that its three angles be equal to two right angles. The omnipotence of God has therefore been actual from eternity, and in the same actuality will remain to eternity."

IV.

If we view Spinoza from the standpoint of the modern era, we see why it is that despite the fact that, in voicing his thoughts, he employed a terminology and a method which are now generally abandoned as scholastic and medieval, he nonetheless embodies the modern spirit, the modern philosophic temper with all its conflicts, doubts and affirmations.

There was a time, not so long ago, when people talked of a conflict between science and religion. This conflict between science and religion is of interest to us here as an indication of a deep cleavage that has been at the heart of the modern spirit. The conflict between science and religion is the result of a desire on the part of modern man to grasp scientific truth and religious truth in a single, synthetic embrace that will do justice to both reason and belief.

It is this philosophic temper that Spinoza gave voice to at the very opening of the modern era in the seventeenth century. When he, in search for what is abiding and essential, examined these, science and religion, he could not accept either, because he found each to be a system of dogmatic postulations and beliefs.

For Spinoza, science is not any particular body of theories, and religion is not creed or a body of creeds: science and religion are for him as universal as the attributes under which they may be subsumed, both leading through extension and thought to eternal Substance. Only, science cannot do so by mere induction from the particular to the more and more general, for that is not

the road to eternal Substance; and religion cannot rise
to God by way of particular creeds, dogmas or cere-
monials. Both, science and religion, must be seen as
following from the eternal perfection of God or eternal
Substance which issues through extension and the modifications of extension in the corporeality of divine being,
and through the attribute of thought and *its* modes or
modifications of the Intellection and Will of the divine
Being: and an adequate understanding of how all things
follow from the necessity of divine extension, and the
divine Will or Intellection, results in an intellectual love
of God than which no greater wisdom or happiness is
possible for man. This involves a transcendence of the
limits of religious creed and dogmas as well as those of
scientific fact and analysis. Spinoza, in fact, aims at
effecting a synthesis of the material and the mental, of
the natural and the divine, of the most real and the most
perfect. The human mind can attain an adequate knowledge of the divine nature because God is not removed
or divorced from the world; in a real sense, though a
subtle one, he *is* that world when viewed from the standpoint of reason or sub specie aeternitatis, that is, time-
lessly. Therefore, according to Spinoza, for us to understand ourselves and the world is to understand God. And
to understand this, in its totality, is the only unqualified
good in this world. Even the ethical core of man must
be sought here, for "The greatest or highest good is the
union of the mind with the whole of nature." Therefore,
according to Spinoza, it is quite correct to say that good
people are those "who have a clear idea of God by
which all their actions are determined", and the wicked

ones are those "who do not possess the idea of God but only the ideas of earthly things by which their actions and thoughts are determined." Because, through the very knowledge of eternal truths, the truths which make all things divine, man becomes an *active agent in the service of the highest good.* That is Spinoza's ethical theory based upon his metaphysics or his philosophy of the timeless.

Thus, the human mind can attain a clear conception or understanding of the nature of divinity. What was needed only was an improvement of the understanding, a perfecting of it for the purpose of achieving its divine capacity. And that improvement of the human understanding may be attained primarily through the realization that our lives depend upon the nature of the object to which we are attached by love; the realization that all our difficulties stem from the fact that men love things which are perishable, while *love for an object which is infinite and eternal feeds the mind with joy* and nothing else, hence a joy which is free from all pain.

Then, too, for improving the understanding we must note the various levels of knowledge, from knowledge by hearsay, to knowledge which is the result of vague experience or loose generalization, to a knowledge which is scientific, of the cause-and-effect type of reasoning — up to the highest grade of knowledge, which is intuitive, or a knowledge which proceeds from divine attributes to the essence of the thing to be known. This highest type of knowledge is for Spinoza a supremely important avenue to divinity. The first and second modes of knowing are dismissed by him as incapable of leading us to the intellectual perfection desired, and the third mode of knowledge, which is the result of cause and effect reasoning is, when taken by itself, insufficient. Spinoza believed in the possibility of our possessing what he calls an adequate knowledge of an attribute of God, by which we arrive at a much more intimate knowledge of things. And he gives us one very illuminating example of the difference between scientific cause-and-effect reasoning and intuitive knowing — the example refers to our knowledge of the union of body and soul. By the third mode of reasoning, he says, we conclude that because we are conscious of sensations, therefore there is union of body and soul, which is the cause of this consciousness of our sensations; *but what that union is we still cannot understand.* However, by the fourth or intuitive mode *we know that the essence of soul is union with body.* This fourth mode of reasoning is not mere inference. It enables us to see at a glance that the meaning of soul is that it and the body are one being. And he devotes several propositions in the *Ethics* to explain the manner in which things are to be understood by the fourth mode of reasoning — the intuitive. Suffice it to say that Spinoza believed in the possibility of our possessing what he calls an adequate knowledge of an attribute of God, by which we can arrive at a more adequate knowledge of things than what scientific cause-and-effect-reasoning can yield. And he aimed to expose what lay at the root of the duality of nature and spirit, of science as the expression of the natural and religion as the expression of the spiritual. His primary purpose was to show that there was a false division here, one that tended to separate knowledge from reverence, science from piety, and religion from God.

Thus it came to pass that Spinoza fashioned his own religion, a religion of essential truth based on a metaphysics of essential causes; science, not as the result of quantity and measurement, religion not based on creed and dogma; for that is why science and religion are never able to get close to each other; but both as involved in the nature of divine Substance, through the parallelism of its attributes: extension and thought; because for Spinoza, the cognition of the true is at the same time affirmation of the divine.

Spinoza was among the first in modern times to view the duality of the scientific and the religious from the standpoint of the unity of thought: for he knew that the human mind had its origin in the divine intellection and hence could arrive at a knowledge of the divine decrees of eternal Substance which was in reality a knowledge of universal natural law — without the binding and blinding influence of the dogmas of supernatural religions. The result, according to Spinoza, is for man to achieve *intellectual love,* or that state of happiness which is not the reward of virtue but virtue or perfection itself.

Thus, as mind or reason is for Spinoza the chief part of man's nature, our moral development advances with our intellectual attainments; for there is no separate sphere of theology on the one hand and of morality on the other. The divine *is* the moral; and he who is closest to God is closest to morality. This it is that Spinoza finds to be essential, and the true fruits of understanding the divine order come with our being able to accept the inevitable with equanimity. Thus alone do we escape from bondage to the world — *by understanding it,* for thus alone, by understanding, do we become most truly ourselves and free. An adequate knowledge of ourselves and the world will so transform our nature as for it to express our divine essences, because "the value of ideas and the actual power of thought are to be measured by the value of their objects"; and these objects can be so widened as to include the most comprehensive and real of all. It is then that we attain intellectual love of God which confers immortality upon him who attains it and upon the mind that enjoys it.

"Blessedness", says Spinoza in concluding his *Ethics,* "consists in *love towards God, which love springs from the highest kind of knowledge . . . this love is virtue itself."*

Such is Spinoza's scheme of salvation. He sums up by insisting again on the power which "clear and distinct knowledge" has over the affects, and concludes as follows:

"Moreover, clear and distinct knowledge begets a love towards an immutable and eternal object, of which we are really partakers; a love therefore which cannot be vitiated by the defects which are in common love, but which can always become greater and greater, occupy the largest part of the mind and thoroughly affect it."

It is in the light of the foregoing that we may understand the concluding propositions of the Fifth Book of the Ethics, those wonderful propositions which bear the unmistakable stamp of inspiration upon them. Goethe refers to these propositions in his Autobiography. "The mind," he says, "which worked upon me so decisively, and which was destined to affect so deeply my whole mode of thinking, was Spinoza's. After looking in vain to find a means of development for my strange nature, I at last fell upon the *Ethics* of this man. Of what I read out of the work and of what I read into it, I can give no account. Enough that here I found a sedative for my passions, and that a free, wide view over the material world seemed to open before me. But what especially bound me to him, was the great disinterestedness which shone from every proposition. That wonderful expression, "he who loves God truly must not desire God to love him in return", with all the preliminary propositions on which it rests, and all the consequences that follow from it, filled my whole mind. To be disinterested in everything, but especially in love and friendship, was my highest desire . . . The all-composing calmness of Spinoza was in striking contrast with my all-too-turbulent activity. Spinoza's mathematical method was the opposite of my poetic imagination and my way of writing, and the very precision which was always considered not adapted to moral subjects made me his enthusiastic disciple, his most decided worshipper. Mind and heart, understanding and feeling sought each other with an eager affinity, binding together the most different natures."

What are these propositions at the close of the fifth, and last, book of the *Ethics* that so enthralled Goethe? "He who clearly and distinctly understands himself and his emotions loves God, and loves Him better (and the more) the better (and the more) he understands himself and his emotions."

"This love of God, above everything else, ought to occupy the mind."

"God is free from passions, nor can He be affected with any emotion of joy or sorrow." Hence, as a corollary, "properly speaking, God loves no one and hates no one."

"No one can hate God", not even if we consider Him as the cause of sorrow; for "in so far as we understand the causes of sorrow, it ceases to be a passion — that is to say, it ceases to be sorrow."

"He who loves God truly cannot strive that God should love him in return."

"This love of God cannot be defiled, either by the affect or emotion of envy or jealousy, but is the more strengthened the more people we imagine to be connected with God by the same bond of love."

"There is no affect or emotion that can be directly contrary to this love and able to destroy it, and so we may conclude that this love of God is the most constant of all the affects or emotions."

"As each person, therefore, becomes stronger in the highest kind of knowledge, the more conscious does he become of himself and of God, — that is to say, the more perfect and happier does he become."

"From the highest kind of knowledge there necessarily springs the intellectual love of God."

"The intellectual love of God, which arises from this kind of knowledge, is eternal."

"God loves Himself with an infinite, intellectual love."

"The intellectual love of the mind towards God is the very love with which God loves Himself, not insofar as He is infinite, but insofar as He can be made manifest through the essence of the human mind considered under the form of eternity — that is to say, the intellectual love of the mind towards God is part of the infinite love with which God loves Himself."

"There is nothing in nature which is contrary to this intellectual love, or which can negate it."

A thorough understanding of Spinoza's main ideas leads us to understand also the admiration which subsequent generations showered upon him. Through a better understanding of himself and his affects or emotions man's active power is constantly increased. This means joy; and joy, accompanied by the idea of God as its cause, results in a love of God. This love becomes broader as we attain a knowledge not only of ourselves and our emotions but also of individual things, an understanding of individual things by the kind of knowledge which is "intuitive" and which "advances from an adequate idea of the formal essence of certain attributes of God to the adequate knowledge of the essence of things," — that is to say, a knowledge of things through a knowledge of God's attributes.

The intellectual love of God, then, involves the discovery of universal law, or divine attribution, and the understanding of the world of objects as subsumed under it. This law may be as wide as the universe, as eternal as God, as infinite as God's own infinite nature; and the higher we rise in our intellection the closer we approach it. Then, says Spinoza, may we attain that *mentis acquiescentia*, that peace of mind, that timeless repose which the mind feels in the contemplation of the eternal order of the universe.

V.

No account of Spinoza's conception of God may be considered complete without proper note of the problem of *eternity*; for Spinoza's is the profoundest insight into the nature of eternity to which the human mind has attained. And so closely related is eternity to God in Spinoza's philosophy that the one without the other is inconceivable.

Even as Immanuel Kant achieved a masterly analysis of the nature of *Time*, so did Spinoza give us an account of *Eternity* which stands as a monument to his creative metaphysical mind.

1. The distinction, Spinoza tells us, between eternity and duration arises from the fact that we conceive the existence of *Substance* as entirely different from the existence of *modes*. (Epistle XII).

2. But "Eternity is an attribute under which we conceive the infinite existence of God. Duration is an attribute under which we conceive the existence of created things insofar as they persevere in their actuality." (Cogitata Metaphysica).

3. "From our division of being into that the essence of which involves existence, and that the essence of

WHAT THE GREAT PHILOSOPHERS THOUGHT

which involves only a possible existence, there arises the distinction between eternity and duration." (Cogitata Metaphysica)

4. "By duration we can explain only the existence of modes, but by eternity the existence of Substance, thas is, the infinite enjoyment or realization of existence." (Epistle XII).

5. Further, as the duration of a thing is its whole existence (for "to whatever degree you deprive a thing of duration to that degree you deprive it of existence") so eternity is that "infinite existence" which coincides with the real essence of God; "which is attributable only to God, and not to created things, no, not even if they endured forever."

This "infinite existence" which coincides with the real essence of God is not something which is super-added to God — it is not something that God enjoys or possesses, it is the divine being.

"We cannot affirm that God enjoys existence, for the existence of God is God Himself."

Duration is, indeed, the enjoyment of existence, but eternity is existence itself.

It is this *infinite realization of existence* that must be our clue to Spinoza's conception of eternity. Most philosophers who had speculated on the nature of eternity prior to Spinoza, and the generally accepted notion of eternity upon which their speculations were based, conceived of eternity as something that happens or accrues after existence had been taken away from a thing or being, i.e. after a complete emptying of existence; while, for Spinoza, eternity represents the very opposite of this:

namely, the infinite enjoyment or realization of existence. What *duration* is to *conditioned* existence, that *eternity* is to the *necessary* existence of God; it is its essence, and surpasses in quality the duration of conditioned existences (since it is infinite existence) by as much as infinity surpasses finitude.

Therefore Spinoza tells us: "By the term eternity we explain the duration of God", but "Since we cannot attribute duration to God, we call Him eternal."

Eternity, then, is existence *par excellence,* existence in an eminent degree, *infinite* existence, or, as Spinoza's formal definition reads: "existence conceived necessarily to follow from the definition, i.e. the essence or nature of the eternal thing."

And Spinoza here lays bare the source of the mistaken notion that eternity can be explained in abstraction from the nature of God or perfect being: "as if eternity could be understood apart from the contemplation of the essence of God, or indeed as if it were anything other than the divine nature."

Evidently, the ultimate view of eternity must be something *more* than a certain abstract intellectual order, which is but an empty *schema* for eternity. For Spinoza, eternity is the most real existence since it is identical with essence: it is *essential existence.*

Now it still remains for us to inquire into the unique nature of this infinite existence — or eternity — which is not to be conceived of as mere persistence or duration, "even if it endured forever." Has the human mind any experience of such a manner of existence? Since we are devoid of any experience of such existence, we may be forced to accept that which is relatively unreal — duration — in its place. This would, it is true, give us a certain intellectual order as a substitute for eternity but the mind would not attain thereby an *inward apprehension* of the nature of eternity.

According to Spinoza, man can have such knowledge; but we must realize that any such knowledge is possible only insofar as that which is known has been removed from the sphere of finite duration and elevated to a level of wholeness and inclusiveness, which is characteristic of eternal being.

For Spinoza, temporal existence is the same as nonexistence: it perishes by reason of its very fragmentariness, while the ideal of perfection is the same as eternity itself; and existence at any level of being approaches perfection and eternity the more it gains in comprehensiveness and universality and thus expressing the divine essence.

In brief, there is a real, concrete, positive sense of eternity; eternity as a whole of creation, and this must be conceived not only negatively as timelessness but as a creative universal whole, independent of time and duration: a necessary order of being in which content and quality merge in concrete universality. And the real knower, the man in possession of intuitive knowledge, comprehends every particular object and event as an instance of this concrete universality of existence which is eternity. He seeks in each individual instance the context of the concretely universal. In fact, a thing only then attains true reality when it becomes an object in an all-embracing intuitive science. It is this which confers eternity upon it, for it then becomes a portion of that undivided and indivisible universal whole which is divine Nature.

A complete and totally comprehensive intuitive knowledge of this type is the prerogative of God, who alone enjoys infinite existence, but we too may attain a knowledge of the whole of nature as a single universal Individual. Hence *our* knowledge, though it will never be as full and complete as God's, can nevertheless be adequate as far as it goes; so that even within the limited sphere of *thought* and *extension* the incompleteness of the range and scope does not preclude an adequate intuitive apprehension of that limited portion of the universal divine content which is thus made available to man.

"For the mind", says Spinoza, "feels those things that it conceives by the intellect no less than those that it imagines. For *demonstrations* are the eyes of the mind whereby it sees and observes things."

The objects of Reason are those basic universals in all finite being, the "fixed and eternal" things of which Spinoza tells us in his *Treatise on the Improvement of the Understanding*. Spinoza there explains that "mutable singulars depend so intimately and essentially upon the fixed and eternal things that they cannot either be or be conceived without them."

And thus it is that the finite mind of man is enabled to attain the highest kind of knowledge, *scientia intuitiva*, which views things as eternal individual objects having their abode within and flowing from the divine Nature. The complete, perfect Reality it is that we must apprehend and respond to; and then we too are eternal. If we fall short of this, and are to the degree and in the measure in which we fall short debarred from that Reality — to that degree we are subject to death and have our merely finite duration in the order of time. Insofar, however, as we do make contact with the infinite universality of immutable truth, we ourselves partake of eternity.

And that, too, is Spinoza's conception of immortality. As Caird well expresses it: "The immortality which is sanctioned by Spinoza's principles is not a quantitative, but a qualitative endowment, — not existence for indefinite time, but the quality of being above all time." (Caird: Spinoza, p.291).

———

Spinoza, thus, in drifting away from the orthodox conceptions of God, arrived at a mathematically-inspired view of the world, a world which in its entirety, its infinity and eternity is divine. Hence he could say *"Deus siva Nature"*, God *or* Nature, interchangeably. But even as his "God" was naturalistic, so was his "Nature" divine. Therefore he could rise to the final stage of his philosophy, mystical, intuitive and rational, where the intellect is saturated with love, but a love which knows but one ultimate object of adoration: the divine rationality at the heart of universal being.

Spinoza died in 1677, at the age of 45. A century passed without too much notice being taken of his thought. But then, suddenly, the intellectual world awoke to the splendor and grandeur of Spinoza's philosophy. The great intellects of Europe began to see what this lonely and lofty Jew of Amsterdam had striven to achieve. Spinoza, they found, had so distilled and purified the concept of God as to reach the essence of a *rational religion*, a religion tinged with the mysticism of Reason itself. He was satisfied to worship the God of this religion intellectually, that is, through an attempt to understand His nature, and hence to love Him, a worship of God which follows from a knowledge that God is *eternal*.

Spinoza realized further, that true love can come only with adequate understanding, and a true love of God only with an adequate understanding of His eternal and infinite Being and what necessarily follows from His nature. Hence he counselled all men to this intellectual love of God. In fact, he gave the world *a new religion*, a *philosophic* religion, freed from all the infantile anthropomorphisms of the older religions. This religion was the result of an understanding of the essential Being of God, Nature or Eternal Substance. He felt that this would call out from man's own essence that *in man* which too is divine. And then only could man rise to his true stature, and in the light of his adequate understanding and intellectual love of God, he would love his fellow-man, *necessarily, inevitably* and truly.

Hence his *"Ethics"* which follows from his metaphysics.

Spinoza's new religion, then, is not Christian, and it is not Hebrew; it is a Religion of Reason — perhaps the religion of the future. And one can worship here too —

in Spinoza's Temple — the Temple of the Universe, for that is for him the true object of worship: the Universe, the totality of Being, Nature, God, or Substance.

And the means to be employed for that worship — knowledge; with *love* as the emotion and *perfection* the reward.

This transition from the ordinary religions to Spinoza's, he conceived of as in fact a transition from human bondage to human freedom.

We clearly see, then, that God is to be loved, says Spinoza, *"not insofar as we imagine Him as present, but because we understand that He is eternal."* This is not easy to grasp unless we first live with Spinoza in the elevated regions of his thought and get accustomed to the atmosphere of those higher altitudes wherein he felt so much at home. It is then, however, that we find Spinoza exhorting us to a love of God so intense, so profound, as to leave no doubt in our minds that for him, as he tells us, "God is the beginning and end both of knowledge and of conduct" and that "the highest life is that which is lived in full consciousness of Him."

Spinoza then, who was repeatedly accused of being an atheist, appears indeed as a "God-intoxicated man," for it was his sublime and, one might say, almost unapproachable conception of the divine nature which caused the German Romanticists to speak of him as "a holy outcast," and Renan to say of the Spinoza House: "It was perhaps from here that God was seen most near."

KANT

KANT

(1724-1804)

I.

For Immanuel Kant, greatest of German Philosophers, the existence of God, the Immortality of the soul, and the Freedom of the will, were *the* three factors of most important concern for man. Yet neither of these could be either affirmed or denied, proven or disproven, accepted or rejected with certainty, by our understanding.

These three, God, Freedom, and Immortality, are all-important, according to Kant, because on their reality depends the value of human life. And yet, we could not say for certain that God exists, that we are immortal, that man has a free will; nor could we affirm with certainty that God does *not* exist, that man has *no* free will, that we are *not* immortal. Hence, we are left in suspense regarding these ultimate theological, psychical and moral questions; on these, though, we stake the value of our lives and our very happiness. For, if God be not in *some* sense real, if immortality be not in *some* sense true, if man be not in *some* sense free, then our lives have lost their sacred meaning.

But it may be difficult for us to prove that God is real, that immortality is a fact, that our will is free; even as it is difficult for us to prove, by merely observing the course and progress of human life and human events, that we are more than animals, destined for a higher goal than brute existence. We are here face to face with problems that baffle our keenest intellectual weapons! Shall we say that they are insurmountable? Or can we tap some deeper sources within us for hidden powers with which to attack these problems!

This is the way the matter shaped itself in the mind of Kant approximately 175 years ago. Everything was much the same then as it is now. Men everywhere were fighting, dying for the cause of liberty; nations were struggling for liberation and independence; individuals were battling against tyranny and oppression. There was poverty, misery; there was war, disease and death;—and there was high idealism too: beauty, art, science, and love; and there were men of good will. Kant looked into all this with his keen, penetrating intellect, which Schopenhauer later called the most philosophic head that nature ever produced. And Kant asked himself: *"Where in all this can I find God?"*

When he was finished with his inquiry, the whole intellectual horizon had been transformed; the philosophic firmament was aglow with the fiery brightness emblazoned by his volcanic spirit.

"If the citizens of Koenigsberg," said Heine, "would

have had the least presentiment of the full significance of Kant's ideas, they would have felt a more awful dread in the presence of this man than of an executioner, who can but kill the body. But the good folk saw in him nothing more than a Professor of philosophy, and as he passed them at his customary hour they greeted him in a friendly manner and set their watches by him."

It is to the great men of Kant's day and of succeeding generations that we must turn for a true estimate of his thought.

Schiller said: "The fundamental ideas of Kant's philosophy will remain a treasure forever, and for the sake of these alone we ought to be grateful for having been born in this age."

With equal enthusiasm, Fichte writes: "Kant's philosophy will in time overshadow the whole human race and call to life a new, more noble, and more worthy generation."

While for Schopenhauer, "to think with Kant and according to his manner is something that cannot be compared to anything else, for he possessed such clear and quite peculiar thinking as has never been granted to any other mortal" . . . When "thinking with Kant's own head . . . we feel as if we had been miraculously lifted out of the dreamy existence in which we are here lost, and as if holding in our hands the very elements out of which that dream consists."

Finally, we may mention Jung Stilling who writes to Kant: "You are a great instrument in the hands of God . . . your philosophy will work a far greater, far more

WHAT THE GREAT PHILOSOPHERS THOUGHT

general, and far more blessed revolution than Luther's reform. As soon as one has comprehended the Critique of Pure Reason, one realizes that no refutation of it is possible . . . its beneficent effects will bring back the religion of Jesus to its original purity, when its only purpose was — holiness."

What did Kant do to deserve all this praise?

First, he *demolished* and *destroyed*, he tore down the intellectual edifice of human reason: science — religion — the basic ideas of "nature" — even the world of common sense, — until he was left with the bare concept of humanity and the moral imperatives of the free individual. Then he *re-built* and *re-constructed* what had been most precious in the old edifice on new and firm foundations of *rational faith*, and of unquestionable certainty. Hence he said: "I had to remove knowledge in order to make room for faith."

Kant was convinced that what was needed, first and foremost, was an examination of the powers and limitations of human Reason. Hence he occupied himself primarily with the question as to *how* we know and *what* it is that we know. He found that we only know objects, knowledge is always knowledge *of an object,* an object *of* or *for* knowledge. Now, this object of knowledge comes to us through our senses — in sense perception.

Our senses report the presence of the object to us, or, as Kant puts it, we "sensuously intuit" the object. But anything thus given in sense perception is a *something* in space and in time: it must occupy a *particular space* at a *particular time.* According to Kant, space and time are our *only* means of "intuiting" objects sensuously. They are *our* two pure forms of sense perception. *Space and time are conditions for our apprehending physical reality, and they are unreal apart from our minds.* That is to say, objects, in themselves, have the characteristics neither of space nor of time. They are fashioned *by us,* by our minds, by the forms of space and time into external, material things. And that is how they appear to us when we sensuously perceive them. Hence, to be an object is to be something external and material in space and enduring in time. When we have thus molded an object into an external, material, i.e. spatial and temporal *phenomenon,* we are ready to *understand* it. But, just as sense perception has forms which are those of space and time, so the understanding has its forms too; these are the *categories* of the understanding. By means of these categories we form a *conception* of the object perceived.

Thus, to the space and time characteristics of sense perception we add the "categories." And our acquaintance with objects is the composite result of our imposing the "categories" of the understanding upon the "intuitions" of sense. (These pure forms of sense (space and time) and of the understanding (the categories) Kant calls *a priori* forms, meaning thereby that they are in our minds prior to any experience of objects.)

But, by this imposition of the forms of sense and the categories of the understanding we gain only a knowledge of objects as they *appear to us.* We arrive, then, at a knowledge not of things as-they-are-in-themselves, but of things as we understand them — a world of finite, conditioned, material, and causally-related objects. These Kant calls *"phenomena", or appearances.*

Suppose, though, that we want to get *behind* the appearances. Suppose we want to obtain a knowledge of reality as-it-is-in-itself, a knowledge of *infinite, unconditioned* reality, that is, *God;* or, a knowledge of the world as a whole, the *universe;* or a knowledge of things - as - they - are - in - themselves, *noumena,* i. e. of things as they are *prior to the imposition of our forms of sense and the categories of our understanding.* Suppose, further, that we want to know the nature of the *soul,* which is by definition *free* and *immortal;* and other such ultimate "objects" of the metaphysician's quest as eternity, infinity, etc.

All of these have *no basis in sense perception;* hence they cannot become "objects" of knowledge. They are ideas, ideas of our Reason; but we cannot *know* them, since, as we have seen, knowledge, for us, must be of *objects* and so a knowledge of what has been stamped by our forms of sense, and the categories of our understanding. The ideas of our Reason, however, such as God, Freedom, and Immortality, are out of space and out of time, infinite, not subject to causal law; the categories of our understanding cannot be applied to them. In other words, these — God, Freedom, Immortality, etc. — *transcend the limits of our understanding.* Our Reason struggles to know them in vain; there ensues a conflict of opposing and contradictory ideas regarding their nature, which Kant calls "antinomies" of Reason. Thus it comes about that we can just as well prove, by Reason, that there *is* a God as that there is *no* God; that the world is eternal and hence had *no* beginning in time as that it *did* have a beginning, or rather, that it *had* to have a beginning in time, etc., etc. These are Kant's *antinomies of Reason*. Because of these antinomies or contradictions into which Reason falls, when it seeks to solve problems that transcend the powers of our understanding, Kant concludes that these problems are forever insoluble, because their "objects" can find neither a representation in sense nor a conception in thought. They are *transcendent* objects, beyond the power of our understanding to grasp or "know."

However, to these *transcendent objects* our Reason feels irresistibly drawn; so that no matter how sure we may be of our inability to form any satisfactory conclusions respecting their nature, we can never refrain from indulging in a *dialectic* of Reason concerning them! That is, *we can never cease striving to know them.* We meet, in experience, with the *conditioned, finite world* of our understanding, and our Reason seeks an *unconditioned, infinite source* to account for this finite, conditioned world as it *appears* to us in "nature." But this transcendent, infinite and ultimate world *can never become an object of knowledge* for our understanding. Hence, our Reason is driven always to alternate between *two* worlds: a world which we know but which is not real (the physical) and a world which is real but which we can never know (the metaphysical). Therefore, along with the logic of the physical, material world, which is the logic of our understanding, our Reason fashions what Kant calls a logic of *"illusion"*, or *Dialectic*. It is by means of this Dialectic of Reason that we strive to know the *unconditioned,* the *supersensible,* the *eternal* and *infinite* — God, Freedom and Immortality. But these transcendent "objects" can never be *known,* nor can the problems connected with them ever be solved. No objective presentation of them in sense perception is possible, no conception can be formed of them by the understanding, and our Reason is only led to contradictory conclusions regarding their nature. This constitutes Kant's Critique of Pure Reason: *we cannot know objects, but only the appearances of objects;* and we cannot know what lies behind the appearances because we are not equipped to know anything but appearances, "phenomena". We reason always from cause to effect and from effects to causes, in a world which exists for us in space and in time, and we thus arrive at our concept of "nature." It is *we* who make nature *"natural."*

No wonder, said Kant, that we cannot find God in our scheme of things, or that we cannot understand how our wills can be free, or our souls immortal! In a world of space, time and causality, we cannot expect to find the *non-*spatial which is spirit, the timeless, or *eternal* which is immortality, the *un*caused or first cause which is God. Our reason only lands us in "antinomies" when we try to understand these things; we naturally find ourselves confronted by conflicting assertions: that there *is* a God, that there is *no* God; that we *have* a free will, that we have *no* free will; that we *are* immortal, that we *cannot be immortal.* We can prove all these with equal logical force and conviction, *because they are not susceptible of rational proof or disproof.* Their "objects" lie *beyond* the sphere of nature, outside of the realm of space and time.

To seek in the world of the conditioned, the *un-conditioned*; in the realm of determinism, the *undetermined*, the *free* act, or the *immortal soul,* is to invite disaster for our faith in God, our hope in a future life and for the self as a *free moral agent!* We can know only phenomena, appearances; therefore our chance of securing knowledge lies in restricting ourselves to the finite sphere and in relinquishing all claims to anything beyond it.

But, if pure Reason can in no way grasp the transcendent world of God, Freedom and Immortality, these "objects" may find their reality established, and all questions concerning them solved, by the *practical or Moral Reason;* for here, *in the moral nature of man,* we are prompted to act in accordance with a *different, higher* Reason; and through the categories of this higher, Practical (Moral) Reason, we can find substantiation for the ideas and ideals of our pure Reason: *God, Freedom and Immortality*.

Thus, what our understanding could not *know,* and pure Reason could only *think,* our Moral Reason can *postulate* as real and certain. In the moral sphere these transcendent "objects" — God, Freedom and Immortal-ity — have a validity of their own: they become real; they are *made* real by the ideal, moral nature of man; for, says Kant, while theoretical knowledge can only "determine the object", in practical, moral knowledge "we make the object *real* also."

Kant explored this realm of the "practical" or moral, this ideal world, with a thoroughness and exhaustiveness such as had never been attempted by any thinker before him. He found that the supreme, absolute Being, the ideal of Reason — God, in the transcendent sense — who could never become an "object" for the understanding — can be postulated as *real* and *true* in a totally different objective sense by the practical or moral reason of man. For, it is here, in the domain of the Moral Reason that the possibility is offered us for substantiating the reality of those very ideals which pure Reason could not theoretically establish. If, in the sphere of the theoretical understanding, we are in the end confronted by an inscrutable world, this in no wise precludes the existence of another rational domain, the moral, where we ourselves can *produce a world*, a moral world which is not bound to the senses. We can only arrive at this moral world, however, after we have secured complete independence from all external things, for this moral world and its problems spring from ourselves; and as members of this moral world, we must act without reference to any subjective ends. Hence, even the pursuit of happiness must be disregarded in this realm, because in that pursuit man always becomes attached to something outside of himself. We must realize, says Kant, that what really counts *here — in the moral sphere* — is not the making of ourselves happy but "how to make ourselves *deserving* of happiness." The moral law which governs this sphere, the unconditional command as to what we *ought to do*, the voice of conscience, the idea of duty — all of these prove that the essence of morality lies in the fact that *we do certain things solely for their own sake*, and *without regard to consequences*. The moral law speaks to us *unconditionally*; there are no exceptions or amendments to it. It is, as Kant calls it, "a categorical imperative" of our moral reason. Here, then, is the *unconditioned*, for which we have been looking in vain in the realm of the theoretical understanding! Here it is, says Kant, in the moral law, which directs our free will with confidence and authority, for it is *our own will* that makes the moral command into a duty! Within our innermost selves we find an intelligible source which commands our empirical self as a moral imperative.

"What a creature is man! Small, small indeed when set over against the great moral law whose demands his conduct is so often and so far from realizing; great, immeasurably great, insofar as he cooperates with that moral law, recognizes it and in it his own innermost will and being; and thus becomes himself the law-giver and the founder of a new, a moral world." It is in the light of this, that we may understand Kant's well-known words: "There are two things that fill my mind, the oftener and longer I dwell upon them, with ever-renewed admiration and awe: the starry heavens above me and the moral law within me. Neither is veiled in mystery or lost in immensity. I need not seek them beyond my sphere of vision and merely *surmise* that they are there. I see them before me and link them immediately with the consciousness of *my* existence . . . *The moral law begins from my invisible self, my personality,* and exhibits me in a world which has true infinity . . . ".

And when we obey this moral law we act in such a way that the maxim we follow could at any time be erected into a principle of universal legislation. Even natural inclinations must be renounced, for we must act *contrary to natural inclinations,* since the moral law demands a higher legislation than the natural inclinations permit. To be moral, man must become autonomous, .ie. independent of nature. "It is autonomy which gives dignity to human nature . . . If reason in man is to serve the same ends which instinct serves in animals, it cannot lift its possessor above the merely animal state."

And for this capacity, freedom must be presupposed; freedom of a rational will to build a new world through the moral nature of man. "You *can* because you *ought*," and you ought, because you can! The causality of nature, however, is inexorably opposed to freedom. For, says Kant: "In the contemplation of nature, experience gives us rules ready to hand . . . in regard to moral laws, however, experience (alas!) is the mother of illusion; and it is inadvisable to derive what I *ought to do* from that which actually *is done* (or to let this fetter my action in any way)."

What makes life really worth living, says Kant, may be found here, in this ideal, moral realm: "If justice should perish, it would no longer be worthwhile to live on earth." Here, then, we find our way to the subterranean depths of reality and the answer to the question as to the meaning of human life. "We can think of nothing anywhere in the world — no, nor even out of it, which can be considered unreservedly good, except a good will . . . All goodness that does not stem from a morally good disposition is nothing but illusion and wretchedness . . . "

This is Kant's faith; from these foundations of morality he deduces the being of God and the immortality of the soul. A higher reason in man, stemming from his free moral will, postulates a cause for the whole of reality which is distinct from nature and which can consummate the exact agreement of happiness with morality. We must postulate this supreme intelligence which, though unintelligible to our theoretical understanding, is, for our moral reason, an indispensable reality; — or we can have no faith in ideality and no possibility for the harmonization of holiness, which is the highest good, with happiness.

Whether there be a God whose existence we can prove or not, *we ought to act as though there were a God, as though we have a free will and as though we were immortal.* Kant's purification of religion lies in this, his supreme achievement: *to base all faith upon morality,* and this latter to have its foundation in *a priori principles* which are as certain as the *a priori* principles of mathematics! The task therefore, that Kant set himself, was to show that *"reason can be practical (moral), i.e.* that it can of itself determine the will independently of anything empirical"; that the moral command which is, for Kant, the basis of religious faith, is *an absolute imperative of reason.* The moral law legislates a new code whose foundation is the principle that "the only unqualified good in this world is a good will." The result is the highest ethical command: *"treat humanity, whether in thine own person or in that of another, always as an end, and never as a means."*

What is this but a *divine command?* How could our moral reason arrive at this divine insight unless it were itself divine? "The moral law," says Kant, "exhibits me in a world which has *true infinity;*" not the false infinite of the theoretical understanding. Here is the *real* miracle, the miracle of morality: *conduct without regard to consequences,* based upon *a causality of freedom;* and this in turn presupposes the unconditioned and absolute. Upon these miracles, of our every day selves, we may found religion, religion without theological dogma, religion based upon the assertion of a greater good than the principle of self-preservation, a greater love than the chemical love of nature, a love which seeks the happiness of others; and perfection for ourselves!

With Kant, therefore, religion is primarily "the recognition of our duties as though they were divine commands." The moral consciousness, the "still small voice" of conscience, is the only, and sufficient, basis for religion.

The world of spiritual reality now opens before us in all its glory. Kant's philosophy may be called the *anatomy of the Ideal.* Nature, of itself, it teaches, can never yield God, Freedom and Immortality. Nay, it is utterly opposed to these ideal notions. What we need, therefore, is a transition from a wisdom of living by nature to a wisdom of living by ideality. Hence, over against the life of the worldly-wise, that is, those whose reason has made a compromise with the demands of natural existence for the sake of survival, Kant extols the life of Ideality in the very midst of the life of nature; and he finds the rational basis for this ideal life. His affirmation of Ideality is a negation of mere existence. For, it is the ideals that transcend the mere will-to-live that make life desirable, significant and timeless. What is more, Kant points the way to the actualization

KANT

of these ideal possibilities in the life of every individual, where it may bear immediate fruit. For there is a causality of the moral world, which the ancients called "Nemesis" and the Christians "the judgment of God;" for Kant, it is a *causality of freedom*.

It is this causality of the moral world, and its imperatives to ideality, that stands opposed to natural inclinations; for the higher reason of man aims at freedom from the tyranny of space and time.

Kant realized that there were ideals, guiding principles of human reason which may be true even though they are logically untenable and physically impossible. God is the summit of these ideals. For Kant, these ideals of Reason *must* be true. He gave eloquent expression to them by exploring them, appraising them, avowing them, and making them *real* — in their own unique manner, in their own *supersensible* sphere. To think with Kant is to *affirm* these ideals in the most adequate manner in which they have ever been uttered. "Philosophy," says Will Durant, "must always be different hereafter, and profounder, because Kant lived."

"I say", says Kant, "that it is necessary, according to Reason, to assume happiness in the same measure in which one has rendered himself deserving of it in his conduct . . . In a moral world, such a system in which happiness is proportionate to morality, may be considered as necessary . . . Happiness must be distributed in exact proportion to morality. This, is, however, possible in an intelligible world *only*, under a wise author and ruler. Such a being, together with life in such a world, which we must consider as future, reason compels

us to admit, unless all moral laws be idle dreams . . .
Hence it follows that God and a future life are two sup-
positions which . . . cannot be separated from the
obligation which reason imposes on us . . . I am therefore irresistibly forced to believe in the existence of God
and in a future life. And I am sure that nothing can
make me waver in this belief, since I should thereby
overthrow my moral maxims, the renunciation of which
would render me hateful in my own eyes."

II

Few lives have been outwardly less spectacular than
Kant's, few inwardly more significant! He searched for,
and found, a way to the depths of nature and man.

Kant instituted a Critique of scientific theory and
scientific knowledge which is probably the most dev-
astating of its kind ever devised by any philosopher.
And religion, morality, and aesthetics too, were first
demolished, and later reconstructed, by Kant in his
three "Critiques". Nothing in the world of thought or
conduct, indeed nothing in the whole realm of values
escaped the piercing shafts of his Criticism, or remained
the same after his monumental analysis. In this sense,
his life was not only very significant but extremely ad-
venturous. No one who has not properly mastered Kant's
"Critiques" can hope to understand the philosophies that
succeeded them, in the nineteenth and twentieth centuries.

But, outwardly, his life ran its course, as Heine remarked, like the most regular of regular verbs, though it was studded with oddities and peculiarities of the most interesting kind. For example, despite the difficult nature of his published works, his lectures were extremely popular; and, despite the fact that he never left Koenigsberg during the entire 80 years of his life, he became the most famous of philosophers even during his lifetime. His education was at first pietistic, and the simple faith inherited from his mother, based upon religion as a matter of deep, inner piety, simplicity, and holiness, as well as obedience to the moral law, remained a characteristic of his life to the very last. Hence, despite his critical attitude toward conventional religiosity and his scepticism toward the accepted proofs for the existence of God and the immortality of the soul, he was nonetheless a deeply religious man.

Born at Koenigsberg in 1724 (where he also died in 1804), Kant was of Scotch descent. His father was a saddle maker. After an early pietistic training, he entered the university of Koenigsberg, at the age of 16. Already, he was practically left to support himself, for there were three sisters and another brother in the family. Both his parents were dead when he was 22, and Kant had nothing but his Latin, Greek, mathematics and physics to rely on for a living — which he did; for during the next nine years he earned his way through life by tutoring in private families. In 1755, disgusted at being a private tutor, we find him back at the university in Koenigsberg, where he remained for the rest of his life. He never married, and his faithful servant, Lampe, awoke him at five o'clock every morning for thirty years. Kant, he testified, never failed to respond to his call, though he instructed Lampe to use force if necessary to awaken him. From early morning until one in the afternoon he worked uninterruptedly, at which time he would repair to a restaurant, varying the locality every few days so as not to be stared at by sightseers who flocked to Koenigsberg to see — Kant! In the late afternoon, without exception, fair weather or foul, Kant, followed by Lampe, always with an umbrella under his arm (just in case it might rain), took his daily hour's walk, so punctually, it is said, that the good folk of Koenigsberg were in the habit of setting their watches the moment Kant appeared at his door, precisely at 4 o'clock. Then came the evening with its hours of meditation. Kant, it is said, gazed upon a neighboring church steeple while thus meditating. By ten, he was in bed. Visitors would come often for dinner and listen to his sparkling conversation in his own home and at the home of friends where he was always a welcome visitor. But he never would allow the conversation to turn to philosophical matters, reserving these more serious subjects for his lectures and books.

At first, his lectures were primarily of a scientific nature, dealing especially with physics and astronomy. The most famous of his works along these lines was his *A General Natural History and Theory of the Heavens* (1775), wherein Kant for the first time propounds the nebular hypothesis for the origin of planetary systems. In addition, he wrote and lectured on anthropology, tides and their influence on the rotation of the earth, the effect of the earth's rotation on winds, the causes of earthquakes, the influence of the moon upon weather, volcanos on the moon; and, he had his own theory as to the origin of man, believing that the various races developed from a common original human species; while he speculated, also, on the peculiar closeness of the anthropoid apes to the human kind, and the possibilities for their developing a semi-human level of intelligence; he discoursed readily on the importance of a world federation of states, a United Nations for the insurance of perpetual peace, on which subject he also wrote a small volume entitled *On Perpetual Peace.*

We can picture Kant sitting there among his friends at the dinner table, talking sprightly and excitedly about the geopolitics of his day, revolutions, monarchies, democracy and wars; and we may see him also with our mind's eye at his high desk in his classroom at the university with barely anything visible of his small, lean, flat-chested body — except his enormous head from which there issued those "world-annihilating" thoughts which were now, by the time he was fifty-seven (in 1781), beginning to be debated in all schools of higher learning — the problems of knowledge, causality, God, science, space, time, and the moral nature of man.

Kant is by now convinced that lack of proper judgment is unfortunately something which lies beyond the possibility of cure:

"Although the teacher may offer, and, as it were, graft into a narrow understanding, plenty of rules borrowed from the experience of others, the faculty of using them rightly belongs to the pupil himself, and without that talent no precept that may be given is safe from abuse . . . Deficiency in the faculty of judgment is really what we call stupidity, and there is no remedy for that. An obtuse and narrow mind, deficient in nothing but a proper degree of understanding and correct concepts, may be improved by study, until it may even become learned. But even then there is often a deficiency of judgment and hence we often meet with very learned men, who in handling their learning betray that original deficiency which can never be mended." (Critique of Pure Reason: Transcendental Analytic).

And he had, by this time, said some very striking things about the need for Criticism, a Critique of all knowledge and all beliefs:

"Our age is the age of criticism, to which everything must submit. Religion, through its sanctity, and law, through its majesty, want to withdraw themselves from criticism; but by so doing they arouse just suspicions, and cannot claim that sincere respect which reason grants to those only who have been able to stand the test of its free and open examination." (Critique of Pure Reason)

Six years later, in the Second Edition of the *Critique of Pure Reason*, he tells his world that the schools must prevent "by means of a careful investigation of the rights of speculative reason" what "every man who has once risen to the height of speculation" knows will sooner or later occur, namely, "the scandal which . . . is sure to be caused even to the masses, by the quarrels in which metaphysicians (and as such, theologians also) become involved, if ignorant of our critique, and by which their doctrine becomes in the end entirely perverted. Thus, and thus alone, can the very root be cut off of *materialism, fatalism, atheism, free-thinking, un-*

KANT

belief, fanaticism, and superstition, which may become universally injurious . . . "

But his chief aim is to institute that universal critique of reason in order to insure the emergence of his Idealism which he conceived as transcending all the three types of abstract thought to which his age was addicted: abstract rationalism, abstract empiricism, and dogmatic religion. Hence he was not intent upon writing a new philosophic system; he was satisfied merely to point the way to *purification of morality and religion by a critical examination of the powers and limitations of human reason in all fields* — scientific, moral, religious and aesthetic. That was the aim of his *three* Critiques: Of *Pure Reason* (Science); of *Practical Reason* (Morality and Religion); and of *Judgment* (Aesthetics: A theory of the Beautiful and the Sublime, and of "Purposiveness" in Nature).

Kant had given voice to the position, which for him was the only position consonant with the ideal nature of reason itself, namely, that what Reason may truly call its own must follow from the demands of the ideality of reason itself.

The outcome of the Kantian Criticism was the revelation that a philosophy which bases itself on ideas may be as far from the truth as a philosophy that bases itself on the data of the senses. And that *only when ideas serve to promote ideals* may their truth-value be affirmed on their own merit; that ideals are the guideposts of human progress and moral development, and that only by serving adequate ideals can philosophy, as well as religion, perform their true functions and become the foundations of concrete spiritual unfoldment.

Between the basic assumption of materialism, of the reality of matter, and the basic assumption of idealism, of the reality of ideas, Kant's philosophy, for the first time, proclaims the reality of ideals. *And his greatness lay in this realization of the basic reality of ideals.* It is for this reason that he speaks of the need for a "practical", i.e. moral philosophy, and *the priority of the practical or moral reason over the theoretical.* All the great philosophic problems henceforth gain their meaning and significance in the light of the ideal necessities of the practical or moral Reason. So that, for the questions: does God exist? is freedom a fact? is immortality true? Kant asks: Is it necessary for the ideality of the "practical" Reason that God should exist, that freedom be a fact, that immortality be true?

Philosophy and religion must be seen to work on the material of the common and diffused ideality of the human spirit, and their task to map out the road to spirituality. For Kant, dogmatic religious doctrines were no longer binding, and reason itself was to yield spiritual truth; for religion was primarily a result of the ideals of the moral Reason of man.

And, as for Christianity: "Christ", says Kant, "has brought the kingdom of God nearer to earth, but he has been misunderstood, and in place of God's kingdom, the kingdom of the priest has been established among us." Creed and ritual have taken the place of the good life, and all kinds of "pious nonsense", says Kant, is preached as "a sort of heavenly court service by means of which one may win, through flattery, the favor of the ruler of heaven." The work entitled *Religion within the limits of Pure Reason,* published when Kant was 69

years of age, expresses these views in the boldest possible terms. Kant, true to his philosophy, bases religion
on morality and derives it solely from that divine source.
Hence he rejects all except moral values from the revealed books of religion, berates all attempts at the
suspension of natural law either by prayer or by miracle,
and flays the awful spectacle of reactionary governments
uniting with the church for purposes of political oppression. For it is then that the acme of perversion is
reached: the clergy, whose aim ought to be to guide and
console a suffering humanity with faith, hope and charity, becomes instead an instrument in the service of
theologico-political intrigues and oppression.

Kant's religion was far above the narrow limits of
any dogmatic belief; though it included all honest faith
and purity of heart, for it was the result of a *good
will*.

"Religion within the limits of pure reason" in which
these views find expression, consists of a series of papers
which Kant now wished to publish. To the first of these
papers "On radical evil" — there was no objection to its
publication from the censor; it may be printed, he said,
since "only deep-thinking scholars read the writings of
Kant." But the second paper was refused publication
by the College of Censors at Berlin. Kant then submitted
his work to the theological faculty of his native city,
and the book was published in 1793. On October 1,
1794, a royal cabinet order was issued charging Kant
with "distorting and degrading many of the chief and
fundamental doctrines of Holy Scripture and of Christianity". All of the theological and philosophical instruc-

tors at the university of Koenigsberg were commanded
not to lecture on his "Religion within the limits of pure
reason". Kant was now 70 years old. He went home to
his study and penned the lines: "All which one says
must be true, but it is not necessary to say openly all
that is true". After that, he wrote his letter of defense,
announcing, at the same time, his readiness "as his
Majesty's most loyal subject" thenceforth to abstain from
all public discourses on religion. As soon as King Frederick William II died, however, he felt he had the right
to express himself publicly again. He, therefore, wrote
and published (Der Streit der Facultaeten) "The Conflict of the Faculties", wherein he defended freedom of
thought for philosophers, and expressed his disgust at a
despotism which tried by compulsory law to procure
respect for that which could only be respected with
perfect freedom. He tried to resume his lectures on the
philosophy of religion but by this time his bodily and
mental force was gone. He succumbed to a weakness of
old age, which deprived him of his mental powers at
the very moment when his philosophy was celebrating
brilliant triumphs at all universities.

For Kant, religion as well as philosophy must embrace
the entire human race, because ideality and moral responsibility is the common birthright of all humanity.

Comprehension and proof for the things of the spirit
do not lie within the bounds of the natural; on the
contrary, nature itself becomes an object of human experience through the creative powers of the reason of
man. For the spirit, or moral Reason, reality does not

come unfashioned and uninformed by ideals. And *"practical"* therefore, for Kant, means not the application of power but the *working out of ends, spiritually satisfying ends that serve ideals.*

Human life is not lived in a pure "reality". The condemned criminal awaiting pardon, the lover confident of the devotion of the beloved, the bereaved turning to faith in the hope of a life beyond the grave — all these pin their hopes on the idealism of their fellow-men and a moral order to help them through the most crucial tests of reality.

Man lives in nature but not always by nature. He breaks in upon the compulsion of natural necessity and enacts the truths of ideality in the midst of the inexorable realities that confront him in nature. By this exercise of freedom he in fact becomes free. And it is this in man, the ideal possibilities of the human spirit, that Kant's philosophy seeks to explicate and affirm. These, too, are the grounds for belief, for Kant; for these possibilities of the human spirit, expressed in moral conduct, and through moral conduct in the conviction of a divine order to the universe, are the only grounds for belief in God and a divine purpose to creation. These ideal possibilities also it is that can save man, as indeed they *have saved* him in the past, from the danger of an all-destroying barbarism.

———

Kant made an epoch-making discovery: "that reason can be practical," i.e. *moral.* As moral reason, it can direct our lives by molding our will and fashioning a world of objective truth and reality that is independent of sense and unassailable by logic; a world of our own creation, ruled by a causality of freedom and a world to which we are bound by the ties of our selves as free moral agents.

This world, governed by its own categories, and freed from bondage to "nature," space and time, matter and causality, *we* construct in *the act* of realizing the moral ideal: when we do something for the sake of duty, because we know, through our higher reason, that it is the right thing to do, the thing we *ought* to do, and not when we function as "natural" beings and do what by nature we *must* do.

Between the *must* of nature and the *ought* of morality, there lies the distance that separates man as a conditioned animal existent and man as a free moral being. It is in this sphere, of the moral, that the world of the free will, the immortal self, and the being of God, find confirmation in deed, and verification in act. It is here that religion may thrive, that the ideals of reason can find ground for sustenance, and that a binding sense of obligation to principles of moral ideality makes of us creatures of true infinity. For, "the moral law within and the starry heavens above" find their point of union here, in the self which, as moral, is infinite, and is at one with the infinity of the universe.

KANT

III

The philosophy of Kant presents a twofold difficulty. Not only is his metaphysical subject-matter of unusual depth and therefore difficult to understand, but in addition he has been accused of often obscuring the intricate meanings which he seeks to convey by a language that is involved and abstruse in the extreme.

But there are innumerable instances of clear and lucid expression wherein the sublimity of Kant's conceptions is matched by the beauty and relative clarity of his speech.

Some of these, especially those relating to morality and God, I have listed here. The reader, who so desires, may brave the difficulties of the following pages.

"The *summmum bonum* is possible in the world only on the supposition of a Supreme Being having a causality corresponding to moral character. Now, a being capable of acting on the conception of laws is an *intelligence* (a rational being), and the causality of such a being according to this conception of laws is his *will;* therefore the supreme cause of nature, which must be presupposed as a condition of the *summum bonum* is a being which is the cause of nature by *intelligence* and *will*, consequently its author, that is God. It follows that the postulate of the possibility of the *highest derived good* (the best world) is, at the same time, the postulate of the reality of a *highest original good,* that is to say, of the existence of God. Now, we have seen it as our duty to promote the *summum bonum;* consequently, it is not merely allowable, but a necessity connected with duty, that we presuppose the possibility of this *summum bonum;* and as this is possible only on the condition that God exists, it inseparably connects the supposition of this with duty; that is, it is morally necessary to assume the existence of God." (Critical Examination of Practical Reason: Dialectic of Pure Practical Reason)

"We must assume a moral World-Cause (an Author of the world), in order to present to ourselves a final purpose consistently with the moral law; and in so far as the latter (the moral law) is necessary, in the same degree and on the same ground, the former also must be assumed as necessary; i.e. we must assume that there is a God." (Critique of Judgment: The Moral Proof)

"That man is morally *unbelieving* who does not accept that which though *impossible* to know it is *morally neces-sary* to suppose." (Introd. to Logic)

"This moral argument does not supply any *objectively-valid* proof of the Being of God; it does not prove to the skeptic that there is a God, but it does prove that if he wishes to think in a way which is in conformity with morality, he must admit the *assumption* of this proposition under the maxims of his practical Reason." (Kant's Critique of Judgment: The Moral Proof, Second Edition).

"The moral law is, for the will of a perfect being, a law of *holiness*, but for the will of every finite rational being, it is a law of *duty*, of a moral constraint, which determines his actions by *respect* for this law and reverence for its duty." (Critical Examination of Practical Reason: The Analytic of Pure Practical Reason)

"There is one thing in our soul which, when we take a right view of it, we cannot cease to regard with the greatest astonishment, and in regard to which admiration is right, or even elevating, and that is the original moral

capacity in us. What is it in us (we may ask ourselves)
by which we, who are constantly dependent on nature by
so many wants, are yet raised so far above it in the
idea of an original capacity in us that we can regard
all these wants as nothing, and ourselves as unworthy
of existence, if we indulge in their satisfaction in opposition to the law which our reason authoritatively pre-
scribes; although this enjoyment alone makes life desirable, while reason neither promises anything nor threatens. The importance of this question must be deeply
felt by everyone, even those of the most ordinary ability
. . . and even the incomprehensibility of this moral
capacity, which proclaims a Divine origin, must rouse
man's spirit to enthusiasm and strengthen it for any
sacrifices which respect for this duty may impose on
him. The frequent excitement of this feeling of the sublimity of a man's moral constitution is especially to be
recommende d as a means of awaking moral sentiments
. . . and so to restore the original subordination of the
springs of action to morality and to the restoration also
of the capacity for good in the human heart in its
primitive purity." (The Philosophical Theory of Religion:
On the Origin of the Evil in Human Nature)

"Conscience is not a thing to be acquired, and it is
not a duty to acquire it; but every man, as a moral
being, has it natively within him. To be bound to have
a conscience would be as much as to say to be under
a duty to recognize duties. For conscience is an inevitable fact, not an obligation and duty. When, therefore,
it is said: this man *has* no conscience, what is meant is,
that he pays no heed to the dictates of his conscience.
For if he really had none, he would not take credit to

himself for anything done according to duty, nor reproach himself with any violation of duty, and therefore he would be unable even to conceive the duty of having a conscience . . . only observe what follows from what has just been said, namely, that there is no such thing as an *erring* conscience. No doubt it is possible sometimes to err in the objective judgment whether something is a duty or not; but I cannot err in the subjective, for if I erred thus, I would not have exercised practical judgment at all, and in that case there would be neither truth nor error. *Unconscientiousness* is not want of conscience, but the inclination not to heed its judgment. But when a man is conscious of having acted according to his conscience, then, as far as regards guilt or innocence, nothing more can be required of him: he is only bound to enlighten his *understanding* as to what is a duty or not; but when it comes to action, then conscience speaks involuntarily and inevitably. To act conscientiously cannot therefore be a duty, because, in that case, it would be necessary to have a second conscience, in order to be conscious of the acts of the first.

The duty is only to cultivate our conscience, to quicken our attention to the voice of the internal judge, and to use all means to secure obedience to it . . . " (Preface to the Metaphysical Elements of Ethics).

"A man may be to me, an object of love, fear, or admiration, even of astonishment, and yet not be an object of respect. His humour, courage and strength, his power due to the rank he has amongst others, may inspire me with sentiments of this kind, but still inner respect for him may be wanting. *Fontelle* says:

KANT

'I bow before a great man, but my mind does not bow.'
I would add, before an humble plain man, in whom I
perceive uprightness of character in a higher degree
than I am conscious of in myself, *my mind bows*
whether it choose to or not . . . Why is this? Because
his example exhibits to me a law that humbles my
self-conceit when I compare it with my conduct: a law,
the *practicability* of obedience to which I see proved
by fact before my eyes. Now, I may even be conscious
in myself of an equal degree of uprightness, and yet the
respect remains. For, since in man all good is defective,
the law made visible by an example still humbles my
pride, my standard being furnished by a man whose
imperfections, whatever they may be, are not known to
me as are my own, and who therefore appears to me
in a more favourable light. *Respect* is a *tribute* which
we cannot refuse to him who merits it, whether we will
or not; we may indeed outwardly withhold it, but we
cannot help feeling it inwardly." (Critique of Practical
Reason: Analytic of Pure Practical Reason)

"Though *fear* first produces *gods* (demons), it is
Reason by means of its moral principles that can first
produce the concept of God . . . Also, the inner *moral*
purposive destination of man's being supplies that which
natural knowledge is deficient in, by directing us to
think of the final purpose of the being of all things
(for which no other principle than an *ethical* one is
satisfactory to Reason), the supreme Cause (as endowed)
with properties, whereby it is able to subject the whole
of nature to that single design (for which nature is
merely the instrument), — i.e. to think of it as a Deity."
(Critique of Judgment: Moral Teleology)

"The speculative employment of reason *with respect to nature* leads to the absolute necessity of some supreme cause of the world: the practical employment of reason with a *view to freedom* leads also to absolute necessity, but only *of the laws of the actions* of a rational being as such. Now it is an essential *principle* of reason, however employed, to push its knowledge to a consciousness of its *necessity* (without which it would not be rational knowledge). It is, however, an equally essential *restriction* of the same reason that it can neither discern the *necessity* of what is or what happens, nor of what ought to happen, unless a condition is supposed on which it happens — or ought to happen. In this way, however, by the constant inquiry for the condition, the satisfaction of reason is only further and further postponed. Hence it unceasingly seeks the unconditionally necessary, and finds itself forced to assume it, although without any means of making it comprehensible to itself, happy enough if only it can discover a conception which agrees with this assumption. It is therefore no fault in our deduction of the supreme principle of morality, but an objection that should be made to human reason in general, that it cannot enable us to conceive the absolute necessity of an unconditional practical law (such as the categorical imperative must be). It cannot be blamed for refusing to explain this necessity by a condition, that is to say, by means of some interest assumed as a basis, since the law would then cease to be a moral law, i.e. a supreme law of freedom. And thus, while we do not comprehend the practical unconditional necessity of the moral imperative, we yet comprehend its *incomprehensibility*, and this is all that can fairly be de-

manded of a philosophy which strives to carry its principles up to the very limit of human reason." (Fundamental Principles of the Metaphysics of Morals)

"Two things fill the mind with ever new and increas-
ing admiration and awe, the oftener and the more steadily we reflect on them: *the starry heavens above and
the moral law within.* I need not search for them and
conjecture that they are real, as though they were veiled
in darkness or were in the transcendent region beyond
my horizon; I see them before me and connect them
directly with the consciousness of my existence. The
former (the starry heavens) begins from the place I
occupy in the external world of sense, and enlarges my
connection therewith to an unbounded extent, with worlds
upon worlds and systems on systems, and moreover into
limitless times of their periodic motion, its beginning
and continuance. The second (the moral law) begins
from my invisible self, my personality, and exhibits me
in a world which has true infinity, but which is traceable
only by the understanding, and with which I discern that
I am not in a merely contingent but in a universal and
necessary connection, as I am thereby also with all
those visible worlds. The former view of a countless
multitude of worlds annihilates, as it were, my importance as an *animal creature,* which after it has been
for a short time provided with vital power, one knows
not how, must again give back the matter of which it
was formed to the planet it inhabits (a mere speck in
the universe). The second, (the moral law) on the
contrary, infinitely elevates my worth as an *intelligence*
by my personality, in which the moral law reveals to

WHAT THE GREAT PHILOSOPHERS THOUGHT

me a life independent on animality and even on the whole sensible world — at least so far as may be inferred from the destination assigned to my existence by this law, a destination not restricted to the conditions and limits of this life, but reaching out into the infinite." (Critique of Practical Reason: Methodology of Pure Practical Reason — Conclusion)

"Morality is not the doctrine how we should *make* ourselves happy, but how we should become *worthy* of happiness. It is only when we add religion that there also comes the hope of participating some day in happiness in proportion to our endeavor to be not unworthy of it." (Critique of Practical Reason: Dialectic of Pure Practical Reason)

———

"It is a FUNDAMENTAL PROPOSITION, to which even the commonest human Reason is compelled to give immediate assent, that if there is to be a *final purpose* furnished *a priori by* Reason, this can be no other than *man* (every rational being in the world) *under moral laws.* (I say deliberately under moral laws . . . Only of *man under moral law*s can we say, without transgressing the limits of our insight: his being constitutes the final purpose of the world. This harmonizes completely with the judgment of human Reason reflecting morally upon the course of the world). For if the world consisted of mere lifeless, or even in part of living but irrational beings, its existence would have no worth because in it there would be no being who would have the least concept of what worth is. Again, if there were intelligent beings, whose Reason were able only to place the worth of the existence of things in the relation of nature to themselves (their well-being), but not to furnish of itself an original worth (in freedom), then there would certainly be (relative) purpose in the world, but no (absolute) final purpose, because the existence of such rational beings would always be purposeless. But the moral laws have this peculiar characteristic: that they prescribe to Reason something as a purpose without any condition, and consequently precisely as the concept of a final purpose requires. The existence of a Reason that can be for itself the supreme law in the purposive reference, in other words, the existence of rational beings under moral laws, can therefore alone be thought as the final purpose of the being of a world. If, on the contrary, this be not so, there would be either no purpose at all in the cause of its being, or there would be purposes, but no final purpose.

"The moral law, as the formal rational condition of the use of our freedom, constrains us by itself alone, without depending on any purpose as material condition; but it nevertheless determines for us, and indeed *a priori*, a final purpose towards which it constrains us to strive; and this purpose is the *highest good in the world* possible through freedom." (Critique of Judgment: The Moral Proof)

HEGEL

HEGEL

(1770-1831)

I.

God or the Absolute Idea

When Hegel was graduated from Tuebingen in 1793, his certificate of graduation commended him for his proficiency in theology and languages, and his good character, but rated him low in philosophy. The verdict of history, however, was to be a different one. In 1818 after the publication of his *Encyclopedia of the Philosophical Sciences* (1817) he was appointed to the Chair of Philosophy at the University of Berlin. From then on, to the end of his life, Hegel was the undisputed ruler of the philosophical world. He died of cholera in the year 1831. Paulsen says: "Never did philosophy assume such a lofty tone, and never were its royal honors so fully recognized and secured as (through Hegel) in 1830."

George Wilhelm Friedrich Hegel was born at Stuttgart, Germany, in 1770, the son of a minor government of-

ficial in the State of Wuerttemberg. He became a tire-
less student and an avid reader; making notes and
analyses of all the books he read and copying out long
passages from them. An early motto of his was to the
effect that culture begins with self-effacement; but Hegel,
far from effacing himself, put the stamp of his personality on the entire intellectual map of his age and, indeed, of his century: the nineteenth century produced
no philosopher comparable to Hegel.

His studies in Greek literature resulted in an enthusiasm for Hellenic culture which was a characteristic mark
of his thinking to the end of his days. "Religion", he
says, "we have from the East . . . but science and art
and all that makes life satisfying, and elevates and
adorns it, we derive, directly or indirectly from Greece."

Hegel's leaning toward philosophy already showed itself when he was only 15 years of age. At 20, he began
to reflect on the relationship of love and reason as a
clue to the nature of reality. He found in the phenomenon of love a strange quality: a movement, a passing
out of one's self into another, and, a subsequent en-
richment. And as he kept thinking about this unique
characteristic of love, its power of leading one out of
one's self into another, and the resulting enhancement
of the person who had thus gone out of himself and
returned into himself again, Hegel's horizon widened
until the relationship of the human and the divine too,
appeared to him such an estrangement, and a subsequent
return; and this was, he thought, *the truth of life*.
Christ, as God-Man, seemed to him also to express such
a relationship and, under the influence of this notion,

he wrote a *"Life of Jesus"* in 1795, at the age of 25.

Hegel's interests, however, were not confined to philosophy alone. He was attracted to history and the philosophy of history. In fact it is at the point of intersection of the two, history and the philosophy of history, that there centers, in the main, the intensity of his thought.

Hegel found, in natural reality, in history, as well as in the life of Mind or Spirit, a *process* by which *thesis* and *antithesis* oppose one another, and are then reconciled in a higher unity which is the *synthesis of opposites.* This process constitutes the development or *unfoldment of the Absolute* or God. Through opposition truth is born, and this movement of opposites is *Dialectic;* dialectic is the soul of the process, both in the real and in the ideal, in Nature as in Mind. The beginning is the Absolute Idea which the conflict expresses; the end is the Absolute Idea which the conflict realizes; and the totality is achieved through *stages of reality* which are at the same time *categories of thought.* Thus, rising from the simplest idea, the idea of being, through matter, organism, consciousness, self consciousness, reason, right, morality, social morality, up to the realm of the *Absolute Spirit* which is comprehended by *Art, Religion, and Philosophy* — we have a continuous ascent through *the dialectic of opposites* which is the dynamic principle at the core of thought as well as at the heart of things; so that every particular has its truth and its reality only by being a *moment* in the development of the Absolute Idea or God.

This is Hegel's notion of divinity. The Absolute Idea is the ultimate divine Idea and since it *is* an idea, it can be comprehended by thought and most comprehensively by philosophy; for "to *think* is to bring out the *truth of the object.*"

Hegel has an unbounded trust in Mind or Reason. The divine itself is a *dynamic Idea,* to be grasped in its totality only by the Absolute or God himself; but we need not despair merely because we are finite, for the so-called "subjective" mind of man may comprehend the objective nature of reality. Indeed, the main aim of philosophy is to reveal the infinite *in* the finite, *to show how the infinite arises out of the finite.*

"It marks the diseased state of the age when we see it adopt the despairing creed that our knowledge is only subjective, and that beyond this subjectivity we cannot go . . . truth is objective . . . *the objective world is in its own self the same as it is in thought."* Being and Thought are one.

In thinking an object we follow through its inner development, we discover its dialectic, its antecedent theses and antitheses and their resulting synthesis — in short, we follow the very being of the object, its growth and development; at every particular instant that object or event has an historical significance as a finite moment of the Infinite.

Hegel's Absolute is the end and aim of all progress, growth and development in the world. His God is a *dynamic process.*

The Absolute, or God, reveals Himself in every moment of relative existence, and every moment of relative existence has therefore an absolute significance. To know God is to comprehend the Whole, the *Absolute Idea as it unfolds* its infinite Being. This is Hegel's formula for avoiding the dilemma of former metaphysics which, either with the rationalists, found it impossible for the finite *subjective* human mind to know a foreign *objective* reality, or, with Kant, abandoned altogether all hope of ever knowing the world-in-itself, the so-called world of true Being.

Thus, what for Kant had been an inherent *fault of Reason,* namely, that it could find proofs for both the theses and the antitheses, is for Hegel a *universal formula of truth;* for only in the clash of thesis and antithesis is truth and reality born. This is Hegel's law of development, in logic, in nature, and in the realm of Mind or Spirit. It is this *clash of opposites* that constitutes the *law of development,* the law of *dialectic necessity.* In the system of rational reality, every particular existent has its truth and its reality only as a *moment* in the process of development of the Absolute, or the Whole of Reality. Only as such is any existent concretely real and only as such can it be adequately comprehended.

For Hegel, the conditioned *gives rise* to the Unconditioned, the phenomenon is the abode of the noumenal, the finite of the Infinite, and history is the battlefield of the Absolute. God, the Absolute Idea, reveals Himself everywhere as *active reason.* God is the active Subject that ever creates in process of unfoldment the objects of our physical world as well as the realities of our spiritual, mental world.

To be an unfinished fragment, an uncompleted part of the Whole is to be an abstraction; *the movement of*

thought it is that makes the world real and concrete.
The divine activity is the Logic of Reality, for God is
a creative Mind or Spirit — an *Absolute Idea,* striving
toward wholeness, reality and concreteness. The aim of
philosophy is to understand the world in terms of the
Absolute, the phenomena of the world as moments in
the unfoldment of the Absolute Idea. Hence, "all being
is thought realized and all becoming is a development
of thought."

As Windelband says in his *History of Philosophy:*
"In this (Hegel's) system of reason every particular
has its truth and reality only as a *moment* in the development of the whole. Only as such is it real *in
concreto,* and only as such is it comprehended by philosophy. But . . . if we think it in its isolation, in which
it exists . . . only according to the subjective apprehension of the understanding, then it loses the connection
with the whole in which its truth and actual reality
consists: then it appears as accidental and without reason.
But as such, it exists only in the limited thinking of
the individual subject. For philosophical knowledge, the
principle holds that what is rational is real, and what
is real is rational. The System of Reason is the sole
Reality."

God or the Absolute Idea becomes manifest in Nature,
first in its most immediate or abstract form as *pure
being;* then it passes through the sphere of mediation or
otherness, until the level of *synthesis* or self-reconciliation
is achieved; that is when the Real triumphs over the
partial and incomplete by annulling all previous antagonistic elements.

But this means, for Hegel, *a reconciliation of the divine Mind with itself.* The alienation of the Absolute Idea is thereby overcome and the divine Idea is, in that moment of its *becoming,* poised for the next higher state of Being. Thus, Hegel pursues the contradictions in the nature of reality and in thought as the creative elements of the Real. For reality is a metaphysico-theological process of becoming, the aim of philosophy being to discover its antithetical elements and to overcome the limitations of finitude whether these be found in the mind of man or in the nature of things.

II.

The Function of Dialectic

The difficulties involved in understanding Hegel revolve around his desire to have philosophy become one with the divine mind. In this respect he set himself an impossible task, but this aim — of having philosophy become one with the divine Mind — is nonetheless central to his entire mode of thinking. For Hegel, the contradictions of thought are the creative contradictions of reality; but reality manifests the divine Mind or the Absolute Idea; hence the contradictions which our reason discovers in reality are ultimate contrarieties in the nature of divine Being: they are the stresses and strains involved in the creative unfoldment of divine rationality. This is what makes Hegel's "dialectic" different from any other type of dialectics previously expounded by philosophers, and it is the key to the discovery of contradictions and oppositions not only in the nature of the Real but in the Absolute itself.

Dialectics has had a long history in Western philosophy. We have to go all the way back to the ancient Greeks to find its origin and first usage. In Heraclitus (c. 536-470 B.C.) we meet with perhaps the first definite formulation of this principle. Heraclitus speaks of "the strife of opposites" which he conceives as the very core of the universe. For him the opposition and strife in the nature of things expresses a metaphysical as well as a physical characteristic of reality. Opposition and contradiction is not merely a surface manifestation but a deep-seated inner conflict in the very nature of the-dynamic process of *becoming, development, flux and change.* There is thus, for the first time in Western thought, a central role assigned in the nature of reality to those oppositions and contradictions which the human mind feels as a basic ingredient of its own thinking. This is Hegelianism pure and simple as far as the dialectic method is concerned. No wonder that Hegel said that there was not a single sentence in Heraclitus that he could not have utilized as part of his own logic! The dialectic of Heraclitus is all-powerful and omnipresent in the universe; but there is nothing divine about it: it is merely nature's way of achieving the ever-new and to it is due the fruitfulness of nature's processes.

Zeno (c. 490-430 B.C.) also believed in dialectics, but for him it was of a purely negative nature, an instrument of thought by means of which to refute the positive naturalistic dialectics of Heraclitus. Zeno belonged to the Eleatic School, the philosophy which was static as compared with the dynamic philosophy of the Heracli-

teans. The Eleatics believed in a pure, changeless Being,
an immutable ultimate Reality; and they held that the
metaphysical oppositions and conflicts of the philosophers
of change (the Heracliteans) only led to contradictions.
These contradictions are contradictions in thought: they
have no metaphysical status, no creative function in the
nature of things, and they lead not to truth but to error.
However, it was by dialectical reasoning that Zeno too
tried to show, through his paradoxes, that motion and
change are inconceivable attributes of the real: for the
Real is, for Zeno, immutable Being.

Plato discovered a dialectic of his own which was *his*
key to divine Reality. For Plato too, dialectics is only
a method; in his case, it is the method of arriving at
the eternal Ideas of a static world of changeless Eleatic
Being. Dialectics was an instrument which he fashioned
out of the Socratic method of discussion for the sharpen-
ing of the logic of reason and the adapting of it to
perform the function of a ladder of ascension to the
transcendent world of the eternal, divine Ideas.

In Plotinus the Platonic dialectic is further amplified
in his (Plotinus') mystical way: "What, in sum, is
Dialectic?" asks Plotinus. And he answers: "It is the
Method of discipline that brings with it the power of
pronouncing upon the nature and relation of things . . .
Dialectics treats also of the good and the not-good, and
of what is eternal and what not eternal, and of these
not by seeming knowledge but with authentic science
. . . it has abandoned all the realm of deceit and
falsity and pastures the Soul in the 'Meadows of
Truth' . . . Philosophy is the supremely precious but
Dialectic is the most precious part of philosophy. It does

not consist of bare rules and theories; it deals with verities . . . Wisdom and Dialectic have the task of presenting all things as Universals and stripped of matter for treatment by the understanding." *(The Enneads)*.

For Kant, dialectic is a "logic of illusion", which presumes to lead us to a transcendent world of supersensuous reality: infinite, timeless, spaceless and divine. But actually it leads nowhere except to contradictions and impossible conceptions.

Such was, in brief, the history of Dialectics up to the advent of Hegel. *By altering the concept of dialectics Hegel also changed the course of philosophy;* and, it may perhaps be true to say, the course of history. With Hegel, the use of the dialectical method is not only dynamic and evolutionary, but epistemological as well; for it is through this strife of opposites that Hegelian dialectics points not merely to a process in the nature of things, determining a given objective reality, but it leads further to the realization that this object of knowledge is *produced in the process* of knowing, the process of dialectical development. Thus, knowing and being, thought and reality are one. Further, this process is infinite and divine. Hegel's is thus the most comprehensive of all types of dialectics and appears as *Absolute Idealism,* which means that Reason is not, in his case, confined to man alone, that he is not concerned merely with *human* reason but with a *divine rationality* which is diffused throughout matter and mind, Nature and Spirit. Hence *Hegel's is a rationalistic, pantheistic fusion of philosophy and theology.* The opposites that confront each other in thought, the theses and antitheses of logical disputation have, for Hegel, not only a metaphysical quality as characteristic of the nature of Reality; they are also the *attributes of a divine, creative rationality.*

"Logic is the science of the absolute Idea, the concrete Whole in the abstract medium of thought . . . It is the unison of universal Being . . . with its being . . . in this individual subjective thinker, who knows this unison as the Truth."

Perhaps these factors may explain Hegel's exclamation: "to be a philosopher one must first be a Spinozist." For it is the pantheistic mystical-rationalism of Spinoza's relatively static conceptions which Hegel adopted for the corner-stone of his dynamic dialectical philosophy.

For Hegel, the finite as such is false because it is incomplete. The business of thought is to transcend the finite. The transcendence of the finite, however, means to follow it through dialectically in its development towards the Absolute Idea. It is thus that philosophy, which is human, attains the divine: by tearing down the barriers between itself and God — the barriers of finitude. And the dialectics of thought is the means for such a demolition of the barriers of the finite. Philosophy thus, in transcending, through dialectics, the finitude of the human mind achieves at the same time a total transcendence of the finite; for in this very process reason ceases to be human and attains a divine metaphysical status in the nature of things. And that is what Hegel means by striving to have philosophy become one with the divine Mind: he went one step further than Spinoza whose aim was a view of the universe from the standpoint of eternity; Hegel's is an attempt at explicating the thoughts of the divine Mind from the lowest to the highest levels of Nature and Spirit. Hence, Hegel's philosophy is not only rationalistic and mystical but also theological throughout.

In his subtle, mystico-rational analysis, Hegel finds the entire sphere of the finite to be a self-alienation of God from Himself. In this finite sphere both nature and the human mind have their origin. As such both human reason and nature stand opposed to the divine Mind. But by dialectical necessity this antithesis is overcome in the forward progress of the Absolute Idea toward its infinite fulfillment.

Hegel has been called, and with justice, the last and greatest of the Scholastics. He too conceived the world as an emanation of divine consciousness and harbored a supreme faith in the power of reason to transmute this divine emanation into elements of rational thought. For Hegel the entire world-process is the coming to *explicit consciousness of the immanent rationality of the divine content in the real world*. He conceived it as the aim of philosophy to trace the ever higher levels of development of this Absolute consciousness, in the forms of existential being, of thought, of Nature and Spirit. And the rationality of the world-process is revealed through the immanent dialectic of its content. Thus what for Scotus Erigena was an eternal creation within the divine nature and an eternal return of all created things to God, was, for Hegel, an eternal *process of affirmation and negation in an Absolute Reality* wherein all its forms are but stages or moments of the

Absolute Idea. These forms, moments or stages of the Absolute are aspects of the divine Nature that pass continually out of themselves in order to appropriate the otherness of things and then return into themselves in fuller consciousness of themselves as moments of the divine process.

There is a close dependence of philosophy on religion in Hegel which is matched by an equally close relationship of the finite with the infinite, the real and the ideal, the human with the divine. With supreme confidence in the power of reason to tap the sources of eternal truth, Hegel made the great leap. "All finite things," he said, "involve an untruth; they have a notion and an existence, but their existence does not meet the requirements of the notion. God alone is the thorough harmony of notion and reality."

What Hegel attempted is what the great mystics of all ages tried to achieve: to transmute the externality and otherness of things by elevating them out of the subjectivity in which they appear in human thought, into their true being in an absolute, universal reality. Only, for Hegel, unlike as in other mystics, *the Absolute is Mind,* and the process of transmutation is a *thought-process* by which the outwardly "real" is absorbed as an element of a *divine progressive rational consciousness.* Other idealistic philosophers and mystics found in the subjective character of our thoughts an insurmountable barrier to the attainment of universal truth: hence they dreamed of a supra-rational approach to the divine. For Hegel, on the other hand, the fact that ideas and notions are *our* ideas and our notions does not in the least detract from their power. They are elements in a universal world-process which in its essence is both rational and divine. More than any other philosopher, Hegel found in the universalizing creativity of our thought the reflection of a divine intelligence, an Absolute Mind or Spirit which is engaged in constantly relieving itself of finiteness.

For Hegel, the key to the philosopher's insight lies in the realization of the identity of Reason with the Real: that Reason and Being are one and the same, for both express a developing process of an infinite divine reality; that only in the inevitable opposition and conflict and the ensuing synthesis of antithetical notions do we find the very principle of the evolution of matter, life, mind, history, religion and philosophy; and that only in this clash of opposing notions is the truth to be found. All is *becoming*, a process in which nature and mind form the beginning and end of the world's rational unfoldment.

III.

The Power of Hegel's Thought

By a strange coincidence, the philosophy of Hegel, which has been pronounced dead and beyond resurrection innumerable times since the decline of Idealism in the 19th century, has not only survived as a potent factor in contemporary philosophic thought, but has had an almost incalculable influence in the political sphere, so that "Communism and Fascism, Pragmatism and Ex-

istentialism, to name only the most outstanding movements in politics and philosophy, are incomprehensible
without Hegel's philosophy." *(The Philosophy of Hegel
by Carl J. Friedrich, Prof. of Government, Harvard
University)*

Not to speak of other perversions of Hegelianism
which have followed it like a shadow, repeating what
has so often happened in the case of the great teachers
of mankind. Their original doctrines could not long survive in their pristine purity without a falsification, to
which great thoughts have always been subjected by their
misguided followers. Hegel's vast and all-inclusive system
of idealistic philosophy with its innumerable aspects, currents and cross-currents, could not escape that inevitable
degeneration which led, in his case, to the "Hegelians
of the Right", "Hegelians of the Left", "Neo-Hegelians",
— all of whom were intent upon discovering in the
philosophy of Hegel what was there merely as a transitory aspect of his phenomenal mind, or, more often,
was not there at all! For Hegel had, despite all his
complexities, *one* very essential, deep-rooted aim, namely,
to refer all things, all events, all thoughts, all logic
and all reality, all existence and all of human aspiration
to a divine Being, a God who made himself known
always, ever and continuously, unceasingly, in Nature,
in the world's history, in the mind of man and in the
universally diffused Mind or Spirit in which the progression of the Absolute Idea makes itself manifest.

*There were cosmic purposes of a universal significance,
and these were reflected in the mind of man:* this was
Hegel's ideal message. But the materialistic followers of

Hegel degraded this into: "The ideal is nothing else than the material world reflected by the human mind." (Marx).

That was in the nineteenth century. In the twentieth, a new understanding of Hegel's immense significance for the human spirit is everywhere in evidence: "the philosophy of Hegel", writes W. T. Stace, "is not something simple, invented out of nothing by himself and flung at random into an astonished world . . . it is not the pet theory of some erratic genius, nor is it merely one theory among many rivals. The true author of it is, not so much Hegel, as the toiling and thinking human spirit, the universal spirit of humanity getting itself uttered through this individual. It is the work of ages. It has its roots deep in the past. It is the accumulated wisdom of the years, the last phase of the one 'universal philosophy'."

And the poet, Walt Whitman, senses a far wider meaning to Hegel's ideal philosophy than any conceived by prosaic minds:

"Roaming in thought over the Universe, I saw the little
 that is Good steadily hastening towards immortality
And the vast all that is called Evil I saw hastening to
 merge itself and become lost and dead."

This Whitman wrote with passionate understanding immediately following his study of Hegel and in comment upon Hegel's philosophy.

What is this "work of the ages" with "its roots deep in the past . . . the accumulated wisdom of the years, the last phase of the one 'universal philosophy'," which, according to Stace, Hegel contrived to perfect?

HEGEL

It is the basic realization of all philosophic idealism, whether Platonic, Aristotelian, Spinozistic or Kantian, that the intelligible is the real and the real the intelligible. But there remained a persistent dualism in the thought of those who had preceded Hegel, a duality of Nature and Spirit, of Freedom and Necessity, of the Finite and the Infinite. Hegel reconciled these supposed contraries. He made the great discovery of the true meaning of Spirit as Self-consciousness. The fundamental essence of man is self-consciousness. But man does not live alone in circumscribed isolation. His quest of truth as well as his moral consciousness forces him to go out of himself and find kindred life with which he may unite and identify himself. This means that the finite consciousness of man is only complete when it lives morally as well as through knowing.

Human self-consciousness is only a phase of the total Self-consciousness which is God, who reveals himself not only in the human spirit but in nature; indeed in all that is. For, according to Hegel, the truth of nature is to be found in Spirit. And so too with man who, at first, is apparently nothing but nature. The end of man is realization, *self*-realization; the end of each individual is to become a free, self-conscious spirit. The universal consciousness is thus reflected and objectified in the individual consciousness.

Hegel has his own explanation for the emergence of this individual self-consciousness. The self is confronted by an environment which it must overcome. To realize itself, the Self must overcome and annul all oppositions.

This overcoming and transcendence of all opposition which is fundamental to the realization of self-consciousness involves the self in relationship with the world — natural, human and divine. Hence, Hegel's idea of renunciation is not the ascetic one of the mystic, nor the anti-naturalistic one of Kant. To attain the highest degree of self-realization, even of the moral self, nature is not to be renounced, as Kant held, but to be *overcome. Man must transform nature, spiritualize it.* He must thus give rise to a spiritual environment the immanent life of which is the universal Reason or Consciousness. The universal consciousness informs and vitalizes the environment in which the spiritual self is actualized.

In other words, man must elevate his environment, natural and otherwise, so that the individual good becomes the universal good. That is Hegel's ideal of the function of man as part of society. "The History of the world", he writes, "with all the changing scenes which its annals present, is this process of the development and actualization of Spirit — this is the true theodicy, the justification of God in history. Only *this* insight can reconcile the human spirit with the course of universal history — namely, that what has happened and is happening each day is not only not without God, but that it is essentially His work."

This is Hegel's high idealistic conception of history. But he does not stop with this. Aiming higher still, he sees in the life of man the unfoldment of a process and the development of a purpose whose significance is timeless:

HEGEL

"What Spirit is," says Hegel in a passage which may be noted for its astonishing lucidity, considering the depth of the subject, "what Spirit is, it has always been essentially; distinctions are only the development of this essential nature. The life of the ever-present Spirit is a circle of progressive embodiments, which looked at in one aspect still exist side by side, and only as looked at from another point of view appears as past. The grades which Spirit seems to have left behind it, it still possesses in the depths of the present."

In conclusion: Hegel's ideal for man is self-realization or the attainment of freedom; but self-realization is attainable only through the individual's making the life of the world his own. An ever fuller, ever wider life of the spirit becomes actual for man as he expands his individuality to include his family, his society, his state. For some individuals, however, the spiritual life may include the life of humanity, so wide are their interests, so vast their ideal scope, so universal their faith, so cosmic their religion. But at whatever level self-realization is achieved it is only possible because the human spirit has its life in an infinite Spirit which is the immanent life and movement of all human activities. As Caird says: "Every pulse-beat of the life of the spirit is the expression and realization of the life of God."

IV.

The Moral and the Ethically-Social

Hegel's philosophic interests are so varied as to defy description. He sees the philosophic spirit at work in any adequate interpretation of nature, history, art, religion, and even philosophy itself. Indeed this is its primary objective. Hegelianism may be called the philosophy of philosophy.

In Hegel, even as in Aristotle, the end is theological. For Aristotle, the Deity "thinks itself and its thinking is a thinking on thinking." *(Metaphysics)*

Hegel's conclusion, similarly, is that "self-consciousness, which knows the pure knowledge of pure inwardness to be spirit, is not merely intuition of the divine, but the self-intuition of God Himself."

On the other hand, for the soul to find itself, it must traverse the tension of the medieval mind which is torn between opposing forces and at variance with itself; torn between the opposition of the eternal and the changing and temporal. Conscious of his desires as a natural human being but striving for the divine, medieval man is "a personality confined within its narrow self and its petty activities, a personality brooding over itself, as unfortunate as it is pitiably destitute." This is what Hegel called the unhappy or Contrite Consciousness. The modern spirit transcends this inner conflict and tension through an awareness of the power of Reason whereby a higher level of understanding is achieved but which is made possible only because of the prior unhappy Contrite Consciousness of medieval man.

HEGEL

As Josiah Royce says: "The thesis, then, in terms of which Hegel defines his Absolute is that the absolute self is aware of itself as a process involving an inner differentiation into many centers of selfhood."

In the perfecting of the rational self, however, two stages are first to be achieved, the *moral* and the *ethically-social*. With reference to the *moral* individual, Hegel in his own way substantiates Kant's ideal principles. The moral law of Kant is restated by Hegel to read: "Be a person and respect others as persons" *(Philosophy of Right)*. But the total personality, for Hegel, needs not only *self*-realization but *social* realization as well. Here too a dialectical movement is discernible. From the first stage of what is right, or mere *legality*, wherein the personality is submerged under contractual obligations, the individual emerges through his subjective *moral will*, best denoted by the term *conscience*. He now stands opposed to that which is merely legally right and there comes into being an ethical-social system wherein the moral imperatives become social ideals and find objective realization in ethical institutions. These are the social forms of family, community, and the ideal State. This ideal State of Hegel's actually rules out both Communism and Slavery. Because Hegel expressly teaches: 1. That slavery in any form is absolutely immoral; for the moral dignity of individuals debars anyone from becoming the property of another. On the other hand, the possession of private property of every other kind is a condition for the self-realization of individuals, because every person has the inherent right to own something. But that does not mean that all property must be equally shared by each and every member of society. Hegel says that people vary in their ability to possess and use private property as much as they vary in other respects. Furthermore, this private property one may use and dispose of at will, namely, through contracts. But there are certain things which belong to one and yet which one cannot rightfully relinquish possession of or transfer to another. Thus one can readily dispose of one's belongings which are in the nature of material things, but one cannot dispose (morally) of one's life or that of another. Suicide is inadmissible under any and all circumstances.

Personalities are related to one another externally through property rights — that is the implication of the legal relationship wherein, through an abstract conception of the Right, personalities gain an objective expression. But that is far from exhausting the depths of personality; for, there is an inward subjective aspect in which man seeks possession of himself rather than of outer things. This, however, is what we mean by *Freedom*, the freedom of the personality expressed through conscience in the fulfillment of duty. There is a complete inwardness to the personality of a free individual which expresses itself through purposeful conduct, responsibility and intention. This is the grade of moral behavior and pertains to the will and its motives purely as such, regardless of benefits to be derived from the action. Hegel, however, does not go the full length of Kant's formal idealism; because for him the moral will in choosing a way of conduct must take into account all the *consequences* which are to accrue from the deed. Hegel prop-

oses a line of conduct that will issue in concrete consequences, despite the fact that he regards conscience as
"the deepest internal solitude." Moral conduct thus, for
Hegel, is completely the result of man's sovereign practical reason, conditioned by his inner conscience; but at
the same time he demands that conscience adjust itself to
the social community, so that there is for him, an enlightened conscience which seeks the good according to
the light of man's inner moral freedom but must adapt
its judgments for the good of all. Hence Hegel's morality
bars both narrow utilitarianism as well as extreme subjective idealism. Nonetheless, the depth and profoundity
of the inner certitude of moral conscience as to what
is right as well as to what is wrong never escapes his
keen penetration. Thus, he writes: "In a self-certitude,
which exists for itself and knows and decides for itself,
both morality and evil have their common root." (Philosophy of Right)

For Hegel, there bloom out of these deep subjective
moral sources the whole series of social-personal moral
values expressed in the objective institutions of the family, the ethical community and the State. Thus the child
somehow remains imbedded in the adult, the youth in
the mature person, and the individual attains his ethical
maturity ultimately as a citizen of an ethical society by
which he identifies his own life with that of his people.
For Hegel, this is true patriotism: the individual's readiness to allow his own spiritual self to unite with the
spiritual in others for the sake of a general enhancement of life through social fruition. And he spotted the
implications of his ethical theories on a grand universal

scale, quoting Schiller's exalted remark: "the history of the world is the world's court of judgment," but only after he had paid his respects to the German Empire as the highest state of man in the historical progression of mankind.

V.

Hegel's Philosophy
of History, Art and Religion

Viewing thus the individual in the light of universal history, Hegel rises to his next important level of *philosophy of history*. The course and progress of civilizations reveals to him a universal spirit in evolutionary historical unfoldment. First the Orient, then Greece and Classical Antiquity, followed by the Roman Empire and ending with Germanic civilization. Hegel's contribution here is immensely significant in that it points to a pattern in history disclosing its inner meaning which is indeed the inner meaning of humanity itself: "the history of the world is nothing but the development of the Idea of Freedom." All particular historical events, all periods, civilizations and cultures in the course of human development reveal an inner purpose to the history of man; it is the aim of individual as well as universal Freedom.

But the highest expression of the human Spirit, that which signifies most intimately the universal Geist — for Hegel both the divine Mind, the acme of universal Spirit, as well as the mind of man — is reached in the realms of Art, Religion, and Philosophy, the regions wherein the Absolute Spirit finds expression in three ultimate forms of manifestation: the beautiful, the religious, and the supremely rational or philosophy, which Hegel held to be the highest synthetic achievement of the human and the divine, uniting a philosophy of the fine arts with a philosophy of religion and fulfilling their deepest aspirations in an absolute philosophy.

With Aristotle, Hegel placed the life of Mind above moral excellence; for Hegel, too, regarded the Absolute Mind or Spirit as the highest reality revealing through its development an opposition of subjective and objective which is overcome through the development of spirituality.

Of the three forms of Absolute Spirit, the first is Art. Aesthetics is the philosophy of fine art. Art expresses the Spirit in sensuous form. But there is a deep meaning that seeks expression or outlet through the forms of art. It is this inner meaning and significance of the fine arts which transcends the forms of their sensuous representation. Seeking ever more concrete meaning, here as elsewhere, to the abstract forms which the spirit assumes in its unfoldment, Hegel finds in the fine arts a progression away from abstraction and inadequacy in the three stages of symbolic art, classical art and romantic art.

The *symbolic* is vague and relatively inarticulate, therefore indefinite and abstract, such as is to be found in oriental statues of the gods wherein there is a deformation of natural organisms as, for example, gods represented in human form with twenty arms. Symbolic art thus, while giving vent to spiritual yearning does not attain to any degree of true concreteness through its sensuous forms, nor does it achieve any adequate expression of its Idea through its sensuous representations.

This harmonious relation of inner significance and outer embodiment or perfect equivalence of Idea and expression is attained by *classical* art. There is here, in Greek art, a perfect equalization of Idea and formal expression. Greek sculptures achieve a precise utterance of what is in the mind of the creative artist; so that from this point of view Greek or classical art attains the highest degree of perfection in expressing the Idea in sensuous form. But, for Hegel, that is not sufficient, for the Idea can never rest content with sensuous manifestation or formal sensuous expression. It cannot be confined or limited to sensuous representation. It overflows the bounds of any artistic sensuous embodiment. In short, the true aim of art in its most exhaustive significance is to strive towards philosophy, to raise universal problems. This is achieved by *romantic* art, which indeed is full of problems and whose art-works provoke all sorts of interpretations—pointing in direction toward philosophy, transcending the sensuous molds in which it finds expression but remaining truly itself, that is, pure art nonetheless.

And Hegel launches upon an historical survey which shows how oriental art is purely symbolic, Greek art primarily classical and Christian art romantic in content. Hegel further classifies the arts themselves into those which are predominantly (1) symbolic: architecture; (2) basically classical: sculpture; and (3) saturated with romanticism: painting, music and poetry.

His contribution to aesthetics alone would place him in the ranks of the most noteworthy among philosophers who dealt with the problems, the history and the meaning of art.

The next stage in Hegel's triad — art, religion, philosophy — is *religion*. In the realm of religion, also, the progression is again from the sensuous to the spiritual: "the Greek god is the object of naive intuition and sensuous imagination. His shape is therefore the bodily form of man."

Now, for Hegel, the importance and supreme significance of romantic art lies in the fact that it is in romantic art that the insufficiency and inadequacy of the aesthetic experience is most fully realized. The conflicts that romantic art expresses and the manifold problems that it provokes is the key to this realization of the insufficiency of the aesthetic; and this reaches its highest point in tragedy, the highest form of poetry. Thus, it is in poetry, i.e. tragedy, that the transition is made from the sensuous to the spiritual, from art to religion.

Religion stands midway between art and philosophy; it still gives us God in the form of images, figurative speech, and sensuous representations. Philosophy, on the other hand, recognizes the ultimately real — the divine — as *thought*. Hence philosophy pursues the fundamental rationality, the divine rationality, which is the same as ultimate reality, as this finds expression in particular individual things. But this is a level of high intellectual maturity, when religion turns into philosophy. The profound insight of religion as to the divine essence of all reality is thereby not relinquished but the further insight is gained, through philosophy, that that essence is rational. Thereby religion is retained while its sensuous basis is transmuted into spiritual thought.

Hegel traces this philosophical insight in the nature of religion itself in his historical survey of the evolution of religion. At its lowest level, the level which Hegel called "the religion of nature", man seeks through magic, worship, and prayer, to control natural forces and to exploit nature's powers to his own advantage. Next comes the stage wherein God or the deity is conceived by religion as infinite power or boundless force. In the Chinese religion this power is represented by T'ien, the Chinese God of endless universal being and power. In the Hindu religion Brahman is this formless, boundless reality. In Buddhism the resulting deity is nothingness. These are all forms of the religion which Hegel calls the religion of nature. Higher stages, wherein religion attains to the conception of the divine as spiritual individuality are those of the Zoroastrian, wherein God is Light or the Good in conflict with Darkness or Evil; the Syrian, which Hegel calls the religion of pain; the Egyptian which is for him the religion of world mystery. These are all permeated by an element of *hope*, for Ahura-Mazda will eventually triumph over Ahriman and annihilate his evil designs; the Syrian Phoenix comes to life again; and Osiris (the Egyptian) dies only to be reborn and live again. These are all religions which are suffused with spiritual meaning since their Gods already possess spiritual individuality. Hence this is the second stage in the evolution of religion, following upon the "nature religions." In this second stage, however, there is a higher level as represented by the three great religions which provide the basis for the advent of Christianity: the Jewish religion which Hegel terms the religion of sublimity, the Greek, which is the religion of beauty, and the Roman which is the religion of utility.

All of these reach their culmination in Christianity, the Absolute Religion which does for religion what the Hegelian philosophy does for philosophy. Christianity elicits the truth of religion in figurative representations, the same truths which the Hegelian philosophy finds as basic to all philosophy, through thought.

In Christianity, Hegel discerns the religion of the Absolute Spirit. The same convictions which one finds in the philosophy of idealism may be discovered in the fundamental doctrines of Christianity, wherein God is represented as a free self-conscious Spirit.

In the Trinity, Hegel finds the threefold self-manifestation of the divine. First, God the universally all-embracing Spirit; second, God as infinite particularized self-manifestation; third, God as the Holy Spirit or individualized eternal love. There follows God's self-alienation which in the finite becomes the sinfulness of man and his redemption through the death of Christ achieving the ultimate reconciliation between the finite and the infinite. Thus Hegel conceived three spiritual kingdoms as the essence of Christianity: the kingdom of the *Father*, or God, eternal Being; the kingdom of *the Son*, or God as manifesting Himself in the finite world which is the self-alienation of God the Infinite Being, an estrangement which issues in a reunion; and the kingdom of the *Spirit*, or God in His living presence in the church, which is the spiritual communion of men of godly spirit.

Christianity gives us the highest possible utterance of religion as figurative representation of the divine Absolute Spirit. But the full expression of this infinite and eternal Absolute Idea can come only through the rational thought of philosophy. Philosophy may thus be called the final synthesis of all spiritual experience.

"Hegel", says Windelband in his *History of Philosophy*, has set "the highest task that has ever been set to philosophy: *to comprehend the world as a development of those principles . . . which form the content of the divine mind.*"

Philosophy is, consequently, for Hegel: "the highest, freest, and wisest phase of the union of subjective and objective mind, and the ultimate goal of all development."

But philosophy too has its history and unfoldment in progressive realization. The history of philosophy is the dialectical unfoldment of philosophic truth. It tells the epic story of Absolute Spirit at the highest phase of its development; it expresses "the dialectical rhythm of the spiritual world." (Tsanoff: *The Great Philosophers)*
Here, in his *History of Philosophy*, Hegel follows the dialectic of philosophic thought through ancient Greek and medieval Scholastic philosophy as well as in the modern antithesis of empiricism with rationalism and its resulting synthesis in the Kantian Criticism.

After Kant, according to Hegel, philosophy culminates in his own philosophy which is the "final result" of the self-expression of the Absolute Spirit or Universal Mind.

But, by Hegelian dialectical necessity, the elements of opposition and conflict found fertile soil in Hegel's own thought — the contrarieties in his own system causing a split among his followers into the "Hegelians of the Right" and "Hegelians of the Left." For the first, those of the right, the theory that the real is rational, seemed to substantiate the existence of Providence and to justify a politics of absolute obedience since Hegel, for them, saw in the Prussian Government the latest expression of the Absolute; and for those of the left, it culminated, with Marx, in a philosophy of history wherein a struggle between the opposed classes in society must lead by Hegelian necessity to "socialism." Marx inverted the Hegelian dialectic. Instead of Hegel's Absolute determining history, he (Marx) found in the stress of economic forces and in the struggle of the masses all ground for change and development. And these basic economic forces determine also the changes in the realm of mind and spirit. so that the currents of the spiritual life itself, aesthetic and philosophic, were the result of fundamentally material, social and economic forces clashing dialectically for supremacy on the battlefield of human history.

But the original Hegelian insight into the metaphysics of reality and the life of mind and spirit has sustained its influence through the insight of its founder, and today, in the twentieth century, when the perversions of Hegelianism of the right and of the left, Fascist and Communist, will have spent their force, the true greatness of Hegel will loom on the horizon as an eternal light to guide the human spirit in its upward struggle toward the divine. Perhaps one day in the not too distant future humanity will echo the words of Hegel who, with the absolute certainty of inner conviction said: "thought and thought alone has eyes for the essence, substance, universal power and ultimate design of the world."

KIERKEGAARD

KIERKEGAARD

(1813-1855)

The discovery, and subsequent popularity, of Kierkegaard in the twentieth century, is among the most important of literary and philosophic events in our age. It was George Brandes, the great Danish critic, to whom many such discoveries are attributable, who first made Kierkegaard known to the world; but even he did so only some twenty years after Kierkegaard's death. The fact that during his lifetime Kierkegaard was considered eccentric, fanatical and "fantastic", is not surprising, for even today his basic ideas strike a dissonant chord in many a "modern" soul.

He was a most unusual man; sensitive to the point of intolerance and courageous to the point of being dangerous. A hundred years elapsed before the English-speaking world became acquainted with this unique thinker. His thoughts have now been completely exhumed and re-evaluated, and Kierkegaard has been adjudged a literary and philosophic "find" of the first magnitude.

Reinhold Niebuhr has called him "the profoundest inter-preter of the psychology of the religious life . . . since St. Augustine," while the Soviet Philosophical Dictionary has devoted several columns to a vehement denunciation of his philosophy.

Kierkegaard was indeed a genius of no ordinary rank; a revolutionary spirit in the truest sense of the term and, as he opposed the accepted religious and philosophical ideas of his day, so does he, even in our age, run counter to much that is by tradition considered sound philosophy and theology.

His anti-rationalism, his desire to rescue the individual from becoming absorbed in an undifferentiated mass immersed in dogmas, religious or scientific; his stress upon the ethical core of man, and upon each individual as a living entity, responsible, in deed and in thought, directly to God; his devotion to the concrete, suffering, willing and aspiring existence that is man, and his desire to bring man back to a consciousness of true religiosity and essential Christianity — all of these factors have won him many admirers and adherents. Kierkegaard now occupies a commanding position in the forefront of twentieth century philosophic and religious thought.

Merely to take note of the immense variety of his subject-matter, is already to become aware of the impressive scope of Kierkegaard's mind. There are diaries, novels, a dialogue, abstract philosophic discourses, the psychology of despair, a critical analysis of the equalizing tendencies of modern times, sublime religious utterances; and, last but not least, piercing irony and biting satire.

KIERKEGAARD

In each case, we come upon not merely objective criticism, but keen introspective analysis. Hence the anguished, revealing lines that dot his pages: . . . "what a painful thing thus to be sacrificed!" And, despite the diversity of his interests, we meet an unbroken continuity and unity of design in his thoughts, as in his life. Indeed, it may be said that one single *motif* permeates his entire outlook:

"The thing is to understand myself, to see what God wishes *me* to do; the thing is to find the truth which is true *for me*, to find *the idea for which I can live and die*; . . . what good would it do me to be able to explain the meaning of Christianity if it had *no* deeper significance *for me and for my life*; what good would it do me if truth stood before me, cold and naked, not caring whether I recognized her or not . . . an *imperative of understanding . . . must be taken up into my life* . . . that is what I now recognize as the most important thing. That is what my soul longs for, as the African Desert thirsts for water." *(The Journals)*

II.

To the world at large the name of Kierkegaard has become almost synonymous with Existentialism. The reason for this is that it was Kierkegaard who first introduced the category of *existence* into modern philosophy in a new and a specifically "existentialist" meaning. He laid stress upon a uniquely religious sense of existence: existence as that of the finite, suffering, responsible and guilty individual who must make a crucial decision when he comes face to face with God, a fundamentally *moral* decision, involving man's deliverance and salvation. The "existence" that he refers to therefore, is that of the self who can possess eternity instantaneously and as readily lose that divine experience, lapsing into utter despair when, becoming involved in the temporal, he allows eternity to slip from his grasp. Kierkegaard's conception of the individual is that of man standing alone as a person before God, an individual quite distinct from all other men and from the world. This conception is essentially religious and it implies a transcendent being in the soul of man. Later existentialists (such as Heidegger and Jaspers) made philosophic concepts of these transcendent, religious notions of the self. From Kierkegaard's religious position they have swerved to agnosticism (Heidegger) and even atheism (Sartre and Camus). Others again, (Gabriel Marcel, Nicolas Berdyaev, Martin Buber and Jaspers), have re-opened the religious aspect. Indeed, it has been pointed out that the new existentialism of these men is modern man's avenue to religion, primarily by way of the despair, the fear and the anguish following upon the moral and spiritual collapse of Europe after two world wars; but Kierkegaard evinces these experiences in all their religious and moral connotations, one hundred years earlier.

Kierkegaard's philosophy is essentially a protest against Hegel and all those who think they can pierce the Absolute by pure thought. And, in the manner of all anti-intellectualism, he employs his own dialectical and logical reasoning to combat rationalism.

The standpoint of Kierkegaard, and of the existentialists generally, is a branch or extension of the anti-intellectualism that swept over Western thought following the reign of rationalism in Europe and ending with the Absolute Idealism of Hegel: the anti-rationalism in Schopenhauer, and later, in Nietzsche, Bergson and William James.

In the tradition of men of profound religious conviction, Kierkegaard passed through an intensity of inner, individual suffering. The questioning spirit that finds expression in Kierkegaard is religious therefore in a very orthodox sense; his main concern is how one can be a true Christian in an un-Christian world. To achieve this, Kierkegaard felt that he had first to clear the ground of all attempts to improve upon Christianity, such as had been made by Hegel and the Hegelians. They overlaid existence with thought and buried the individual under a heavy burden of ideas. That was not the way to God, for Kierkegaard. He saw in man primarily an existing individual and only secondarily a thinking one. Existence is prior to thought for Kierkegaard. The *Cogito ergo sum* (I think, therefore I am) of Descartes must be altered therefore, to read: *Sum ergo cogito* (I am, therefore I think). The individual as an existing entity, with all his suffering, anguish, despair and possibilities of redemption, is Kierkegaard's concern. How can one reach the inner core of individual existence? Like Kant, Kierkegaard felt that he had to "do away with knowledge in order to make room for faith."

The certainty of *knowledge* is, for him, a certainty concerning that which is merely possible, a certainty regarding the *hypothetical:* while *faith*, which admittedly is uncertain, deals with the *actual*, not with the merely possible.

The actual, existing individual can be reached only through faith; faith which is "objectively uncertain" but whose objective uncertainty has true and actual existence at its base.

The Hegelians wanted to contact the divine by means of thought?

That is not the way to God! The way is through fear, anguish, trembling, despair — thus only can the self become ripe for facing God! One must first pass through the dark night of the soul to arrive at *true self-consciousness* and thence to *God-consciousness.*

Science tries to pierce the Ultimate by "objective" truth? There is no objective truth. Truth is subjective!

III.

In Copenhagen, on May 5, 1813, there was born to the Kierkegaards, Soren, the last of seven children. He was reared in a strictly orthodox Lutheran home, under cheerless and depressing conditions. His father, of peasant stock, was a lonely and melancholy man. One day, towards the end of his life, he informed his son, Soren, that a curse lay upon the family, for he, as a young shepherd, had once cursed God for his hapless existence.

KIERKEGAARD

Soren's childhood was an unhappy one. In fact, childhood, as ordinarily understood, never existed for him. As he says: "I started with reflection . . . ; I am reflection from beginning to end." As a youth he was ridiculed and mocked at in school and at the University of Copenhagen, for he always seemed at cross purposes with the other students, primarily because of his pungent wit and fierce polemics.

When he entered the university, in 1830, the Hegelian philosophy was at the height of its reign. Ten years later, in 1840, he passed his examination in theology, then entered the seminary for pastors, and only one year thereafter he delivered his first sermon in church. The year, from 1840 to 1841, proved to be of great importance in his life, for it was during this year, 1840, that he became engaged to Regina Olsen, an engagement which was broken off in 1841. Regina married Schlegel and Kierkegaard was to mark out an entirely new course for his life due to this shaking event. His literary career now became extremely prolific in results, his polemics more pronounced, and his conflicts with the Church more vehement; and he set himself up as the defender of pure Christianity. Henceforth this was to be his chief aim and he embarked upon this task with missionary zeal. But these conflicts, so vital to his spiritual self, broke his physical body. On October the 2nd, 1855, as he was walking in a Copenhagen street, he collapsed. He was removed, in an unconscious state, to Frederiks Hospital where he died on November 11 of the same year.

Thus, at the age of 42, there expired the lonely thinker, Kierkegaard, who was destined to play a commanding role in the thought of the twentieth century, one hundred years later. Kierkegaard had anticipated, in his mental and spiritual life, in the middle of the nineteenth century, the self-same conflicts, enigmas and paradoxes, the same anguish and despair which was to weigh on some of the best minds of the twentieth century as a result of the uncertainty, disillusionment, degeneration and decay of post-war Europe. Hence the immense influence of his thought wherever translations of his works appeared, first in Germany, then in Italy, in France, and finally in the English-speaking countries.

The unprecedented interest in Kierkegaard's works, despite the many difficulties in the way of their assimilation, such as the fact that he wrote under various pseudonyms each of whom attacks the problem from a new, and sometimes conflicting, point of view; the mixture of the philosophic, the aesthetic and religious; and his almost fanatical zeal in unmasking the Christian world in order to lead men back to a truly Christian life — these and other disturbing factors of a literary, psychological and even psychopathological nature are serious impediments to a grasp of Kierkegaard's essential message, which was to apply an *existential philosophy to Christianity* and thus to satisfy the deepest needs of the religious consciousness. For Kierkegaard, the individual and his soul-experiences as a suffering and anguished existent, always subjective and facing inward, was the sole object of interest, and he therefore rejected speculative philosophic thought with reference to religion and especially as regards Christianity. His main problem was *how to become a Christian;* both of these, *to become* and *to become a Christian,* were, for Kierkegaard, intertwined. Existence, for Kierkegaard, was real only as expressed in a particular individual; and Christianity had to appeal to the individual with his wants, desires, suffering, torments and moral aspirations.

For Hegel, every particular existent was significant insofar as it revealed the universal embodied in it. For Kierkegaard, every intuition of reality, every situation, every deed was significant solely *for the singularity of the individual involved therein.* To *be,* to *exist,* is to resist its opposite, non-being and dissolution. All objectivity, and all objective thought, refers to something outside the thinking, feeling, willing subject and his particular existence. Therefore he writes: "systematizers and objective philosophers have ceased to be human beings and have become speculative philosophy in the abstract, something which belongs in the realm of pure being." *(Concluding Unscientific Postscript).* What Kierkegaard means, of course, is that the particular, existing individual with his intimate sufferings, guilt-consciousness, and desire for redemption, and not the pure abstract being of the absolutist metaphysician, is his chief concern. In fact, the individual existent is all that matters for him. This was the new sense of "existence" which Kierkegaard propounded and tossed into the lap of philosophy following the other meanings of *existence,* ancient *(as pure being),* and medieval and scholastic (as *pure essence)* which had dominated philosophic thought for two thousand years; and it sought to link the concrete, particular, individual with the moral and spiritual imperatives of the Christian life. Kierkegaard felt that this (the true Christian life) was to be found nowhere in the Christendom of his day — neither in the Christian theologians nor in the Christian philosophers.

Religion in general and Christianity in particular are subjective realities, concrete spiritual experiences demanding passionate avowal and commitment, and ending in a complete transformation of the self.

The powerful religiosity at the core of Kierkegaard's being asserts itself in a unique and, one may say, unparalleled manner. Two great problems confront his soul, to which an answer *must* be found: 1. How to *become* a Christian, and 2. how to *become again one's true self before God*. He sees the Christian world as a complete failure. His contemporaries were not Christians, nor were any of the other so-called Christians, during the entire period of Christian history, — echoing thereby the sentiment of Nietzsche: *"the last Christian died on the cross."* — The men who call themselves Christians, were all *potential* Christians. But Kierkegaard is concerned with the vital problem as to how one can become a Christian *in reality*, not merely potentially but *actually*. "Actually" means, for Kierkegaard, in this instance, for each individual to make his own decision and to *become a Christian because he wills to do so*, and not because he has been baptized — which was a decision not his own — or for any other reason except the important one, namely, *to make of one's self by one's own will and decision a Christian*. This involves Kierkegaard in the larger problem of religion, philosophy and humanity. One is not born a man, a philosopher, or a Christian.

KIERKEGAARD

We *become* human, philosophers or Christians. All of these involve a task imposed upon us, and all of them, as well as many others of a simliar nature, and of the most far-reaching implications, are involved, for Kierkegaard, in the problem: *how to become a Christian!* And all of these questions, including the last one, stem from the grand, general question: *how to rise from unauthentic to authentic existence.* If we can answer this, we shall have dispensed with all pretense: we shall have ceased to *pretend that we are human, religious, philosophic, or Christian,* and shall have *become* all of these.

How does one, as an individual, "attain in his lonelines the courage and the dauntlessness of a religious man answerable to God"? That is how the problem shaped itself for Kierkegaard, and the solution of this would be the key to all the other essential problems. For, one becomes a Christian, one becomes religious, one becomes truly oneself *by attaining the courage to answer before God!*

All of this, however, presupposes an individual, true selfhood, essential subjectivity, concrete individuality; and this, in turn, true existence.

How can one truly exist when one has become alienated from oneself, a stranger to one's own inner world of the self? Kierkegaard launches upon a psychological study of self-estrangement. The same fear, dread, or anxiety which obsesses contemporary existentialism is already fullgrown here, in Kierkegaard. And, because we find it here in its pure and original state, it is perhaps more clearly and precisely enunciated by him than by any of the other existentialists. We have in Kierkegaard a thorough psychological analysis (or psycho-pathological study) of the nature of "Angst", the peculiar fear or dread which is perhaps most precisely translated into English as *anxiety*. Kierkegaard devotes an entire volume to this dread which he believes to be the key to that state of alienation, which is the dreaded state of one's leaving one's self, in an internal sense. Hence the "Angst", the fear which yet knows that there is nothing specific to fear. "Angst" is rather that dreaded presentiment of an impending evil, due to a power outside of us which takes possession of our selves; an evil not yet present but soon to come. In Kierkegaard's words: "a desire for what one dreads . . . an alien power, which captivates . . . with a sweet apprehension" . . . hence, "a sympathetic antipathy and an anti-pathetic sympathy", the state in which one's freedom is lost; for, we stand here, in this psychological state, in danger of "an alien power which threatens our dissolution." Hence, "anxiety and nothing correspond to each other . . .". This "Angst", or anxiety, a process of internal alienation of one's self from one's self, becomes despair, which despair is "the sickness unto death."

Perhaps it is here that we may lay our finger on the cause of the immense influence that Kierkegaard has had upon contemporary thought. His psychological analysis of despair is at the root of the entire existentialist psychology; for the scepticism and doubt of modern man leads in the end, similarly, to an inner self-examination and, finally, to despair. Whenever a self, in process of becoming, ceases to bear the proper relation to itself, there arises a spiritual illness, an illness of the spiritual being of man which is *despair*. Actually, however, this state is the result of man's desire to separate himself from the power which gave birth to him, or, what amounts to the same, *despair* arises when man discards his spiritual self and releases himself from the eternity within him. This results in one's having no God and, whenever one has lost God, one has lost one's Self, while he who has no Self lands, inevitably, in despair.

But this state of despair is, nonetheless, a very essential one for every man. Ultimately, it is not a purely psychological state but the forerunner of true existence, true religion and true Christianity. It is, one might say, the beginning of wisdom, and the prelude to emancipation; for it is with this experience that one must start, no matter how dear the cost in suffering and anguish "if one wants to find the Absolute." One must begin, not as Descartes thought, with doubt; to find the Absolute, "one has to start . . . not with doubt, but with despair." From this basis in despair one may find one's way and become one's self again. There is but *one* way: by "becoming again oneself before God." The way to paradise regained (becoming oneself again) after paradise lost (becoming entangled in the objective world) is through what Kierkegaard called *Repetition*. This is the title of one of his most fascinating books. Repetition, in Kierkegaard's usage of the term, becomes one of the discoveries of modern philosophy — a discovery in the realm of the spirit which may turn out to be on a par with Hegel's discovery of the *concrete universal* or Kant's *transcendental unity of apperception*.

For, *Repetition* is the road to salvation — the way of deliverance, the way of "becoming again oneself before God."

Kierkegaard's "Repetition" is the means for healing the rift in the personality which, immersed and involved in the world, becomes a *dual* personality. The essential self is the pure self, the *subjective* self; when this self becomes *objective*, it loses its initial pristine concreteness and reality, its true *existence* and one becomes a mere shadow of a man. By *Repetition* the initial self is regained as a pure subject "again oneself before God".

In short, it appears to Kierkegaard that modern man has lost his true Self. His knowledge does not concern existence and hence is not essential knowledge reflecting the innermost inwardness of the Self. For Kierkegaard, all other knowledge, no matter how broad and varied and certain, is contingent and inessential.

Objective, mathematical, metaphysical or historical knowledge is *abstract though objectively certain*. For Kierkegaard, the existence of the individual self is a matter of total indifference to such knowledge; hence it is of little value, while modern thought is dominated almost completely by such "objective" knowledge.

Finnally, knowledge that disregards the true needs, the anguish and aspirations of the subject, is in reality devoid of truth. Its value as "objective" already stamps it as valueless for the needs of the subject as a truly *existing* entity.

For the individual, as an essential existent, only his own existence is truly real and knowable: Truth resides, for him, in inward, subjective reflection, in the merging of the self with its own subjectivity.

All of the above implies the priority of the religious and ethical over all other knowledge. These alone — the religious and ethical — have access to the inward reality of the truly *existing;* for in the religious and ethical experience it is that existence and truth become one.

In brief, for Kierkegaard, "truth is subjectivity". This, as may be seen at a glance, is at the opposite pole to the tendency of all modern science which, for Kierkegaard as for so many others, leads us to ever more *objective* and ever more *abstract* knowledge. Hence, it teaches us to *know* instead of to *live,* to *be* instead of to *exist.* Existence, for Kierkegaard, means inward apprehension of the subjectively real — or, *self*hood; it applies, therefore, solely to human existence. But Kierkegaard is not interested even in this type of existence as such, that is, of a *finite* human being. Concerned as he is always and primarily with the *infinite* and the eternal, in man and in human existence, he would like to view the finite individual from the standpoint of his infinite potentialities of becoming a truly existing entity, i.e. a being responsible to God and capable of facing the divine in himself without flinching. This implies a completely inward reflection, an analysis of human passion, moral choice, sin and guilt; hence of man in process of becoming himself and therefore of the philosophy and religion of human selfhood, or of man's existing as an individual; not *mere knowledge,* not *only religious beliefs* which may yield objective results, each in their own way. "Subjective thought puts everything in process and omits the result", says Kierkegaard; hence man's thought "must correspond to the structure of existence". The knowledge of that which is internal Kierkegaard calls the "how" as distinct from the "what" of external or objective knowledge: "this inward 'how' is the passion of the infinite, and the passion of the infinite is the truth." *(Concluding Unscientific Post-script)*

If this inner subjective knowledge of "how" constitutes the truth, it is not because it attains certainty. Certainty, on the contrary, belongs to the scientific, the mathematical and logical. Wherein, then, does the validity of subjective truth lie? Answer: not in its certainty but in the fact of "its having a relationship to an existing subject." This, it is true, is not objective certainty of the intellectual sort; it is, rather, *paradox*. From the standpoint of the objective there is no certainty in the realm of the subjective. And Kierkegaard finds in the very fact of objective uncertainty an indication of the paradoxical truths issuing from the deepest recesses of an existing individual. This truth is passionately avowed by the individual, despite its being paradoxical or even absurd. The test of truth here in inner subjective experiencing is rather the fact of its being in consonance with one's entire existence, part and parcel, as it were, of one's very being. Hence, if it appears as paradoxical and absurd — no matter! Perhaps it is truer to say, as regard the subjective and inward in human existence, that something is true *because* it is paradoxical and absurd. This would place it at the opposite pole to objective truth which is the province of intellectual certainty.

Why not the absurd as a test of truth, in this subjective realm? After all, Christianity itself, the Christian faith may appear from the standpoint of objectivity and intellectual apprehension as paradoxical and absurd. Is it not absurd to say: "that the eternal truth has come into being in time, that God has come into being, was born, has grown up, and so forth, precisely like any other individual human being"? This may sound absurd but what could be truer than this "absurdity"? The test of truth from the standpoint of the existential inward being of man must be sought in the realm of faith, and faith may well appear as paradoxical and absurd! Would this fact invalidate faith? Of course not! The truth of inner religious experience consists in its passionate avowal of what it "knows" to be identical with its innermost self.

To be true is to be faithful; even in common speech we realize this when we speak synonymously of being "true", "loyal", "constant", "faithful'. Kierkegaard saw clearly into this sense and meaning of the "true". The "true" resides in the act of one's being true to oneself, which means, to be true to one's eternal self and hence true to God. Indeed, in Kierkegaard's sense of the term, the "true" belongs strictly to the inner essence of a human being; for to be true is the same as to "truly exist", to be true in the presence of God, when we come face to face with the divine. Indeed, it is then that we participate in eternal truth or divine truth. There is so close and intimate a relationship here between the finite self and the infinite, that the two tend to coincide and, to truly exist and exist truly mean the same, for truth and existence are one, and the transcendentally divine finds a clear echo in the innermost existence of the individual self.

In short, Kierkegaard maintains and adopts the position that nothing in the world of objectivity has value, in an ultimate sense, for man. Man alone, the living, suffering, anguished and despairing individual truly exists from the standpoint of subjective reflection. Objective knowledge does not matter. It is not really "true", except in an objective sense, that is, in the sense of objective certainty. But of what value is that certainty in an existential sense? *Existential* refers to the individual self, hence to the subjective mind and soul of man. It is to this that faith makes its appeal, to this inward essence of man religion has meaning and the Christian life must bear for this inner self the significance which it should.

Science leads to abstractions and deals in hypotheses; within that circumscribed area alone are its findings objectively certain. Truth, however, resides in the concrete existence of man, in his free choice as a moral being, in his passionate devotion to eternity, in his being true to himself and in his dauntless courage when he comes face to face with God. Religion can lead us to this that is so essential in the life of man; philosophy, too, must become *existential* for it to be *true*. Hence, the individual human being, as a moral and spiritual entity responsible only to God, must free himself in thought and in conduct, from the levelling mediocrity of the mass and face his eternal destiny as an absolute replica of the infinite and divine.

KIERKEGAARD

IV.

Kierkegaard appears as a phenomenal apparition out of the past to express many of the sentiments of the non-conformist of today. Hence, contemporary existentialism is an outgrowth and extension of Kierkegaard's basic notions and ideas.

In his satirical way *(Concluding Unscientific Postscript)* he tells us: "I conceived it my task to create difficulties everywhere."

After all, there were so many who had made it their business to "make life easier and easier, some by railways, others by omnibuses and steamboats, others, again, by telegraph, and still others by easily understood compendiums and short outlines of everything worth knowing, until we finally arrive at those who are the true benefactors of mankind . . . those who make spiritual existence itself systematically easier and easier, and at the same time more significant." (Kierkegaard refers here, of course, satirically, to Hegel, and other absolutist and rationalistic "system"-builders.) No. He would not make life easier!

He found his vocation rather by way of Lessing's observation that "if God, holding all truth in his clenched right hand and in his left hand the persistent striving after the truth, even including the ever-present possibility to err, said: Choose; I should humbly prostrate myself before his left hand, and say: "Father, give me what is herein contained; pure truth is, after all, only for Thee."

The *pursuit* of truth — that was to be *his* life's work! the persistent striving which is, in reality, "the ethical life view of the existing subject". This is not something metaphysical, nor does it apply to"any individual who exists metaphysically". Kierkegaard does not appeal to metaphysical existents but to concrete, actual, living human beings, to "the consciousness of being an existing individual."

Hence philosophy, for him, must throb with a vitality which will overflow the static conceptions of intellectual apprehension.

In this way, philosophy will appeal to "human beings" and not to "fantastic beings in fantastic language". It will appeal to existing individuals for whom "the ideal of a persistent striving is the only view of life that does not carry within it an inevitable disillusionment." And this approach seems to him so simple as to merit immortal fame which, under the conditions of nineteenth century Europe, could not be accorded this doctrine since it is so "very simple," but "every thoughtful individual must confirm its truth."

Kierkegaard examines the objective and the subjective approaches to Christianity. The truth of Christianity does not depend upon an objective determination; one does not accept or reject Christianity after "objective" certitude and verification has been achieved. On the contrary, such an acceptance of Christianity implies "a disingenuousness which seeks to shirk the decision (as to whether one should become a Christian or not) by an objective mode of approach" to a subjective issue. The subjective decision (to become a Christian) "is precisely the decisive factor" while "an objective acceptance of Christianity is paganism or thoughtlessness."

KIERKEGAARD

To become a Christian is an individual experience. Christianity promises "eternal happiness . . . to one individual at a time"; hence the decision to become a Christian is an individual *subjective* decision. It has nothing to do with the truth of Christianity in the objective sense.

One must be prepared and predisposed to appropriate the infinite good of Christianity; and there is no guarantee that one is "ready for such acceptance" or that the subject has "a real conception of what such a good signifies."

To become a Christian the subject must be "infinitely concerned about himself," for Christianity is concerned solely with subjects and "it is only in subjects that its truth exists" while "objective Christianity has absolutely no existence."

Let those who will speak of universal history (like Hegel), and construct "systems" to explain history, but "there is more Christian joy in heaven" over one simple human being in whom Christian "truth" has found a habitation and a home than over all universal history and the systems devised to explain it. This is the core of Kierkegaard's existentialism.

Such is the spirit of Kierkegaard's thought, and we must not underrate or minimize its importance; nor speak of his philosophy and religion condescendingly. The dead do sometimes live again.

Of course, we, who have been scientifically conditioned, pride ourselves on "objective" knowledge (the very knowledge whose objective certainty is for Kierkegaard a sign of inadequacy as "true" for the subjective consciousness). Hence, to us, the very title *Unscientific Postscript* is abhorrent! But Kierkegaard persists in drawing our attention to what, for him, are very obstinate facts. He says in a remarkable phrase: "No one ever becomes devout objectively". "Devoutness inheres in subjectivity."

Philosophy and science both err in this respect and their error is, for Kierkegaard, a cardinal sin.

The ideal of modern man is *objectivity*. It is "the admired wisdom of our age that it is the aim of the subject to increasingly divest himself of his subjectivity in order thereby to become more and more objective." Thus it comes about that modern philosophy "teaches that the way is to become objective, while Christianity teaches that the way is to become subjective, i.e. to become a subject in truth."

The "intensification of passion to its highest pitch" which Christianity wishes to achieve is an effect produced on subjectivity; love, too, is a determination of subjectivity; while "faith is the highest passion in the sphere of human subjectivity."

By a strange coincidence we have, in Kierkegaard, a curious mixture of Socratic irony, Nietzschean iconoclasm and Augustinian religiosity: the fierce, polemical criticism of the one, the profoundly religious zeal and conviction of the other, plus the methodical questing of the third, are all in evidence here, in Kierkegaard; and, in every instance, it is one or the other of their methods that he employs. So, too, with reference to the problem of God.

We *must believe in God*, said Augustine, lest we run

the risk of spending our lives without finding Him or completing the term of our existence without having found Him. We cannot afford to wait indefinitely for confirmation and proof. *Kierkegaard goes even one step further than Augustine. Objective proof for the existence of God is neither possible nor necessary,* he tells us. On the contrary, it is precisely after the dialectical logic of reason "brings passion to the point of despair" that the individual can "embrace God with the 'category of despair'" which is *faith.* It is then that the postulation of the being of God ceases to be a mere postulate and becomes "a life-necessity". Indeed, "God is then not so much a postulate as the existing individual's postulation of God is a necessity."

Kierkegaard here solves the Kantian postulation of God by the practical (moral) reason of man through *his* Critique of what he calls the "approximation-process by which it is proposed to bring God to light objectively." This, he says, is impossible — "in all eternity impossible" — as impossible for him as for Kant, because *God is a subject, and therefore exists only for subjectivity.*"

Whoever has come to realize this and therefore chooses the subjective approach to God is aware of the futility of the logical (dialectical) approach to the divine; he knows the futility of one's trying to "find God objectively"; and, further, he feels the painfulness of such attempts, their wastefulness in seeking God objectively, "since every moment is wasted in which one does not have God". And, miracle of miracles, the moment he becomes thus aware of his needs and of the futility of objective modes of satisfying them, the individual "that very instant has God" — "not by virtue of any objective deliberation but by virtue of the infinite passion of inwardness."

All of this is, of course, Augustinianism with a vengeance, and mysticism with an Hegelian underlining; but it is also Kantian Criticism with a passionate avowal of the spiritual and the divine. For this reason it is *vital*, and vital for our age that has definitely lost the sense for subjectivity and positively worships at the altar of "objective" truth. Kierkegaard brings us to the realization that there is no such thing. For the existential being that is man truth is an *inward subjective experience* which he possesses, and is possessed by, the moment he is truly himself, hence truly at one with God, when the finite in him relinquishes its hold and he is once again free to embrace the infinite and divine, to be himself again, to come face to face with God, morally, inwardly, spiritually.

———

This is the meaning of Kierkegaard's contrast between the objective and the subjective approaches to the spirit and to God. On the one hand, the passionate desire for God is completely alien to the approximating logic of so-called "objective knowledge", while he who is impelled "by the urge of passion" (for the divine), for him of subjective awareness and subjective knowledge every day is "a deadly peril, and the decision (to come face to face with God) so infinitely important and so instantly pressing that it is as if the opportunity had already passed unutilized." Thus, says Kierkegaard, when we come to add up both sides of the ledger, to find out on which side there is more truth, "whether on the side of him who is in quest of God objectively and pursues the approximate truth of the God-idea; or on the side of one who, driven on by the infinite passion of his need of God, feels an infinite concern for his own relationship to God . . . the answer cannot be in doubt for anyone who has not been demoralized by the aid of science."

Kierkegaard has no regard for *men*, only for *man*, *this* man, *this individual*. The herd does not concern him, only the *one*, who can stand up *against the herd!* And *this* man alone is capable of the religious experience. He it is who counts — for *he* must make his peace with God, and he alone can do so. He can regain the eternity which everyone of us loses when he enters the world and becomes attached to it and its false ideals, is lost in error and sin, and lands inevitably in despair.

Then must we seek ourselves anew and then only can we find ourselves in relation to God, in *my* relation to God. And any hindrance in the way of such an intimate union with the divine, Kierkegaard attacked with all the merciless logic, satire, wit and humor at his command. Hence his biting irony, his fierce tirades, his violent invectives, his derision and abhorrence of all those who, directly or indirectly, obscure the real issue — for Kierkegaard the *only* issue: How to become a Christian.

He was, no doubt, too severe in his criticism and one-sided in his attacks — unjust and unforgiving too. And he himself knew it: "Severity first", he writes in his

Journals, "severity first, that is to say, the severity of the ideal, and then gentleness . . ."

This is Kierkegaard; this is what he lived for; and, perhaps, therein lies also the secret of his persistent vitality: sincerity, honesty, purity — wherever God and eternity, wherever religion and Christianity are concerned.

In Kierkegaard's own concluding words of his magnificent sermon on "The Unchangebleness of God":

"Thou, O God, who art unchangeable. Thou art always and invariably to be found, and always to be found unchanged. Whether in life or in death, no one journeys so far afield that Thou art not to be found by him, that Thou art not there, Thou who art everywhere. It is not so with the well-springs of earth, for they are to be found only in special places. And besides — overwhelming security! — Thou dost not remain, like the spring, in a single place, but Thou dost follow the traveller on his way. Ah, and no one ever wanders so far astray that he cannot find the way back to Thee, Thou who art not merely as a spring that may be found — how poor and inadequate a description of what Thou art! — but rather as a spring that itself seeks out the thirsty traveller, the errant wanderer: who has ever heard the like of any spring! Thus Thou art unchangeably always and everywhere to be found. And whenever any human being comes to Thee, of whatever age, at whatever time of the day, in whatever state: if he comes in sincerity he always finds Thy love equally warm, like the spring's unchanged coolness, O Thou who art unchangeable!" *(The Unchangeableness of God: Princeton University Press)*

KIERKEGAARD

This is the tranquil Kierkegaard, discoursing on the miracle of God's unchangeableness, and voicing the perennial wonderment of the human mind at His eternal Being. Philosophers have no monopoly on this; nor has any one religion, any sect or creed, any one man or woman. The love of God belongs to humanity, and the knowledge of the divine Being reveals itself in the quest of the human for the divine, or is that quest itself.
